The Embers and the Stars

The Embers and the Stars

a philosophical inquiry into the moral sense of nature

Erazim Kohák

The University of Chicago Press • Chicago and London

The University of Chicago Press, Chicago 60637
The University of Chicago Press, Ltd., London

Paperback edition 1987
Printed in the United States of America

03 02 01 00 99 98 5 6 7 8

Library of Congress Cataloging in Publication Data

Kohák, Erazim V.
The embers and the stars.

Bibliography: p.
Includes index.
1. Philosophy of nature. 2. Ethics. 3. Philosophical anthropology. I. Title.
BD581.K54 1984 113 83-17889
ISBN 0-226-45017-1 (paper)

This book is printed on acid-free paper.

A M. Paul Ricoeur
Une ésquisse d'une poétique
Hommage respectueux

Contents

Prolegomenon

There still is night, down where the long-abandoned wagon road disappears amid the new growth beneath the tumbled dam, deep, virgin darkness as humans had known it through the millennia, between the glowing embers and the stars. Here the dusk comes softly, gathering beneath the hemlocks and spreading out over the clearing, muting the harsh outlines of the day. There is time to listen to the stillness of the forest when the failing light signals the end of the day's labor but the gathering darkness does not yet warrant kindling a lamp. Here time is not of the clock: there is a time of going forth and a time of returning, and there is night, soft, all-embracing, all-reconciling, restoring the soul. On the clear nights of the new moon, the heavens declare the glory of God and the ageless order of the forest fuses with the moral law within. Here a human can dwell at peace with his world, his God, and himself.

In the global city of our civilization, girded by the high tension of our powerlines, we have abolished the night. There the glare of electric light extends the unforgiving day far into a night restless with the eerie glow of neon. We walk on asphalt, not on the good earth; we look up at neon, not at the marvel of the starry heavens.[1] Seldom do we have a chance to see virgin darkness, unmarred by electric light, seldom can we recall the ageless rhythm of nature and of the moral law which our bodies and spirits yet echo beneath the heavy layer of forgetting. The world of artifacts and constructs with which we have surrounded ourselves knows neither a law nor a rhythm: in its context, even rising and resting come to seem arbitrary. We ourselves have constructed that world for our dwelling place, replacing rude nature with the artifices of *technē,* yet increasingly we confess ourselves bewildered strangers within it, "alienated," "contingently thrown" into its anonymous machinery, and tempted to abolish the conflict between our meaningful humanity and our mechanical life-world by convincing ourselves, with Descartes, that we, too, are but machines.[2]

It is not my purpose in this book to condemn the works of technology or to extoll the virtues of a putative "natural" life. I have lived close to the soil for too long not to realize that such a "natural" life can also be brutish, worn down by drudgery and scarred by cruelty.[3] I am aware that *technē,* too, can be an authentically human mode of being in the world, capable of setting humans free to be nature's kin, not her slaves or masters. A life wholly absorbed in need and its satisfaction, be it on the level of conspicuous consumption or of marginal survival, falls short of realizing the innermost human possibility of cherishing beauty, knowing the truth, doing the good, worshiping the holy. A *technē* which would set humans free from the bondage of drudgery, to be the stewards rather than the desperate despoilers of nature, should surely not be despised.

Yet in our preoccupation with *technē* we stand in danger of losing something crucial—clarity of vision. Surrounded by artifacts and constructs, we tend to lose sight, literally as well as metaphorically, of the rhythm of the day and the night, of the phases of the moon and the change of the seasons, of the life of the cosmos and of our place therein. The vital order of nature and the moral order of our humanity remain constant, but they grow overlaid with forgetting. We come to think of a mechanistic construct, ordering a world of artifacts, as "nature,"[4] losing sight of the living nature of our primordial experience in which boulders, trees, and the beasts of field and forest can be our kin, not objects and biomechanisms. Losing sight of the moral significance of nature, we then seek that significance in "History"—only to become trapped in the paradox of a "progress" which sacrifices the fullness of the present to an ever receding future.[5] We are still human, all too human; even amid our plastic gewgaws the moral sense of our being, the bond of love and labor, the vision of truth and justice, all remain constant. Yet that moral sense of our humanity is all too easily obscured by the mechanical order of our artifacts. Though no less there, it seems no longer evident to us as once it did to the Psalmist on a desert night or—perhaps—still to Immanuel Kant amid the sparse pine forests of Moditten.[6] In our daily lived experience, the starry heaven above and the moral law within have been heavily overlaid by artifacts and constructs.

The quest of this volume is one of recalling what we have thus hidden from ourselves. It is a philosopher's book, deeply indebted to the cultural heritage of three millennia of Western thought. It is also a book of philosophy, though in a sense far older than the current acceptation of that term. In a technological age, philosophy, too, tends to conceive of itself as a *technē*. To some writers, it has come to appear as one of the special sciences, whose subject matter is language, whose task is the analysis of arguments, and whose virtue is technical proficiency. Others take philosophy to be a metatheory whose subject matter is the theories of other philosophers and scientists, whose task is speculative construction, and whose virtue is sophistication in the peculiar sense of maximal remoteness from lived experience, so that the author who writes fifth-generation commentaries thinks himself more advanced than the preceding four generations of commentators—and far more so than the naïve observer upon whose original insight they all comment. Both linguistic analysis and theoretical construction are, surely, legitimate tasks. Yet the thinkers whose insight withstood the test of time, from Socrates to Husserl, were of a different breed. They were the perennial beginners, taking the sense of lived experience in its primordial immediacy for their subject matter. Their stance was one of wonder, not of sophistication; the task they undertook was one of articulation—and their virtue was naïveté, a willingness to *see* before theorizing, to encounter the wonder of being rather than enclose themselves in cunningly devised theories.

There is, I think, a reason. For the purposes of manipulating our environment—the legitimate purpose of *technē*—conceptual analysis and the construction of theoretical models are appropriate tools. Here the theoretical construct of, say, a uniform motion in a frictionless medium, though nowhere to be found in experience, is far more useful than Aristotle's experientially accurate distinction between spontaneous "natural" motion and a violent one. When, however, the task is not to effect a predetermined purpose but rather to ask what the purpose is, to grasp the sense of the cosmos and of our being therein, including the purpose of engaging in natural scientific inquiry, then clear, sensitive seeing is in order. *Prima philosophia* cannot start with speculation. It must first see clearly and articulate faithfully the sense evidently given in experience.

So Plato's metaphorical prisoner labors through the stage of *dianoia* or reasoning not in order to construct a hypothesis but to reach the point at which he can *see*, grasp in a direct awareness, the idea of the Good. Almost three millennia later, it is *seeing* that Husserl and Wittgenstein alike call for in the face of the spiritual crisis of the West: not to speculate but to *see* the sense of it all. Reflection and speculation remain no more than cunningly devised fables if they are not grounded in what, paraphrasing Calvin Schrag, we could call the prephilosophical and prescientific matrix of self-understanding and world-comprehension.[7] Though philosophy must do much else as well, it must, initially, *see* and, thereafter, ground its speculation ever anew in seeing.

So I have sought to see clearly and to articulate faithfully the moral sense of nature and of being human therein through the seasons lived in the solitude of the forest, beyond the powerline and the paved road, where the dusk comes softly and there still is night, pure between the glowing embers and the distant stars. I have not sought some alternative, "more natural" life-style nor some "more authentic" mode of being human. Artifacts, I am convinced, are as "natural" to humans as the dam and the lodge are to beavers, culture as "authentic" to them as nature. Nor do I wish to recall humanity to an earlier stage of its technological development. It is, surely, good that there are synthetic medicines to ease the surplus of pain, telephones to break through loneliness, and electric lights to keep the wayfarer from stumbling.

There is, though, something wrong when we use medicine to deaden our sensitivity, when we obliterate solitude with electronics and blind ourselves with the very lights we devised to help us see. There is nothing wrong with our artifacts; there *is* something wrong with us: we have lost sight of the sense, the purpose of our production and our products. Artifacts, finally, are good only extrinsically, as tools. They have no intrinsic sense of their own. A humanity which knew only a world of artifacts might justly conclude that the world and its life therein are absurd.

Too often we have so concluded, having sought the sense of life where it cannot be found, in the products of our artifice. To recapture the moral sense of that life and its world, even the world of artifacts, humans need to bracket it, seeing beyond it to the living world of nature. It takes the virgin darkness to teach us the moral sense of electric light. It takes the beauty of solitude to enable us to grasp the sense of the word spoken over the distance, the crystal-bright gift of pain to teach us the moral sense of penicillin.

Through the years beyond the powerline I have sought to rediscover that moral sense of life, too easily lost amid the seeming absurdity of our artifacts. In writing of those years, I have not sought to "prove a point" but to evoke and to share a vision. Thus my primary tool has been the metaphor, not the argument,[8] and the product of my labors is not a doctrine but an invitation to look and to see. With Husserl, I have sought not to instruct but to point out,[9] to recall what we have forgotten.

My intellectual indebtedness to Husserl and Heidegger, to Plato and to Kant, to Ricoeur and to Rádl, to Masaryk and to Patočka, is, I think, evident enough in the text—and I have sought diligently to acknowledge it in my notes. I should, however, like to acknowledge a different indebtedness as well, to all the neighbors who helped and taught me to survive and to see, to Don and Robin Williston on Binney Hill, to the good people at All Saints', in the woods and along the logging roads, especially to Bonnie and to Larry Poole, wherever he may be, who for years had been a neighbor in the best sense of Luke 10:30–37 and a friend of lean winters. They, together with Borden Parker Bowne and Peter Anthony Bertocci, have taught me that, contrary to Descartes, long before the *cogito* of reflection there is the goodness and the truth of the *sumus*.

Erazim Kohák

Sharon, New Hampshire

I. Theoria

When, in 1928, Martin Heidegger described the human as a sheer "presence,"[1] contingently thrown into an alien context which constantly threatens to engulf him with its instrumentality, he appeared, to many of his contemporaries, to be doing no more than acknowledging an evident truth. Certainly, Heidegger was not speaking in a vacuum. For a century or more, Europeans and their cultural heirs in Russia and America had thought of themselves as privileged beings, persons in an impersonal, material world—and had acted accordingly. Western science described the world in ever more mechanistic, "value-free" terms, wholly alien to a moral subject,[2] while industry ruthlessly exploited the world so described as no more than a reserve of raw materials for human gratification. Still, the impact of Heidegger served notice that, at mid-century, the heirs of Europe's personalistic cultural heritage had come to perceive themselves as absurd aliens in a dead, meaningless world.

Ironically, Heidegger himself may not have intended to present the image of the human as the embattled outsider. Though admittedly diverging from the moral personalism of his two great predecessors, Edmund Husserl and Max Scheler,[3] Heidegger, already in the introduction to his *Sein und Zeit,* insisted that the question he was posing was one of Being as such, to which the being of humans is to serve but as a clue.[4] In his postwar works, the continuity of Being and being-human does stand out prominently and the emphasis shifts: the fourfold presence of Being here becomes a clue to the understanding of being human.[5] In the phenomenology of *Sein und Zeit,* however, the discontinuity of humans and their world is no less present, and it was the discontinuity on which most of Heidegger's readers seized: the emphasis on the *Entschlossenheit,* the resoluteness of humans as *Dasein,* the presence standing out or "ek-sisting" from the tool-system of reality in a defiant self-assertion.

Whether or not such was indeed Heidegger's intent, that was the theme his successors derived from his work and elaborated for some three decades. In the writings of Jean-Paul Sartre and of the thinkers who took their cue from him, notably Albert Camus, the nonhuman appears as also inhuman, absurd and nauseating. Here the descriptions of the natural world, as of the gnarled roots of an old tree or of the protagonist's own hand in *Nausea,* stress its repugnant absurdity. The human finds himself a stranger in that natural world, a nothingness, an outburst of an infinitely lonely freedom in *The Flies,* who exits, followed by the Furies. In the less fanciful categories of *L'Être et le néant*—literally the being and the nihilating, that which is and that which negates, not just the "Being and Nothingness" of the English title—the human is *l'être-pour-soi,* the intentional, meaning-creating project wholly discontinuous from and in a fundamental conflict with the sheer, meaningless mass of what simply is, as *l'être-en-soi.*[6] The human as a moral subject—"man," in the terminology of the age—is said to have no "nature": the ideas of "humanity" and "freedom" and the idea of "nature" appear fundamentally contradictory. The human here is a nothingness, a "godlike," arbitrary freedom to whom—or to which—nature, dead, meaningless, material, is at best irrelevant and typically threatening, to be conquered by an act of the will. In Sartre's rather infelicitous phrase, "existence precedes essence": the human simply *is;* only retrospectively, in terms of what he has been, can he be said to have been something in particular.[7]

Whatever the value of "existentialism" as a philosophy, it is a powerful testimony to the intellectual climate of the West at a certain time. The vision of the human which appeared evident to some of the foremost thinkers of the age—those, at least, who refused to abandon the conception of the human as a moral subject in favor of the human as a particularly complex robot and so continuous with a mechanistically conceived nature—was one of a lonely, arbitrary freedom defying the absurd orderliness of a dead, meaningless reality. The immense popular appeal of existentialist writings testifies to a moment of recognition: the humans of the West in the mid-twentieth century indeed perceived themselves in a great part as perplexed, perhaps defiant aliens in a strange, meaningless universe. Two generations earlier, Nietzsche had proclaimed that God is dead. By mid-century, to a great many Westerners, nature seemed no less dead, and the human, a lonely survivor, himself an endangered species.

That progression is not accidental. Nietzsche's Zarathustra presented the death of God as great good news: though Dostoevsky was clearly mistaken in supposing that if there were no God, everything would be permitted, it did seem that, in that case, nothing would be prohibited. The true implication, however, is deeper. If there is no God, then nature is not a creation, lovingly crafted and endowed with purpose and value by its Creator. It can be only a cosmic accident, dead matter contingently propelled by blind force, ordered by efficient causality. In such a context, a moral subject, living his life in terms of value and purpose, would indeed be an anomaly, precariously rising above it in a moment of Promethean defiance only to sink again into the absurdity from which he rose. If God were dead, so would nature be—and humans could be no more than embattled strangers, doomed to defeat, as we have largely convinced ourselves we in fact are.

That the notion of a fundamental discontinuity between humans and their natural world should have come to appear evident is itself a curious phenomenon. That notion is, primordially, radically counterintuitive. Humans, notoriously, live their lives in and as their bodies whose rhythm is integrated with the rhythm of nature. The cycle of vigor and fatigue echoes that of the day and night, the rhythm of the new moon and the full moon has its counterpart in the rhythm of a woman's body and, less obviously, a man's body as well. The cycle of the seasons harmonizes with the cycle of human life. In the quest for sustenance and shelter, for the sharing of lives and the care of the young, in the eagerness of youth and the fullness of age, the lives of humans intermesh with those of all animate beings. Drawing water at dawn, making ready to break fast, I watch the woodchuck at his grazing: I can sense with all the evidence of primordial awareness that he and I are kin. Resting before the house at dusk, I can see the porcupines with their young beneath the boulders on the opposite bank venture forth: even so I had once led my children on their discovery of the world. Hoeing the beans, I watch their tendrils groping for the strings I stretched for them—so I, too, have groped for support. I can understand the old age of my apple trees, living past their time: perhaps that, too, will be my lot.

I sense my own place in the rhythm of the seasons, from seed time to harvest, the falling leaves and the stillness of winter. Some tasks are, perhaps, uniquely mine, not shared by other dwellers of the field and the forest. I can cherish the fragile beauty of the first trillium against the dark moss, and I can mourn its passing. I can know the truth of nature and serve its good, as a faithful steward. I can be still before the mystery of the holy, the vastness of the starry heavens and the grandeur of the moral law. That task may be uniquely mine. Yet even the bee, pollinating the cucumber blossoms, has its own humble, unique task. Though distinct in my own way, I yet belong, deeply, within the harmony of nature. There is no experiential given more primordial than that.

Sensing the life of the forest around me, I think only a person wholly blinded and deafened, rendered insensitive by the glare and the blare of his own devices, could write off that primordial awareness of the human's integral place in the cosmos as mere poetic imagination or as "merely subjective." The opposite seems far closer to the truth. It is what we are accustomed to treating as "objective reality"—the conception of nature as a system of dead matter propelled by blind force—that is in truth the product of a subject's purposeful and strenuous activity, a construct built up in the course of an extended, highly sophisticated abstraction. It is, undeniably, a highly useful construct for accomplishing a whole range of legitimate tasks. Still, it is a construct, not an experiential given. Humans must suspend lived experience to produce the "scientific world view" of physics.[8] Our direct awareness of nature as the meaningful context of our lives, by contrast, presents itself spontaneously, without a subject's effort. If anything, it requires the very opposite: to suspend effort, to let be and listen, letting nature speak. In a real, though not a customary sense, it is what we mislabel "poetic imagination" that is, "objective," a spontaneous experiential given. It is our image of nature as dead and mechanical—and the image of the human as either a robot or a rebel—that is "subjective," a product of the subject's active imagination rather than a given of lived experience—and actually quite counterintuitive.[9]

The image of the human as a stranger contingently thrown into an alien context is as alien to the spirit of Western thought through history as it is to experience. Through its three recorded millennia, Western thought has been consistently personalistic and specifically *naturalistic*, at least in the generic sense of that term, understanding humans as continuous with and at home in nature.

That generic sense of the term "naturalism" is not, admittedly, readily accessible to our age. As commonly used, the term "naturalism" reflects the late mediaeval division of reality into two realms, conceived of as almost two distinct natures, one "natural," the other "supernatural." Within this bifurcated conception of nature and presupposing it, "naturalism" came to describe the claim that the "natural" component is both self-contained and self-sufficient, perhaps even alone real, so that the human, his works, and his world are to be understood without recourse to the resources of the putative "supernatural" realm. How narrowly or how broadly that exclusion was to be conceived—whether, for instance, it excluded only references to God and "miracles" or whether it precluded all reference to intentional objects, purposes, values, or meanings—would then depend on whether the investigator opted for a "rich" or an "austere" ontology.[10] Thus "naturalism" came to mean a philosophy which accepted as normative of "reality" the reality construct of the science favored by a given "naturalistic'" thinker, as, in random instances, vitalistic biology in the case of a Driesch or a Dewey, biophysics in the case of Schrödinger, or a rather simplistic mechanics of action and reaction in the case of a Hobbes or a Watson.

So interpreted, however, the term is not overly useful. For one, the division of reality into a "super-natural" and plain "natural" realm was a rather short-lived, fortuitous product of a highly specific historical situation. Saint Augustine knew nothing of it, and even Saint Thomas, though in fusing Aristotle with Augustine he was led to distinguish two realms of discourse, prefers to speak of them as philosophical and theological. Only the Averroist thinkers of a century later, most notably William of Occam, introduced a conception of a bifurcated reality, of two truths and two natures, one "natural," the other "super-natural." In the nineteenth century, that distinction came into common use by both Catholic and Protestant thinkers struggling to preserve the autonomy of the spirit against the reductivist science of their time. By the mid-twentieth century, however, the distinction had all but disappeared from philosophical usage. Those Catholic and Anglican writers who, for reasons of tradition, continue to speak of the "supernatural," use the term, somewhat misleadingly, to indicate the dimension of the sacred in a unitary reality and experience, not a second, superior "nature." A philosophy contingent on the bifurcated conception of reality, affirming one of its halves against the other, would be as dated as that conception itself.

Then, too, making our philosophic conception of reality contingent not on lived experience but on the reality construct used by a particular natural science is intrinsically problematic. Even a philosophy of science, if it is not to become a sterile, self-confirming dogmatism locked within a wholly formal system of its axioms and their implications, must retain an independent access to the primordially given nature of lived experience in terms of which it can evaluate the adequacy of the reality construct assumed and used by a particular science. If we were to take "naturalism" to mean—as in fact it has often meant—a philosophy which takes a particular science as definitive of reality, the term could claim only a limited descriptive accuracy, not a philosophical significance.

For the purposes of our reflections, a generic rather than a historical idea of naturalism seems more relevant. By speaking of "naturalism" in a generic sense, which includes but is not restricted to its historical instances, we shall mean any philosophy which recognizes the being of humans as integrally linked to the being of nature, however conceived, treating humans as distinctive only as much as any distinct species is that, but as fundamentally *at home* in the cosmos, not "contingently thrown" into it as into an alien context and "ek-sisting" from it in an act of Promethean defiance. By "nature" in a similarly generic sense we shall mean the nature presented in lived experience, the primordially given cosmic context in which humans find themselves and to which they themselves belong in their bodies and minds, as humans are in fact aware of it, whether thematically or not, in their daily lived experience, not as it appears in the theoretic nature-constructs which seek to capture it. What is at issue between naturalism so conceived and its denial is not the nature of "nature" but rather the place of the human in the cosmos: whether we shall conceive of ourselves as integrally continuous with the world about us or as contingently thrown into it as strangers into an alien medium.

It is in this generic sense that we can speak of Western thought as basically "naturalistic." The conflicts within it hinge, for the most part, on how nature is to be conceived; *that* humans are a part of its order seemed beyond question. That is certainly true of the pre-Socratics. For them, the crucial dividing line, if we can speak of one at all, would run not between humans and nature but between all that is natural, a part of nature as *physis,* the living, meaningfully ordered web of purpose within which each being, humans no less than the stars and all in between, has its appointed task, and, on the other hand, the realm of artifacts, devoid of a life and an entelechy of their own. The order which for, say, an Anaximander governs the life of the cosmos is indistinguishably both vital and moral.

That continuity of the vital and the moral order becomes explicit in Aristotle, as, for instance, in the familiar Book I of his *Politics*. Here Aristotle explicitly equates the moral order with the natural order. The moral order is distinctive only inasmuch humans, unlike their fellow animals, must grasp the order of the cosmos through an operation of the intellect and choose to honor it in an act of the will. While for beings endowed with instinct the operation of the law of nature is automatic, vital, for beings endowed with reason it is voluntary and, in that specific sense, *moral* rather than vital. Its contents, however, remain largely constant: it is the one order which appears either as vital or as moral; it is, in both cases, the "natural" which appears as good and the disruptive or "violent" which appears as evil.

Saint Thomas was able to take over that conception without undue difficulty. Natural law, as he conceives of it, is not the law of some "human condition" or a law specifically invented for humans. It is the law with which the Creator endows all of his creation. The analogies between human and animal societies, which sound so strained to a contemporary reader, seemed entirely legitimate to Saint Thomas and the medievals. The natural and moral "laws" of marriage and marital fidelity, of the love of a homeland, of the rhythm of aging and renewal, all are natural patterns of behavior which we can detect among most animals and which can serve as clues to the natural order of human life as well. Humans are distinctive only in their freedom to know and obey (or ignore and disobey) that natural law—and in their ability to discern, beyond that law, as the idea of the Good, the overarching virtues of faith, hope, and charity, the "theological" virtues which later Scholastics were wont to designate as "supernatural," with unfortunate results.

The vision of the integral unity of the being of humans and that of the cosmos is no less present in the other great tradition of Western thought, which we can trace from Socratic moral philosophy through Plato and the Stoics down to the Renaissance. Socrates shocks younger readers today by his scornful insistence that he has nothing to learn from trees. Surrounded by artifacts which indeed can teach us nothing but what we have programmed into them, we are just beginning to realize that it is precisely the living, growing nature that Socrates scorns that can teach us. Similarly, Plato, Socrates' star pupil, rejects this world, presumably including *physis,* as a cave of shadows in the *Republic* and as a world running backwards in the *Statesman.* It is not difficult to read into Socrates and Plato a fundamental opposition between humans and nature and to re-present them as the ancestors of existentialism in a sense as generic as that in which we are using the term naturalism.

Before we do that, however, we might do well to look again. Neither Socrates nor Plato rejects the idea of a natural order in the name of the sovereignty of an arbitrary human will arrogating unto itself either the powers of creation or those of determining good and evil. The opposition, as becomes clear in Plato's exercise in designing an ideal community, is one between the rational order of the cosmos and the contingent, customary ordering of the human world. The human is not a stranger: he belongs integrally within a cosmic order. The Idea of the Good, the structure of the Ideas, and the reason which reaches out to them are neither "supernatural" nor antinatural, though Windelband, Jowett, and their nineteenth-century contemporaries may have tended so to read them.[11] Rather, they represent the true order and meaning of the cosmos in which nature and humans participate, albeit imperfectly. That becomes evident in the thought of Plato's direct heirs, the Stoics. For them, the *logos* is the order of the *kosmos,* guiding alike the flight of the sparrow and the life of the sage. As the bearer of the *logos spermatikos*—usually rendered "the spark of reason"—the human is anything but a stranger. If there is anything discordant and "unnatural," it is the unruly passions which elude the rule of nature's *logos.*

Christianity could incorporate the Stoic vision of the *logos* which/who was in the beginning and through whom all things were made, just as it could accept Aristotle's conception of a natural order of things, because it is itself deeply "naturalistic" in the generic sense of the term. Heir to the Psalmist who saw the heavens declare the glory of God, calling on a God who became flesh, reconciling the world unto Himself, Christianity did not conceive of nature as a dead, mechanistic medium alien to moral effort, nor of humans as strangers contingently thrown into it. The Christian cosmos is a *creation,* an ordered, meaningful work of God's hands, and the human is set into it as its steward and its integral part. Like the Stoics before them—notably Seneca—

the Christians did contrast the authentic *kosmos* as God created it with the "fallen" nature of everyday experience—acknowledging, by the way, that it was through humans that sin came into the world. By making that distinction, the Stoics and the Christians may have opened up the possibility for a later conception of a meaningless nature, separated from God's grace. Still, even the "pilgrim through this barren land" of Christian piety was not a homeless stranger but a homeward-bound wayfarer, a citizen of a kingdom which included both heavens and the earth. The Christians, repeating each Sunday that they believe in one God, maker of heaven and earth and of all things visible and invisible, could never quite lose sight of nature as God's creation or of the continuity of their own being with that of the *kosmos.*

For all the motifs of the "prison of the body" and of the "pilgrim through this barren land," the ek-sistentialist vision of the human as essentially a stranger contingently thrown into an absurd, alien context—that is, the explicit denial of what we have been calling "naturalism" in the generic sense—remains foreign to the genius of Western thought, basically counterintuitive, and, ultimately, most unproductive, leaving the human in an arbitrary isolation. The question underlying our bewilderment about being human in an unhuman world may well be how we came to convince ourselves of the putative truth of the deeply counterintuitive and counterhistorical notion of the human as a stranger contingently thrown into a meaningless, mechanical world.

There are some obvious answers, frequently given. One is psychological: humans have to dehumanize their world in their imagination in order to be able to exploit it ruthlessly in their actions—and that is surely true. Another is historical: the cataclysm of the two world wars swept away ruthlessly all the familiar landmarks of our customary social world, leaving Europeans feeling bewildered, as strangers in a strange, unfamiliar context. Similarly, the collapse of ancient Rome was surely not unrelated to the dark view of nature associated with Stoicism, nor the theme of the pilgrim to the travails of the Thirty Years' War. An "ek-sistentialist" perception of man and the world is understandably more persuasive after a cataclysm and a useful ideology for the "conquest of nature," as in the period of heedless, ruthless industrial expansion which followed the suppression of the Southern bid for independence in America. All that is true.

In our time, however, the phenomenon has become global and the sense of the depersonalization of nature and of humans within it reaches far deeper. There is much to suggest that, apart from favorable conditions, it is the product not simply of particular greed or a particular cataclysm, but of the convergence of two lines of long-range development, one conceptual, the other experiential. Since the seventeenth century, Western scientific thought—and popular thought in its wake—gradually substituted a theoretical nature-construct for the nature of lived experience in the role of "reality." Far more than we ourselves usually realize, when we make seemingly obvious assertions about "nature," we are no longer speaking about the natural environment of our lived experience, the living, purposive *physis* which humans can recognize as kin and in which they can feel at home. Our statements are far more likely to refer to a highly sophisticated construct, say, matter in motion, ordered by efficient causality, which is the counterpart of the method and purpose of the natural sciences rather than an object of lived experience. Within such a construct, to be sure, there is no place for a moral subject, simply because that construct was not designed to deal with him. As Erwin Schrödinger points out, that construct is not an accident: it is the product of a specific methodological device, the exclusion—phenomenological writers usually speak of the *self-forgetting*—of the observer, the subject with all that pertains to him, value, meaning, beauty, goodness, truth, holiness. As a methodological device, it is a useful and legitimate procedure. Increasingly, however, we have come to treat the construct it yields, useful for the purposes of manipulating our physical environment, as if it were what nature in truth is. Not surprisingly, we have then concluded that, if that is what nature is, the moral subject, if he is not to be simply an illusion, must be a radically nonnatural, "ek-sisting" being.

That conceptual development, to be sure, is not without a precedent. The contrast between an "austere" ontology said to be the Way of Truth and the rich ontology of lived experience, dismissed as the Way of Seeming, is as old as Parmenides. In our time, however, it has come to seem far more convincing because of a second, experiential development. With the expansion of our technology, we have, in effect, translated our concepts into artifacts, radically restructuring not only our conception of nature but the texture of our ordinary experience as well. It is exceptional rather than routine for us to sit before a croft of an evening, watching the all-reconciling night spread out from beneath the hemlocks into the clearing while the stars pierce the heaven above to declare the glory of God and the majesty of the moral law. We spend much of our lives locked in concrete cubicles, blinded and deafened by electronic glare and blare. On a primordial, intuitive level, we preform our conceptions of nature not in an intimate interaction with God's living nature but amid a set of artifacts which conform to our construct of reality as matter, dead, meaningless, propelled by blind force. Heidegger's description of the world of artifacts, the dead *Zeuge*, "gear," surely owed much of its persuasiveness to the fact that most of Heidegger's readers were not woodsmen and tillers of the soil but urban dwellers, artificers in a world of artifacts devoid of life and rhythm of its own.[12]

That is indeed our world, and it is a world in which humans encounter neither the order of nature nor that of the moral law, only the products of their own labor, as Karl Marx, the unwitting prophet of relentless industrialization, so clearly noted long ago, taking the nightmare world of the factory as normative for the "species being" of humans. Actually, our world of artifacts may be no more than the thinnest of layers covering the rhythm of living nature, but it is that layer that we confront in our daily experience. Once we come to take it for "nature," then our impersonal nature-construct appears an accurate description. Then, too, the conviction that humans must conceive of themselves either as complex robots and so in tune with a mechanical nature or as moral subjects in defiance of it becomes experientially compelling. Though the theoretical construct of a mechanically ordered matter in motion may bear little resemblance to the living nature of the field and the forest and so may never have appeared convincing before, it is a faithful reflection of a world of artifacts and as such compelling to a humanity whose experience of nature is restricted to contact with artifacts. To insist, as the existentialists did, that though nature be meaningless, humans are yet bearers of meaning, is a noble but an infinitely wearying position. It was more with a sense of relief than of regret that the West welcomed the new gospel, proclaimed on the authority of science, that humans are not human after all.[13] The generic naturalism of the Western philosophical tradition broke down, I would submit, because the Western conception *and effective experience* of nature broke down first. To recover the moral sense of our humanity, we would need to recover first the moral sense of nature.

There have been thinkers who have sought to do just that, even in our time. To Americans of my generation, Joseph Wood Krutch was one such voice, and in the subsequent generation the ecological movement raised a chorus of voices. To my Czech compatriots, it was Emanuel Rádl who spoke most clearly. A biologist turned philosopher, Rádl had a keen sense of the wonder of nature. That sense of the order of nature led him to an awareness of a moral order. Starting from a moral sense of nature, he went on to write of the moral sense of Czech national identity and of the moral sense of Western culture. In the darkest year of the Hitler war, 1942, when that culture seemed on the verge of disintegration, Rádl, then in the terminal year of a prolonged illness, penciled his philosophical testament, a passionate confession of faith in the genius of philosophy and in the personalistic vision of the world as *kosmos* and of humans as moral subjects therein.[14]

When Rádl's testament, *Útěcha z filosofie,* really no more than a brief, unedited essay, written in anguish and devoid of all the artifices of philosophical sophistication, could at last be published, a year after the war, it sold beyond all expectations, but appeared to many readers as little more than a moving anomaly. The time was charged with existentialist despair and revolutionary technological hope. A conception of the human as a moral subject seemed an outdated bourgeois prejudice: the human as the counterpart of Marxism and nature as a counterpart of technology appeared as the wave of the future. Rádl's assumptions seemed simply wrong.

Rádl's conception of nature is in truth far closer to that of Aristotle than of Galileo and his successors. His basic metaphor is not that of dead matter and violent force but of life with its inherent entelechic order.[15] What he sees about him, whether in his studies of the light sensitivity of plants and insects or in his reflections on biological theories, is not a dead, mechanically ordered force field conceived on the model of the world of artifacts but a living *physis* whose multiform strivings are guided by a hidden yet powerful purpose, each creature charged with its task. The human, too, as Rádl understands him, is a part of the vast cosmic order—and can be so because the cosmos with its vital order is not alien to or discontinuous with the order of meaningful life. In the case of the human, however, the vital order of the creation assumes the guise of a moral order. The human is called to recognize and to choose to obey voluntarily the same cosmic law which instinctually guides the plant, the insect, the animal. In that sense, the command presents itself as moral, not vital. While, however, its operation in humans is thus not automatic, there is yet a law of being human: there is a right and a wrong and the distinction is not arbitrary. While the moral law of being human is not identical with the law of other animate beings—there is, for instance, the fundamental difference between the rule "an eye for an eye" and the injunction to "love your enemy"—neither is it discontinuous with it. Human right and human wrong, too, are instances of what is "natural," consistent with what is harmonious in nature, and of what does violence to it.

Rádl argues vigorously that this had indeed been the guiding vision of Western thought through the millennia. He stresses the continuity of antiquity and the Middle Ages, as well as the essential consistency of the Greco-Roman and the Judeo-Christian heritage of the West in this respect. The radical break, he claims, comes only with the Renaissance and can be traced to a fundamental shift in our conception of what it means to know. Throughout antiquity and the Middle Ages, the idea of knowing had been linked to that of seeing, of a direct grasp, whether in sense perception or in rational intuition. Plato's prisoner, as we noted earlier, passes through the labor of *dianoia,* reasoning, not to construct a conceptual model but in order to *see* the Idea of the Good, not as in a glass, darkly, but face to face. Aristotle, too, for all his divergence from Plato, seeks to *see* the patterns of meaning acted out in nature, not to construct them. His distinction, say, between the spontaneous movement of life and the violent movement of matter impelled by a force, as in the image of the arrow violently propelled skyward and naturally falling to earth, presents a faithful articulation of an experiential given which has its counterpart in the lived experience of the ease of spontaneous movement of our bodies and the strain of their effort. The medievals took over Aristotle's and Plato's conception: up to the Renaissance, when seeking to know, Western thought sought to see clearly and to articulate faithfully the intrinsic structure of experienced reality rather than to construct ideal explanatory schemata and to impose them upon nature.

The technical efficacy and moral sterility of more recent thought, Rádl believes, reflects the decision to focus on the latter rather than the former. The shift, symbolized by Galileo, comes with the recognition that, for the purpose of manipulating our physical environment, ideal constructs with no intuitive counterpart can be far more efficacious than categories articulating the order of experienced nature—and the deeper assumption that the overall purpose of all such activity is basically nonproblematic, so much so that it requires no special inquiry. The Renaissance, indebted to Roman Stoics though hardly sharing their somber mood, thought of it as a "conquest" of nature, a restructuring of nature in the image of Reason. The nineteenth century spoke of "progress." In our time, B. F. Skinner settles for "survival."[16] This way or that, however, the question of purpose remained unasked, overshadowed by the question of efficacy.

Together with the majority of the critics of our technological infatuation, Rádl tends to speak of the Galilean turn in tones of moral indignation. In fairness to Galileo, though, we should note that the shift to the methodology of generating and imposing constructs is not at all arbitrary, a sort of conceptual equivalent of original sin. It is itself a reflection of the structure of lived experience, prompted by the ineffectiveness of experiential categories for certain specific tasks.

There is, for instance, an experiential, "natural" temporality in the rhythm of the seasons and of human life, with the possibility of a "natural" time reference. This natural time is not the imaginary, mathematically reversible sequence of uniform moments, extending infinitely into the past and the future and capable of being treated mathematically as a fourth dimension along with the three spatial ones. Neither, however, is it a merely "subjective" internal time consciousness, private to each experiencer, or a form of sensibility imposed by reason upon experience. It has all the hardness of the real, a logic of its own—the rhythm of vigor and fatigue, of day and night, the cycle of the seasons in the life of nature and humans alike. Its stages, though personal, are not in the least arbitrary. Primordially, human experience simply is not a sequence of discrete events which need to be ordered by a clock and a calendar or by free association within a stream of consciousness à la Proust or Joyce. It is, rather, set within the matrix of nature's rhythm which establishes personal yet nonarbitrary reference points: when I have rested, when I grow weary, when the shadows lengthen, when life draws to a close. Though we may speak that way, it is simply not the case that at "six of the clock" certain events will occur—the shadows will lengthen, my axe will grow heavy in my hands. Stopping the clock does not stop the event. The primordial time reference is the opposite: it is the experience of the evening, lodged in the shadows about me and in the weariness of my arms, which is the primordial given. Only secondarily do we designate it by a clock reference or acknowledge it in an internal time consciousness.

For the sake of managing our environment purposively—say, of dispatching rockets to the moon or of assembling a body of persons for a lecture on temporality—such a natural time reference is, admittedly, not overly effective. Bodies tire at different rates, the darkness comes unevenly in valleys and on mountain tops, under clouds and on a bright day. Here an ideal time-construct, visualized as a uniform sequence of consecutively numbered moments providing an arbitrary but common reference, serves the special purpose at hand far more effectively. It does not, to be sure, articulate any experience: nowhere does such a time line exist in nature. The idea of 1800 hours on 6 June 1981 is a pure artifact, a construct imposed upon nature's rhythm, subordinating and ordering it. Still, for the specified purpose for which it was designed—and on the assumption that we know that purpose independently of it—it is a powerful tool.

The usefulness of such a construct, however, remains inevitably contingent on the prior purpose which brought it into being. The construct becomes problematic already when we seek to apply it beyond the scope of its original intent, as the theory of relativity made evident with respect to the traditional conception of physical time. It becomes even more problematic when we attribute an ontological significance to it, treating it no longer as a construct contingent upon and restricted by prior purpose but as a description of the true nature of reality—while we devalue the temporality of lived experience to the status of mere "subjective" reflection. Good physics makes bad metaphysics.

This becomes painfully evident when the task before us is not one of theoretical reflection but of practical decision. I know of no example more graphic than the dilemma posed by the technology we call "life-supporting," even though, too often, it cannot support life—only prolong dying without relief. A patient without hope of recovery, strapped to the gleaming chrome artifact, no longer lives. He is condemned to witness his own dying. It is a cruel and unusual punishment. When is the right time to flick the switch and let death come? When is the right time to die?

The technical reason which produces the machine cannot teach us its human use. We can speak of a *right* time only in the matrix of natural time, the rhythm of human life and the cycle of the seasons. Here there is a time to be born, a time to rejoice and a time to mourn; there is also a time to die. On an infinite line of uniform numbered moments, however, the very notion of a "right" time becomes wholly unintelligible. Here time cannot be "right." There can be only $t_n \ldots t_\infty$. The decision to disconnect the machine at t_3 rather than at t_6 or t_n becomes arbitrary. To make it, we would need to have recourse to the recognition of the rhythm of natural time, the rhythm of a human life. Having, however, convinced ourselves that our linear time construct alone is real while all else, including our awareness of natural time, is "merely subjective," we have effectively foreclosed such a recourse. Instead, we stand helplessly over the machine and the agony, hoping that a committee will reduce to anonymity the decision which we can no longer make responsibly as moral subjects.

The example of time and temporality can serve to describe Emanuel Rádl's reading of the development of all Western thought since the Renaissance. As he sees it, we have, in effect, mistaken the development of our conceptual technology for a progress of knowledge, step by step substituting our constructs for experienced reality as the object and the referent of our thought and discourse. Those constructs, however, were designed for a particular purpose, that of the manipulation of our physical environment, and the composite image of reality they present is, appropriately, one of a system of manipulanda. In a nature so conceived, from which the dimensions most crucial to lived experience, those of value and meaning, have been intentionally bracketed out as "subjective," there is no more room for a moral subject.

Rádl directs his most emphatic criticism against a mechanistic materialism which, in our time, survives on the level of popular scientism rather than at the leading edge of theoretical physics or philosophy of science. By contrast, he endorses a biological model which, in the work of Bergson and even more pronouncedly in that of Teilhard de Chardin, leads to some rather problematic results.[17] The fundamental thrust of his criticism, however, is deeper than his specific polemic and speaks to the biological as well as the physical model. In principle, Rádl is pointing out that the physicalist model, taking as its root metaphors "matter" and "force," may be at most capable of *reducing* the complexity of life's rhythm to its terms, not of *understanding* it in its complexity. The biological model, taking the process of a life as its basic metaphor, is far more adequate, but still not sufficient for understanding the life of a moral subject. It adds the dimension of temporality which life adds to the inanimate, but it ignores the distinctive dimension of eternity which humans add to the temporality of the animate.

Eternity here does not refer to an endless prolongation of a linear time, as it often does in common usage. It indicates, rather, the awareness of the absolute reality of being, intersecting with the temporal sequence of its unfolding at every moment. For animate being—at least as we conceive of it, unfairly, perhaps, to the animals—all value is basically instrumental, defined by a horizontal reference to a before and an after. As an animal, which he also is, the human is a dweller in time, defining his present instrumentally. Process philosophy, child of the age of "progress," articulated the positive aspect of temporality in the concept of growth, as in the work of John Dewey, or again in a conception of a creation of novelty, especially in Bergson. Heidegger, in *Sein und Zeit,* noted the obverse: being-in-time is a *Sein-zum-Tode,* being toward death, leading the existentialists to conclude that human life is always a failure because the human dies.[18]

As a moral subject—a Person in the technical personalist sense, *Geist* or spirit in the work of Husserl or Scheler[19]—a human, however, is capable of nontemporal reference as well, grasping the moral, noninstrumental value of being. The beauty of a trillium; the truth of an insight, the goodness of a gesture of kindness, or the pain of tragedy have their absolute value, ingressing in time but independent of it. Whitehead sought to capture it with his conception of the "consequent nature of God"[20] in which the absolute being of each moment is inscribed in eternity. Whether or not that metaphor is adequate, the experience is real: Persons are beings capable of appreciating beauty, goodness, truth, holiness, all serving no purpose in time and justified by none, needing no such justification, but ingressing into time—in our earlier term, intersecting with it—as good in themselves. When we conceive of being human as a biological model, even one extended by what Teilhard calls the "noogenesis" of a "noosphere" or by the "immortality" of popular religion,[21] all value becomes reduced to an instrumental status in the course of a "progress," its present validity contingent on the "attraction of an inexhaustible future." While for Rádl the physicalist model fails because it cannot do justice to the temporality of being human, the biological model fails in its turn because it is unable to recognize the dimension of eternity in human life.

Rádl was by no means alone in protesting against the reduction of the personal, moral dimension of our humanity to the merely physical and biological cycle of need and its gratification. Ironically, though, his writings, more than those of kindred spirits from Søren Kierkegaard through Max Scheler to Alfred North Whitehead, demonstrate why the conception of a moral law became problematic. If critical reason lacks the ability to discern the moral in the vital—and reason technologically conceived notoriously lacks that ability—how is the moral law to be made manifest? Rádl looks to custom, to tradition, to bring forth the moral law: what humans have ever believed and observed must *eo ipso* be natural and so moral. Unlike in the works of his vigorous years, in his final anguished testament Rádl comes to sound as an uncritical defender of all that is traditional as also moral. Yet tradition, as the notorious example of slavery graphically demonstrates, can itself be profoundly immoral. In this respect Husserl, identifying the crisis of our culture as a crisis of reason, reduced to the service of technology, may be more perceptive than Rádl. The outcome, though, is the same: a conception of the human as a cluster of matter in motion and of human life as devoid of all meaning, all order other than that which can be derived from the cycle of need and gratification.

It is another Czech thinker who, to me, most clearly points out the cultural corollary of that conception: a reversion of humans to a "prehistoric" level of their humanity.[22] Jan Patočka, who died in 1977 under police interrogation after affixing his signature to a human rights manifesto, is known in the West primarily as Edmund Husserl's last pupil and collaborator, the author of a Husserl bibliography and of studies in the philosophy of history which exhibit a strong kinship with Martin Heidegger. Yet, for all that, Patočka is also Rádl's heir. In his usage, the term "prehistoric" refers less to an age than to a mode of being human which is characterized by a total absorption in needs and their gratification, in production and consumption, untouched by a vision of the Idea of the Good or of a moral law. In the terminology we used earlier, it is a horizontal, wholly intratemporal mode of being, devoid of all vertical reference. A century ago, writers routinely attributed such a purely "animal" existence to "the primitives," quaintly termed *Naturvölker,* natural peoples, by German writers contrasting nature with history (and identifying history with morality, in great part, perhaps, because the application of the "scientific" model had at the time not affected our vision of history as much as it had that of nature). Yet already those very writers, from von Humboldt to Cassirer, were presenting evidence that such peoples do not in truth fit that definition.[23] Far from being merely producers and consumers, they were, eminently, the makers of myths and worshipers of the gods in whose lives myth and worship were anything but peripheral. What they lacked was not the moral dimension of being human but only the nineteenth-century conception of history as "progress"—without which the West might well have been better off.

Far more than the cultures of the *Naturvölker,* it is the culture of consumerism on which both the Marxian and the non-Marxian societies of the historical West are converging which fits most accurately the definition of a "prehistoric" humanity in Patočka's sense. Consumer societies, to be sure, mass-produce "culture" no less prodigiously than electric can-openers, but its significance shifts radically. No longer is it an expression of *cultus,* the awe before the holy, the beautiful, the true, the good. Rather, it, too, becomes a consumer product, a part of the "entertainment industry," subordinated together with all the being of humans and of the society to the dynamics of production and consumption, whether guided by a five-year plan or by the whims of the marketplace.

The logic of that production and consumption, however, grows ever more elusive. Through the ages of humanity's precarious survival on this earth, the meeting of basic survival needs provided a ready justification for productive activity. Were we inclined so to direct our energies, it might still do so: there is more than enough hunger and sheer dismal misery still with us. For the most part, though, we manage to ignore such need. The logic of our production is not that of need but of affluence which lacks such automatic justification. If affluence is to be justified, it cannot be by need but by some greater good, be it meeting the needs of others, caring for the natural world, or creating higher values of culture. Culture, in the noblest and widest sense of *cultus,* has to justify surplus consumption and production.

When culture, however, ceases to be *cultus,* an ideal we serve, and becomes no more than another component of the vast surplus of consumer products designed to gratify our whims, what can justify surplus consumption? Surely not need—what conceivable need could we conjure up for, say, a remote-control tuner of ever larger colored television sets unless the viewer is paralyzed and unable to reach out for a knob? Not the slightest. Yet individually and collectively we sacrifice precious life and resources to producing and paying for just such items—and are constantly assured that we must do so to "stimulate the economy." Production itself has become the justification of ever more absurd consumption: we consume to produce, produce to consume; all other considerations must stand aside.

A humanity which so orders its priorities is indeed reverting to a "prehistoric" stage of development, wholly absorbed in production and consumption—though, as Patočka also points out, with a crucial difference. Unlike the primitive survivor absorbed in satisfying his needs, the sophisticated consumer, though no less so absorbed, is not confronted in his daily doings with the immediate proximity of lived nature and its law. The world with which he deals is a construct embodied in a system of artifacts, devoid of any presence of a Great Spirit such as American Indians encountered in their search for sustenance in the field and the forest. The artifact world, to be sure, also bears the imprint of its maker, but its maker is "man." The consumer society is here realizing the nightmarish vision of Karl Marx, for whom the human is the being who confronts the world and encounters in it only the product of his labor. The system becomes self-perpetuating. The metaphor of a wholly self-contained, man-made world, a "Battlestar Galactica," is quite appropriate. That is the ultimate solipsism embracing our entire species—a world of nothing but humans and their works, devoid of an Alter to confirm the reality of our collective Ego. Nietzsche's Zarathustra proclaimed the age in which God is dead and what had been His creation with Him, humans alone remaining, as an age of liberation. Masaryk, however, once pointed out that the solipsist must kill, whether himself in suicide or others in murder, to reassure himself of his reality.[24] What, then, if the entire species is the solipsist?

The failure of the existentialist revolt made the point that we cannot retain our moral humanity in a defiant isolation. However, the development of naturalism, both in its physicalistic and its vitalistic forms, has made the point that we cannot break out of our isolation by seeking to integrate our being with a nature construct from which we have abstracted the dimension of meaning. A philosophy which would take seriously the task of the "care of the soul" with which Socrates charged it must take the care of nature no less seriously. It cannot take over the nature-construct which represents no more than the theoretical assumptions of a special science. It must approach nature anew, undertaking no less than a phenomenology of nature as the counterpart of our moral humanity.

How, though, can we go about the task of recovering our vision of a living world and of our place as moral subjects therein? There are surely a great many ways. If, however, Husserl's critique of our constructs is at all justified, then Husserl's program might also be appropriate. Perhaps our first step does need to be a bracketing of the thesis of the naturalistic standpoint which, over the last three centuries, has become so familiar as to appear "natural." We need to suspend, for the moment, the presumption of the ontological significance of our constructs, including our conception of nature as "material," and look to experience with a fresh eye, taking as our datum whatever presents itself in experience, as it presents itself and only insofar as it presents itself, using the totality of the given as the starting point, the justification and the ultimate test of all speculative claims. With respect both to ourselves and to nature, we need to suspend all theory and ask, without prior ontological prejudice, just what it is that in truth presents itself in lived experience itself.

That, in any case, is the familiar phenomenological program which Husserl sets down in *Ideen I* and reiterates, with minor variations, in all his subsequent works. The evident estrangement of our scientific theory, especially in the humane sciences, from lived experience gives that program a certain perennial timeliness. Still, almost three generations later, it is hardly new or revolutionary—if anything, it might sound a bit weary. If, however, the implications we have sought to derive from Husserl's analyses of the crisis of Western consciousness are at all sound, then the proposal for phenomenological bracketing does acquire a new, radical dimension, as *not only a conceptual, but a practical bracketing as well,* a bracketing of artifacts. Our constructs, we have argued, are no longer merely conceptual. We have translated them into artifacts which effectively hide the sense of our lived experience from us. The heavens may still declare the glory of God, but we look up not at the heavens but at neon reflected on smog; we walk not on the good earth but on asphalt. Our estrangement from nature is no longer conceptual only: it has acquired an experiential grounding. Figuratively, we are all in the position of the child who has never seen, never mind milked, a cow, and whose lived experience constantly provides an experiential confirmation for the assumption that milk comes from a supermarket cooler. In such a context, the attempt at a phenomenological bracketing, no matter how theoretically sound, will inevitably prove practically futile. The *Sachen selbst,* the very stuff, of our daily experience will reintroduce the very constructs we have bracketed. Though milk may still come from cows, our lived experience reaches only as far as the dairy case. Though we bracket the construct of "nature" as a mechanical system and of the human as the sole source of all meaning, our urban experience will lead us right back to it. In a world of artifacts, "man" is indeed the "measure of all things"; the human as a producer and a consumer is here indeed the source of all meaning amid a mechanical system. If Husserl's program of phenomenological bracketing, his call for a return to the *Sachen selbst,* is to uncover the fundamental sense of the world and of being human therein, it must, I am convinced, look for ways of bracketing not only purely, bracketing constructs, but of practical bracketing of artifacts as well.

In a technological age, to be sure, any proposal to bracket the world of artifacts will inevitably sound suspect, as a nostalgic romanticism longing for a return to a simpler world that never was—and not without reason. There is something disingenuous about Thoreau's retreat to Walden Pond, a condescending self-righteousness which becomes painful when Thoreau propounds his alternative life-style as a model to the Irish laborer John Field, condemned by his lot to drudgery. Count Tolstoy's self-conscious imitation of his *muzhiki* tends to ring as false as the false low ceiling of hand-hewn beams which he had installed in one of the chambers of his palace to create the illusion of a peasant *izba.* It is not simply that few of us would wish to entrust our bodies to the medical treatment of, say, mid-seventeenth-century medicine or our safety to an army equipped with muzzle-loaders—though no one who ever had to submit to on-the-spot medical treatment or watch Soviet tanks rolling into his country could possibly wish either. High technology is indeed irrevocably a part of our life.[25] We could surrender it only at a high cost not simply in luxuries, but in genuinely human values like health and freedom.

The point, however, is more fundamental. Technology, as Martin Heidegger recognized even in the forests of the Schwarzwald, is not only a convenience but also an authentic human possibility.[26] In the freedom which transforms the vital order of nature into the human moral law, consciously grasped and voluntarily obeyed, the human does indeed in a significant sense stand out of nature. He is an artificer not by accident but essentially, and all his works are, in a sense, artifacts. Playing on words, we could say that even the natural, when done voluntarily rather than instinctively, becomes artificial. Technology is the human's achievement, not his failing—even though the use he chooses to make of it may be fallen indeed. If the products of human *technē* become philosophically and experientially problematic, it is, I would submit, because we come to think of them as autonomous of the purpose which led to their production and gives them meaning. We become, in effect, victims of a self-forgetting, losing sight of the moral sense which is the justification of technology. Quite concretely, the purpose of electric light is to help humans see. When it comes to blind them to the world around them, it becomes counterproductive. The task thus is not to abolish technology but to see through it to the human meaning which justifies it and directs its use.[27]

That is why I choose to stress Husserl's conception of bracketing. The task of the critique of artifacts appears to me strictly analogous to the phenomenological critique of theoretical constructs. There, too, the purpose of bracketing is not to abolish theory but to set aside its claim to autonomous validity as an arbiter of reality and to put it in the perspective of the lived experience wherein it is grounded and of the purpose which led to its generation. Husserl insists that he seeks not to deny the validity of the sciences but to affirm it by providing them with an experiential grounding. Even so it is not the purpose of bracketing the world of our *technē* to return, as Thoreau might have sought to do, to some prelapsarian, pretechnological existence but rather to restore its validity by capturing the moral sense which it simultaneously mediates and obscures. The world of artifacts may make philosophic reflection impossible when it assumes an absolute ontological status and subordinates the moral subject to its mechanical order. Bracketed, however, it can also make philosophic reflection possible. Thoreau's retreat to Walden is possible only in the margins of a complex civilization. Only on the fringes of a great city can I live in a forest clearing, yet devote almost all my time to thought and writing rather than to wresting a livelihood from the rocky fields of New Hampshire. The purpose of such a retreat is not to abolish the works of technology but to bracket them, to escape their fascination in order to rediscover their forgotten meaning.

That distinction, so difficult to make in an electrically lit, centrally heated study where book-lined walls mediate between a human and his world, stands out clearly in a forest clearing, a mile beyond the powerline and the paved highway, where the dusk still comes softly, unscarred by neon, and the world of everyday lived experience is still God's nature, not "man's." Life here is not "pretechnological" or "natural" in some romantic sense. A wood stove and a kerosene lantern are still technology, even high technology by the standards of many parts of this world. Even an open cooking fire and a rush light would be that. There is, however, a difference between a participatory technology which lets the human meaning of a subject's act stand out and the automated technology which conceals it, creating the illusion of autonomous functioning.

Heating with one's own wood may be no more "authentic" than central heating, but it offers a far clearer metaphor. Heating with wood is very much a participatory activity. In the year-long cycle, from flagging trees for culling to the rich glow of oak cinders of a winter's night, the subject is constantly present and nature is directly present to him, both in the hardness and in the caressing softness of its reality. Felling, limbing, skidding, bucking, splitting, stacking, kindling and building a fire are all primordially, directly subject acts and experienced as such. There is nothing anonymous about the glow of the stove: its heat can be experienced primordially as a gift of the forest and of a person's labor. Cleaning the chimneys and trimming the wicks, filling the lamps and kindling a light in the darkness, those are no less evidently a person's acts, a person making light. In such a context, the place of the human in the cosmos stands out in unobscured clarity: the love which gives meaning to labor and the labor which makes love actual.

That love and that labor are no less present in an automatically lit and heated urban apartment. Here, no less than in a forest clearing, light and warmth of a winter's night are not automatic. They, too, are the gifts of love and labor. Their sense, however, does not stand out: too many intermediate links intervene. An urban parent may tell his child with equal justification that he goes to work to give her warmth and light, but when that work is not splitting wood or trimming a wick, the claim, however justified, will remain abstract and theoretical, lacking all experiential force. The parent himself may easily lose sight of it, becoming convinced that he must work to "make money" because "they" charge so much for the electricity which, in some better world, would be "free"—paid for, that is, invisibly, by someone's anonymous, invisible labor. The alienation which Karl Marx attributed to capitalism is real enough, no less so in lands governed in his name. It seems, however, far more the by-product of the forgetting which becomes so easy when the intermediate layer of technology obscures the living bond of love and labor between the human and his world, leaving him with no place, no role therein—unless it be that of the consumer whose greed justifies it all.

Diatribes against technology, so dear to the Romantics, are, alas, always deeply justified—and vastly irrelevant. The point is not that "natural" life is good while technology is bad. It is not even that simple technology is good while complex, automated technology is bad. Since the same technology can be used either to destroy or to protect the creatures who share this planet, the problem could be said to be one of the uses of technology. Beneath that, however, the deeper problem is one of forgetting, of the covering-up of the moral sense of the cosmos and of human life therein beneath a layer of artifacts and constructs. Philosophy has many tasks, yet in our age the task of bracketing and seeing, of uncovering the forgotten sense of the cosmos and of our lives therein, may be one of the most urgent.

2. Physis

The Gift of the Night

The night comes softly, beyond the powerline and the blacktop, where the long-abandoned wagon road fades amid the new growth. It does not crowd the lingering day. There is a time of passage as the bright light of the summer day, cool green and intensely blue, slowly yields to the deep, virgin darkness. Quietly, the darkness grows in the forest, seeping into the clearing and penetrating the soul, all-healing, all-reconciling, renewing the world for a new day. Were there no darkness to restore the soul, humans would quickly burn out their finite store of dreams. Unresting, unreconciled, they would grow brittle and break easily, like an oak flag dried through the seasons. When electric glare takes away the all-reconciling night, the hours added to the day are a dubious gain. A mile beyond the powerline, the night still comes to restore the soul, deep virgin darkness between the embers of the dying fire and the star-scattered vastness of the sky.

The night comes softly, almost imperceptibly. The darkness gathers unnoted amid the undergrowth, in the shelter of the hemlocks and beneath the boulders of the old dam, slowly seeping out to cover the ground. There is still light on high. Only down on the ground the splitting wedges, bright and keen through the day, melt with the shards of bark around the splitting block. Then it is time to gather up the tools, to straighten a body bent with the day's toil, and to look up from the darkling earth to the still light sky. It is the time of radiant maples.

The sun has not yet set: though its rays no longer reach down to the ground, they go on shining above it across the treetops, letting the shadows rise up among the trees and fill the valley. Contrary to legend, evening shadows do not fall: they rise up from the thickets as the sun edges toward the rim of the treeline. Only the tallest maples reach up above the pool of shadow and, for a few moments, catch the last rays of the sun. That is their moment of glory. All through the day they had merged with the profuse green of the treetops. Now they exult in the sunlight, radiant clusters above the darkened forest. It is a time to lean back and to give thanks for the miracle of the radiant maples.

Then the shadows rise up and drown the fire of the maples. The trees around the clearing gradually darken, their trunks merging into the curtain of the forest. There is still light in the air, diffused in the particles of dust and the droplets of moisture from the water tumbling over the boulders. There still is light, but a human eye cannot gather it. Neither can the tree trunks, the satin maples, the coarse oaks and the flaking cherries, nor the ageless, lichen-covered boulders. They stand subdued in the gathering dusk. Only the birches, the glorious great birches, focus that light. Their chalk-white bark comes aglow, rising out of the gathering darkness, white, glowing, glorious. Theirs, too, is a moment of immense wonder. I can understand why the good people of Shelburne, in the northern part of the state, erected no marble war monument but chose instead to plant great birches in memory of all who did not return. No monument could speak out the sorrow. Only the birches, glowing at dusk, can do that.

Then the birches, too, merge in the curtain of the forest. There is darkness all around, only high above the sky is still pale, outlining the black lace of the treetops and leading the eyes of humans, earth-bound through the day, up to the heavens. You would watch in vain for the stars to emerge from it. The stars do not emerge: they happen with the suddenness of a pinprick in the celestial dome. Many a night I have watched the sky, knowing full well where the first star would appear, yet have never seen it happen. Perhaps I rested my eyes momentarily, perhaps I let my attention wander. One moment there is only the unbroken sky, growing dark overhead. Then, without a transition, a star is there, bright and clear, then another and another until the entire wondrous dome sparkles with lights. That, too, is a moment of wonder, precious in our time. The stars do not insist: even the glare of a white gas lantern or the reflected glow of neon will drown them out. Only where humans respect the night can they see the wonder of the starry heaven as the Psalmist saw it.

The night has other lights as well. There are the fireflies of a summer night, the flies of Saint John to my ancestors, tracing their paths across the clearing in occulting flashes of cool green light. There are the mushrooms, glowing yellow in the tree stumps slowly reverting to humus. The lights of human presence are warm, a match struck among the trees, the glow of a cigarette, a flashlight. The lights of the night are as cool as the night to which they belong, Saint John's flies, mushrooms, the blue lights on the bog and the silver-white lights which apear, unexplained, deep among the trees. All through one August moon, one would appear each night after the last traces of daylight faded, always in the same spot atop the old dam, a cool, glowing disk the size of my palm. Was it the moon reflected on a damp leaf? A flake of silica in a boulder? Or a tobacco can dropped by a logger? I do not know. Several times I tried to walk up to a night light among the trees, carefully keeping it in view. Each time it would disappear before me. One night I drove in aiming stakes so that I could inspect the spot by daylight, yet I found nothing and gave up the effort. There are things which it is so beside the point to explain! It is much more important to cherish and give thanks for the lights that enrich the night. Explaining, making, those are the priorities of the day which conceal the world around us. In the dusk of a forest clearing, other things matter—to respect first, then to understand, only then, perhaps, to explain.

The night embraces the human and opens itself to him, though not in his role of *homo faber.* It belongs not to him but to its lights—the glow among the trees, the stars, the moon in its seasons. It rises slowly, a huge silver disk behind the tracery of branches across the river, until it swings up over the treeline and floods the clearing with liquid silver. The glow of the moon is less a light than a darkness rendered visible, revealing a nighttime world which light would dispel, a stilled world of hidden kinships. On winter nights, that is the time of silver beeches. All through the day, their gray, green-speckled bark merges inconspicuously with the forest. Only the liquid darkness of the moon brings them out, a silver filigree incredibly delicate in the night. That is the time to wander across the crusted snow, up the moonlit path toward the orchard, past the old cellar hole, watching while all that had stood out clear and distinct by daylight settles back softly in the reconciling darkness. There was day, and there was dusk. It is time to let the night come.

Dusk is the time of philosophy. Daylight, with its individuating brightness and its pressing demands, is the time of *technē*. In its light, the beings of this world stand out in insistent individuality. Even the forest comes to seem an aggregate of trees and human life an aggregate of discrete acts. Their intricate kinship, the deep rhyme and reason of their being, recede from view much as the stars pale before the sun in the daylight sky. It is a matter-of-fact world whose multiplicity calls for the *technē* of doing and theorizing to bridge its discontinuities with acts of utility and constructs of causality. By daylight, nothing conjoins the two white planks, planed smooth, unless it be an eight-penny nail or a construct like "lumber," the *hylē* of ancient Greeks. In the brightness of daylight, even philosophy becomes a *technē,* substituting the precision of analysis and the artifice of constructs for the insight of a philosophic vision.

Nighttime, by contrast, is a time of *poiēsis.* The soft darkness penetrates the soul, fusing all in an intimate unity. The tree trunks, so sharp and distinct by daylight, fuse into the single presence of the forest around the clearing. Only their uppermost branches stand out against the still light sky. Then the sky, too, darkens and the earth and the sky merge under the immensity of the starry heavens. The insistent multiplicity of daylight fades to triviality before the overwhelming vastness of the One. Nothing is left to do, to say: a human can only stand in silent awe and thanking devotion before the immense wonder of it all. Night is the time of poetry, when *dichten* overtakes *denken.*[1] It is the time of deep dreams.

Philosophy, the daughter of poverty and plenty, is born of neither time. It is, most fundamentally, the art of the intermediate vision, of the transition between daylight and darkness when the failing light mutes the insistent individuality of the day but the darkness of the night has not yet fused all in a unity. Certainly, philosophy, like *poiēsis,* must acknowledge the wonder of Being, lest it become trivial. It must, like *technē,* remain no less aware of the distinctiveness of beings, lest it become inarticulate. A philosopher insensitive to the vision of a Heidegger and to the rigor of a Quine would run a grave risk. Still, philosophy must do more; true to its birth, it must discern both the unity that structures the multiplicity and the multiplicity which articulates the unity. Its proper object is neither pure meaning nor sheer being but meaningful being—being animated by meaning, meaning incarnate as being. Its domain is the intermediate range between *poiēsis* and *technē,* its starting point and the condition of its distinctive possibility is the ability to see and grasp the *sense* of being. It is, primordially, the act of discerning the moral sense of life suspended between the poles of the speechless wonder of Being and the empirical datum of beings.[2]

That is why dusk is the time of philosophy. The *technē* of the day can teach us the factual difference between life and death in the order of time and instruct us in the skills of inflicting the one and preserving the other. *Poiēsis* can teach us the profound indifference of life and death in eternity and give us the wisdom of reconciliation to the one or the other. Philosophy must undertake the far harder task of discerning the rightness of time, of time to live and time to die. For if our choice of living and dying—and all the choices of right and wrong, good and evil—are not to be arbitrary, we must discern more than the empirical difference and the poetic indifference of life and death. We need to grasp their rightness, the moral sense which emerges when the fading daylight no longer blinds us to the deep bond among beings but darkness has not yet obliterated their distinctness. It is at dusk that humans can perceive the moral sense of life and the rightness of the seasons.

In the global city of our civilization we have banished the night and abolished the dusk. Here the merciless glare of electric lights extends the harshness of the day deep into a night restless with the hum of machinery and the eerie glow of neon. Unreflectingly, we think it a gain, and not without reason. We are creatures of daylight, locating ourselves in our world by sight more than by any other sense. We think of knowing as seeing. Light and darkness belong among our most primordial metaphors of good and evil. Darkness has ever appeared to us as the shroud of evil deeds. Ever since the dawn of history, humans have struggled to kindle a light against the darkness, making it, too, a place of works of charity and necessity. The unsleeping lights of the Monadnock Community Hospital, casting an auburn glow over the white pines below, may well appear to us as a symbol of human triumph over darkness.

Those lights are deeply good, as good as the labor of all who keep vigil by their glow. To think of them as a triumph over darkness, however, is far more problematic. We have thought in those terms for so long that night has come to appear alien and threatening, an enemy to be banished, no longer a place of our being. Yet half of our time on this earth is, perforce, lived in the night. Might we not do better to teach ourselves to think of the lights we make as a human way of dwelling at peace with the night?

As long as kindling a light meant no more than lighting an oil lamp, that question might well have appeared academic. The night was so vast and our lights so faint within it that we needed have no fear for its integrity. An oil lamp does not violate the night. The house is still dark and at peace, only over the table a golden circle of light inserts a sphere of human doing, at peace with the enfolding darkness. The lights of recent years, gas lights and electric lights, are qualitatively different. They flood the room, giving us the godlike power of banishing the night—without, however, God's wisdom in using it. For the most part, we do not use our lights specifically to illuminate a nighttime task. We use them generically, to banish the night. We flood our rooms with it, even the unoccupied ones, and surround our dwellings with floodlights, creating the illusion of a perpetual day.

Yet we are not only creatures of the light. We are creatures of the rhythm of day and night, and the night, too, is our dwelling place. Darkness enriches even our days. Pure light would blind us: our perception depends on discerning contrasts, the interplay of light and darkness. Without the rhythm of day and night, of going forth and resting, our lives would flatten out in unchanging monotony and our philosophy in an undifferentiated *technē*. It is good, deeply good, to kindle a light in the darkness, though not against it. There must be also night. Philosophy needs to recover the darkness that comes not as a menacing stranger but as a gift of the night, the time of philosophizing.

There is a second task as well—to reclaim the gift of solitude. For most of us, even to think of solitude as a gift requires an effort. We fear solitude no less than we fear darkness, and have striven no less strenuously to banish it from our lives. We are convinced that truth is in communication, as we are convinced that there is seeing only in light—and, again, it is a part of the truth.

Yet a part only. Philosophy must speak, though if it would speak of aught but the turmoil of our passions, it must first hear and see, and that is not a task for crowds and committees. The consensus of a crowd can constitute a conventional world far too readily, far too soon. Husserl's analysis of the intersubjective constitution of "objective" reality is no speculative construction.[3] It is a description. When two or three are gathered together, they seldom have the patience of letting be, of listening and seeing. All too eager to speak, they constitute, in their consensus, a conventional image which they interpose between themselves and the living world around them. The small creature who darts across the clearing is promptly labeled with a name and the identification confirmed: it is a *burundík*—a chipmunk, if there is an English speaker among us—and its behavior explained in biological or psychological categories. Deafened by consensus, we lack the humility to watch the chipmunk, busy at his tasks, to let him present himself. He remains as unseen as the *Ding an sich* in its autonomy,[4] as the fiery crowns of the maples and the silver tracery of the beech to a crowd of revelers trampling through the forest. The intersubjective consensus establishes something very like a collective solipsism. Speakers, seconding each other, constitute a shared, internally determined monad into which the world can enter only in predetermined categories. Within it the human has nothing to save him from his knavery and folly, now sanctioned by the consensus of consenting adults. A philosophy which begins with a consensus will not easily penetrate beyond the shell of our collective monad. To do that, we must first suspend that consensus in the radical brackets of solitude.

Without an Other to lend his conventions the weight of objectivity, a human cannot impose them upon the world quite so easily. Perhaps in the transient quasi-isolation of a book-lined study, a human can fantasize a reality of his making, since there is not only no one to second it but also nothing to challenge it. The deep solitude of the gray wintry ocean or of the summer forest is different. Here nature presses in. It is too vast for the human to outshout it, too close for him to withdraw from it into speculation. The world the human confronts here is not the phenomenal world, a convention of a human community or a speculative construct of studies and laboratories. It is, in a Kantian term used in a thoroughly non-Kantian way, the *thing in itself,* present to be acknowledged, making its own demands.[5] Solitude is the great liberating gift from which philosophy can be born, not as the way of seeming but as the way of truth.

Yes, "two are better than one, for they have good reward for their labor," as the Preacher tells us,[6] and his words have lost none of their validity. All beings need, deeply, the company of their kind. But as it takes darkness to understand the light, it takes solitude to realize how fundamental that need is. In a crowd, the fellowship of kindred beings can appear as no more than a convention—a marriage, say, as a contract for the exchange of services that can be abrogated at will and convenience, lightly entered into and lightly left. In the stillness of solitude, the vision is deeper: the bonds that bind humans to their kind stand out as sacred, a fundamental law of all being, vital and moral alike, precious in its wonder. The bluejay and his mate honor that law, perhaps unknowing, as they build their nest each year in the tangled hemlock. The porcupines know it, in whatever way porcupines know, as they raise their young. It would be a desperately impoverished vision of nature which did not see, acted out in it, the wonder of the intrinsic sense of life. Two *are* better than one: the beauty of the trillium is not fulfilled in seeing alone, only in a vision shared. Only where life is shared can it be fulfilled and renewed. Yet even the wonder of sharing can remain concealed in the everydayness of crowds unless humans dare yield their pride of place as the makers and the measure of all things and are willing to encounter the presence of reality humbly, as dwellers, in the great solitude at dusk.

I know that I cherish the visits of my kind. The stillness of the house fills with human presence. The earthenware pitcher, filled with the fruit of the vine, focuses the open sky and the good earth, the glimpse of the holy and our own humanity.[7] There are songs, the wistful songs of the Moravian plains, the defiant songs of the Slovak mountain lads, songs of memories, songs of the land. A people that had no songs would soon grow one-dimensional. A written text may speak about its subject, but a song recalls it, relives it, shattering the solipsistic enclosure of the here and now.

The visits are intensely good. The evenings seldom end before the moon is high, the forest still and the pitcher empty. But then it is time to kindle the lantern and light the visitors up the path, past the cellar hole and the old orchard and onto the road. They fire up their motorcars, breaking the stillness and blinding the night with their headlights. The logging road that had rested at peace in the moonlight comes alive, suddenly leading to the highway and on to the city where the sounds of human work never cease, the light never fades, and the monadic *Umwelt* of a human community seems to exhaust all reality.[8]

I have chosen to bracket that consensus. I shall follow the path through the cool darkness of the forest to the house. If there is a moon, I shall douse the lantern: the path is intimately familiar. The house will be still once more, at peace with the forest. Only the wine tumblers and the full ashtrays will recall the songs and the people who shared my evening, but those will soon be cleared away. The only sound will be the river outside the window. I shall climb up to the loft, pausing to look at the moonlit forest without, undisturbed by my presence. There are miles of woods all around, still, cool and moon-bright. An owl is awake, but the nearest human is miles away, in a different world. I am alone, and grateful for the gift of solitude.

For solitude, too, can be a gift of the night. The perennial question, "Don't you get lonely, all alone out here?" prejudices any answer by obscuring the distinction between solitude and loneliness. In our deeply ingrained prereflective image of reality, solitude has indeed become synonymous with loneliness, the state of being cut off from all that supports and sustains us, alone in an alien world. Having conceived of that world as dead matter, we think of other humans as the only possible companions. Then stepping out of the intersubjective monad of our human community, even for a passing moment, appears to us to constitute a state of being alone. We fear solitude: in a curious inversion, we tend to suspect pathological motives in those who choose it, prescribing crowds as a cure in the boundary situations in which humans through the ages had diagnosed a need for solitude. We strive, stridently and compulsively, to overcome it, turning on our radios not to listen but to dispel silence, and seeking out human voices in the same way, for the same reason. The solitary walker of our time would deafen the forest with the blare of a monstrous tape-deck. Yet all the while we suspect that the effort is vain. No less a thinker than Paul Ricoeur, in a moving passage in his *Interpretation Theory,* speaks of the "fundamental solitude of each human."[9] I have often pondered that passage. It is, admittedly, a passing comment. The focus of Ricoeur's work is not loneliness but communication. Still, like so much that Ricoeur has written, it goes directly to the heart of the matter. Ours is the age to which the essential loneliness of being-human seems so evident that it requires no elaboration.

On reflection, it seems a puzzling conviction. How could loneliness, the state of being cut off, be the *essential* condition of an incarnate being who already through his body is intimately a part of nature, who is conceived in the loving union of a man and a woman and who learns to speak in a human community with which his very identity is bound up? Certainly, in the life of a being who remembers and anticipates, there will always be contingent loneliness. All of that life and its world cannot be present at once. There will be significant others and cherished parts of the world who are absent, there will be someone who is *not there,* someone beyond reach or not responding. There will be love going out and disappearing in the vastness. We can, as dwellers in time, speak of *inevitable* loneliness. Inevitable, however, is not yet essential. The very fact that we experience the absence of another as a lack, a privation, testifies that it is an accidental, not an essential condition of our being. Only because being human is in its very core a being with others can the absence of a particular other appear as a deprivation.

Conventional explanations of the loneliness of our crowds rely, as a rule, on a catalogue of the objective conditions of life in a technological age. Technology, we are told, has displaced much of the casual daily contact with our fellow humans which is said to have characterized the pretechnological age. Barter and communal self-labor—four men around a threshing floor, bringing down their flails in time, make an appealing metaphor for anyone who has never actually tried it—have been replaced by cash exchange and automated production. Affluence makes possible individual housing, transportation, entertainment, while requiring impersonal, anonymous employment. An assembly line hardly makes for togetherness. We are oppressed by loneliness, or perhaps "alienated," we are told, because we have displaced the communal life of an earlier age with the individualism of a technological civilization.

All of that, to be sure, is true, and since our loneliness is real enough, it might sound like an explanation. We have, however, largely forgot the loneliness and the solitude of an earlier age. Walk the roads of New Hampshire and Vermont, the unpaved roads leading past isolated farmhouses set in a harsh, rocky landscape. Driving a car, you may think of them as constituting an idyllic rural community. Within living memory, however, they were an hour's walk apart. The general store, symbol of communal togetherness in our nostalgia, was two hours away by horse and wagon—a luxury when the strength of the horses was needed in the fields. Walk those roads, walk them long enough to start sensing the distance in terms of weary steps, of a tired team and a heavy load. Then you will sense the awesome solitude of another generation.

Humans in other ages knew as much or more isolation. They surely knew loneliness as well. Yet they seemed neither oppressed by it nor obsessed with escaping from it. What has changed in the way we experience solitude that it has become something to be dreaded rather than cherished?

A different experience, that of fear, may provide a clue. A person choosing to live alone must face the question, "Aren't you afraid, all alone out here?" as regularly as the question about loneliness. It reflects another preoccupation of our time. Objectively, it makes little sense. There are no ferocious beasts in the benign forests that have taken over the abandoned pastures of New England. As for criminals, those you are far more likely to encounter in the interstices of our cities where people, their prey, gather. The people who pose the question themselves bolt and bar the doors of their apartments and with ample reason fear to venture out in the street at night. Few of the solitary houses scattered on the unpaved roads have locks on their doors. A solitary walker following the moonlit wagon road past the bog and up the esker to the shadows of what remains of the old Spring Hill gristmill would have far less to fear than he would on an urban street.

The fear is groundless. Perhaps others who live alone have never experienced it. I know there is no need for it. Still, when I first came to live in the clearing, a fear was often near me. By day, the forest was mine; I was at peace, at ease with it. With the failing light, the mood of the forest seemed to change. I grew alert, tense. Working with a chainsaw at dusk, deafened by its roar and so deprived of the warning of sound, I would often spin around suddenly, half expecting to see . . . I never knew what. As the night closed in around me, I would withdraw into the clearing lit by my fire. Even after I framed the house and enclosed it, I put up curtains: for warmth, of course. Yet I know that more than once I drew them closed to hide the blank, dark windows through which the night was staring at me. None of it made sense. Supposing there were danger, a man in the woods is safer by far in the open, silent in the dark, seeing but unseen, hearing but unheard. I knew that, as I knew there was no danger. Still, I preferred the clearing and the walls of my tent. They were familiar, the darkness was alien. It was then that I wished for the company of my kind.

Today the darkness is no longer alien. The woods have grown familiar in their silences and their sounds. I have grown used to the stillness of the house and the square of moonlight on the loft. The darkness which at first seemed a threatening emptiness has come to be a presence. The loneliness of those long-ago months faded with the fear, transformed into solitude.

That, I am convinced, is the key to the experience. Loneliness is the condition of feeling abandoned amid an alien world, cut off from communication. Solitude is the condition of being alone in the presence of a living, familiar world, willing to listen to it, to see and to understand it in *Einfühlung* and *Eindeutung*, sharing in its feel and meaning. The constructs and artifacts with which we have surrounded ourselves, cited in conventional explanations, do not so much increase our factual isolation, perhaps just the contrary, but they do contribute to making the world seem alien. Typically, we no longer live outdoors, retiring within only for a purpose. Increasingly, we think of ourselves as living within enclosed spaces and do in fact so live, venturing out ever less frequently. Our effective world is a dead one, the darkness of nature's cycle of day and night appears to us alien, an intruder to be banished with lights.

Loneliness, the loss of solitude, is the price we pay. Yet solitude need not be loneliness: it can also be the cure of loneliness. It is not a matter of "learning to live without others," but rather of learning to live with nature and others, not outshouting them with our insistent presence, but being instead ready to see and hear, in love and respect. For, in understanding as in sense perception, it is when we stop speaking that we begin to hear; when we stop staring, things emerge before our eyes; when we stop insisting on our explanations, we can begin to understand. As solitude dissolves the opacity of our collective monad and the dusk lights up the moral sense of life, humans can begin to see.

The pattern, finally, is all too familiar. Having taught ourselves to conceive of our world as dead matter in meaningless motion, we experience solitude not as communion but as isolation amid lifeless, alien surroundings. Having conceived of our world as alien, we dare not trust it: we flood it with lights, blind to all but the products of our own labor therein, absurd in its self-serving futility. To grasp again the moral sense of our being, a second bracketing is needed: the bracketing of crowds which would enable us to recover the second gift of the night, the gift of solitude.

Darkness and solitude are both gifts of the night. There is, though, a third paradoxic gift, perhaps the hardest to accept—the gift of pain. It is a gift to philosophy because understanding is ultimately not only *Eindeutung*, but also *Einfühlung*, sharing not only understanding but also emotion.[10] A human needs to open himself—or, perhaps, needs to *be opened*—to the joy and pain of the other. Along with the paradoxic gifts of solitude and darkness which for three centuries we have taught ourselves to regard as enemies, we need to appropriate a third paradoxic gift, the gift of pain, integrating it into the rhyme and reason of our being.

Like darkness and solitude, pain, too, appears to us as an enemy, a feared intruder in the bright, communal and painless world of our daytime aspirations. Though, theoretically, we are not unaware of its place in the economy of our lives—the pain which warns of potential injury is the example most often cited—we seldom try to understand it. We have committed ourselves, with a passion, to eliminating pain and that is, surely, a most laudable endeavor. There is such a vast surplus of pain in the universe, corroding life and absorbing energy that would be well used for joy, praise, and thanksgiving. Pain *ought* to be relieved: there is something perverse about a person who is capable of feeling infinite compassion without lifting a finger to alleviate the pain. Humankind have, far too often, resigned themselves to bearing pain in the name of wisdom long before they exhausted all possibilities of alleviating it in the name of charity. Surely no human effort is more noble than that which dedicates itself to the reduction of the immense surplus of pain in the cosmos—and no perversion more despicable and pitiable than those relished by the Marquis de Sade and the Ritter von Sacher-Masoch.

And yet, greatly though the works of mercy should be praised, were we to conceive of pain simply as a dread and incomprehensible enemy and of our task simply as one of its elimination, we would condemn ourselves to failure. We should, in our preoccupation, be ruled by pain, living in dread of it and fascinated by it. We should, as indeed we do, cease asking ourselves, "Would it be good?" restricting ourselves to the timid inquiry, "Would it hurt?"—and voluntarily surrender much of the greatness and the goodness of life because it brings pain or effort with it. We should, as indeed we do, drug ourselves to insensitivity—and turn to the horrible blasphemy of inflicting and bearing pain for pleasure or to reassure ourselves that even in our drugged stupor we are still capable of feeling something. For all of that, we should fail, as indeed we are failing, for pain is not an alien intruder that could be shut out of a sunny, companionable, and painfree life. Like solitude and darkness, it is an intrinsic part of the rhyme and reason of all life. Until philosophy can learn to accept it, too, as an intimate part of life, one of the paradoxic gifts of the night, it will remain inherently incapable of seeing and grasping the moral sense of a life which includes it intrinsically. It will remain where not nature but Thomas Hobbes placed it, in the bondage of "two sovereign masters, pleasure and pain," a bondage so integral to the artifact world as to appear "natural." To be free of that bondage, we need not only a different view of pleasure, encountered in the solitude at dusk, but also a radically different vision of pain, not as an intruder who will enslave us unless we banish it, but as kin—and a paradoxic gift of the night. Here philosophy needs to learn from *poiēsis*, whose vision of the profound kinship of pain and joy sees beyond the implacable opposition in which daylight's *technē* places them.

Still, philosophy is not *poiēsis*—its task is not only to sense the dark unity of all being but to discriminate within it. For philosophic reflection, the best starting point for learning to live with and understand pain, accepting it as a gift, may be precisely the recognition of the effort to eliminate and alleviate pain as a moral demand. Humans *may not* consent to the surplus of pain. To give it battle is a common human task, as basic as the distinction of good and evil. Any attempt to reach a philosophic understanding of pain which fails to start with a clear acknowledgment of that basic recognition and commandment must inevitably be suspect. Alleviation must be the first answer to pain.

In the global city of our civilization, that first answer might easily appear as the whole answer as well. The blueprints of the alabaster city we have been building since the Enlightenment include, among its principal features, freedom from darkness, solitude, and pain. The dream of the alabaster city, unsleeping in its perennial day, where mass communication dispels solitude while chemistry and automation render life painless and effortless, is turning into an inhuman nightmare before our eyes, as much and more by its successes as by its failures. In the pain of its collapse, its inhabitants are once again, as so many times before in the history of our culture, turning from the pride of their works to the green, living nature where the world is still God's world and God is never far, where there still is darkness, solitude—and also effort and pain.

Why should that be? I doubt not for a moment the reality of the *vis medicatrix naturae,* the healing power of nature, even on the most mundane levels. The dominant colors of a forest clearing are green and light blue, both of which, as empirical psychology can attest, have a distinctly soothing effect on humans. The decibel levels here are geared to the tolerances of the human nervous system. The effort required by daily tasks, whether drawing water, building a fire, or making wood, provides regular physical exercise and has a beneficial psychological effect as well, building a sense of competence and confidence—the "mastery" of psychological lore.[11] The diurnal cycle, undisturbed by electric power, assures a healthful alternation of activity and rest, while, together with the phases of the moon and the seasons of the year, it gives life a rhythm it lacks in the unchanging urban environment. The environing world of a forest clearing is calm and unjarring, living its own familiar life, so unlike the threatening, unpredictable environment of the artifact world. Want to hear more? Read Tolstoy, Thoreau, Rousseau—or Vergil, long before them.

It is, incidentally, all quite true, good, and useful altogether, yet it is really not to the point. Perceived in terms of its alleged and freely admitted healing power, nature remains locked in the urban perspective, another artifact, albeit one "naturally" produced or created by God rather than man-made, serving an urban purpose much as a mountain village may serve as a "natural" sanatorium for a convalescent. It is to be praised and it is to be valued, yet the nature which presents itself to a dweller in the solitude at dusk is not such a natural artifact. Its tasks are not those of the city and its power is not simply the *vis medicatrix naturae* of the natural sanatorium. Its power is that of absorbing, not of avoiding pain.

There is, in fact, a great deal more rather than less mundane pain in living close to the land. There are the perennial cuts and bruises of the day's work, the hands and the ankles mangled in working with wood and stone, the raw, chapped hands of the winter, the blackflies and mosquitoes of the summer, the joints aching with dampness in the spring and fall. Nor is relief nearer. In the logging season, it would take a major disaster to bring work to a standstill for a trip to the hospital. Many of the injuries which keep urban emergency rooms busy warrant no more than a kerchief pressed to the wound and a wave of the hand. It is not that pain hurts less here. It does not, nor do wounds reopened by the strain of continued work heal more quickly. The pain simply *matters less.* There is so much more that matters. When humans no longer think themselves the measure of all things, their pain is no longer a cosmic catastrophe. It becomes a part of a greater whole.

The power of absorbing pain is not the healing power of nature which the convalescent seeks in "nature's sanatorium." It is the far more precious gift of a changing perspective, undoing in a small part the ill effects of Descartes's and Kant's Copernican revolution. Alone among artifacts, source of their meaning and of all value, the human is indeed the center of his universe—and his pain, be it a bruised hand or a bruised heart, appears to him as an event of cosmic significance, as if God the Creator had burned his hand creating a volcano. In the solitude at dusk, the world which presents itself to the dweller is not a world of his making, nor does it derive its meaning from him. He is not its center but a dweller within it.

There is pain, but there is also so much more. Even the task of avoiding or alleviating pain, while no less basic, acquires a wider context. It becomes a matter of judgment: is the relief, good in itself, worth the price it would demand? Is the comfort of the drug worth the loss of sensitivity it exacts? Is avoiding the discomfort of the cold worth the price of giving up the sight of the January full moon rising behind the bare darkened trees? The point in each case may be moot but the question is at least raised. Perhaps our urban lives are so poverty-stricken also because the question appears answered: we have taken it as evident that the avoidance of pain, discomfort, and effort is our one, all-overriding task. Displacing ourselves from that Hobbesian bondage can have a liberating effect.

That recognition, however, can be taken as no more than sound prudent advice, acceptable within the limitations of a hedonistic calculus, without a radical displacement. We can and often do conclude that some things, though troublesome, are worth the trouble. The gift of the night is of a different order, a reconstitution of perspective in the face of the sorrows of finitude. It includes all the pain of life broken and love laid waste, of the helplessness of longing and the remorse of guilt, the hopelessness and pity of pain and destruction which cannot be undone, all the grief that a human can neither accept nor avoid. It is the pain of the spirit, but a human is a spirit incarnate. The pain spreads from the spirit to the mind and on to the body, settling as an aching lump on the chest and pressing on the heart. It is a pain that cannot be cured, a crushing pain that must be borne, so much of it in the lives of humans that, to Unamuno, it became life's very sense, the tragic sense of life. There is so much pain.

Following the strategy of ordinary pain, humans can try to escape grief, but all the strategies of escape share a common trait: the price is our humanity. Humans are beings who can remember and bear responsibility for their acts and enter in shared feeling and understanding into the life of the other. They can escape the burden of pain only by giving up those traits—committing, in effect, a suicide in body, mind, or spirit. Even forgetting cannot but be a self-destruction: a human escapes the grief of loss only by surrendering the truth, beauty, and goodness of what is lost. The more intensely he remains human, fully human, the more insistently does the pain go with him.

The sorrow and the pain go with him even when he leaves behind the neon and the asphalt: if the solitude at dusk is not to be the place of self-loss but of discovery, it must be a place of remembering, not of forgetting. Away from palliatives and distractions, the pain does not subside: it stands out in all its purity, purged of all self-justification and self-pity. What remains is pain, pure and clear as a bright crystal. There is no distraction, no escape. And yet something does happen, slowly, silently. The grief does not grow less beneath the vast sky, only it is not reflected back. Artifacts reflect grief. Having no meaning other than that with which humans endow them, they are charged with their pain. The forest is different. It lives, it absorbs the grief. On moonlit nights, the river, low in the summer, turns to silver, cascading over the dark, half-exposed boulders. It absorbs the grief that hangs suspended over the clearing, bearing it downstream from the land, washing the land clean, dispersing the pain into the cosmos. The river, the silvery, dreamlike river, absorbs the grief.

A human alone, surrounded by the gleaming surfaces of his artifacts, cannot bear the pain. He can do that only when the grief can disperse, radiate out and be absorbed. Fellow humans and their works, bearing the same burden, cannot absorb it. Grief and remorse are reflected from them, ever reinforced, until the human, crazed by pain, strikes out and kills those around him or himself, or both. Murder and self-murder are the futile, desperate human ways of dealing with the vast surplus of grief that is never lifted off, reconciled.

To reconcile, that is what the forest does, silent and accepting, as if God were present therein, taking the grief unto Himself. When humans no longer think themselves alone, masters of all they survey, when they discern the humility of their place in the vastness of God's creation, then that creation and its God can share the pain. For the Christians, the Cross symbolized that reality; confronted with it, the human is not freed of grief, but he is no longer alone to bear it. It is taken up, shared.

That is the age-old wisdom of the Book of Job, not of the folktale of the good man tested and, ultimately, rewarded for his faithfulness with even finer progeny and kine, but of the meditation on suffering which a later writer inserted into it. Job's counsellors exhaust all the conventional explanations; the zealous young Elihu offers the best that the rabbinic orthodoxy of his time had to offer. Yet that is all still the conventional wisdom of the collective human monad. When God speaks, the framework is different. He speaks not of pain but of the vastness of the creation, of the gazelle in her mountain fastness and the mighty creature of the deep sea. God is not avoiding the issue. He is teaching Job the wisdom of bearing the pain that can neither be avoided nor abolished but can be shared when there is a whole living creation to absorb it. That healing power then is no longer the *vis medicatrix naturae*. It is the *vis medicatrix Dei*.

When the human, in the solitude of dusk, surrenders his pride of place and learns to bear the shared pain, he can begin to understand the pain that cannot be avoided as a gift which teaches compassion and opens understanding. Seen out of pain, the porcupine in the clearing is no longer the object of our sovereign biological observation. He becomes a cherished fellow being who helps bear the pain. As solitude dissolves the monad of our conventions, pain borne and shared dissolves the monad of our pride and self-righteousness. Happiness, to be sure, can also be generous, but as it opens to the other, the opening tends to be unidirectional. In its generosity, happiness can also be insensitive and self-righteous. Pain borne and shared, not imposed on the other but freely accepted by him, teaches the human his own insufficiency, his own need and, with it, gentleness. It opens him to receive, in empathy, the gift of the other, not in censure but in gratitude and love. The blindness of time, judging in terms of what happens to aid or to hinder, must yield to the wisdom of eternity, which sees, behind time's pleasures and annoyances, the eternal value of every fragment of what is good, true, beautiful. It is when solitude dissolves the collective monad and pain borne and shared teaches the human to accept gratefully a gift freely offered that philosophy can begin to see the moral sense of the creation, of nature, the human's place therein, and of the God of it all. It is not simply in wonder but in love that philosophy begins. The paradoxic gifts of darkness, solitude, and pain are the radical brackets, the brackets of practical reason, which enable philosophy not only to speculate but to see.

Philosophy, as the ancients knew, begins with wonder. That wonder, though, is not puzzlement. It is, far more, the openness of one who no longer clings to the confidence of conceptual and technological mastery. It is the openness of one willing to see, to hear, to receive. Whatever the flaws of phenomenology—and they are a legion—there is a greatness in its courage of leaving the safety of preconceptions behind in its act of radical bracketing. It is, though, not only concepts that blind us but also the artifacts in which we have embodied them. That is why a radical bracketing must be a practical one, reclaiming the gifts of darkness, solitude, and pain. Those gifts enable us to see.

The Gift of the Word

There still is night, beyond the powerline, where the silvery moonlit river transforms pain into a gift. In the purity of the starry night, humans can see not only the mundane fact and the vast wonder, but also the *sense* of being. Nor see only: they can also speak of it. For here words are not intruders, interposing themselves as a veil between humans and being. That may so appear when we conceive of being on the model of our artifacts, as dead matter impelled by blind force. For if we conceive of being as meaningless, then there is no meaning to which our words could point. Inevitably, they appear arbitrary. Discourse would have first to create meaning and to impose it on the meaningless world so that, as Jacques Derrida[12] would have it, a discourse could describe nothing but the meaning it itself brought into being. Discourse can be more than the monologue of our species within its collective monad when, in the solitude of dusk, we recognize that what surrounds and penetrates us is not merely being but, primordially, meaningful being. As Paul Ricoeur reminds us,[13] something must be for something to be said—there must be meaning to which our words point, not as intruders or impositions, but as expressions of the meaning that stands out at dusk. The word is not philosophy's handicap. It, too, is a gift.

That, to be sure, is not a view with which most philosophers of our time would feel comfortable. Perhaps not since the days of Gorgias, at least as Sextus Empiricus reports his views, has Western thought labored under so profound a fear that, even if there were truth and humans could know it, they could never communicate it. The word, in our time, appears not as a gift but as a burden, concealing rather than revealing. Philosophers of a century ago seem naïve today, not in their views but in the innocence of their unquestioning confidence in their ability to speak of philosophy in univocal assertions. There is something wistful about the uncritical optimism with which Husserl speaks of "seeing clearly and articulating faithfully," as if the latter were no more than a matter of care.[14]

In that assertion, Husserl identifies, though perhaps unwittingly, the two cornerstones of the perennial, elusive vision of philosophy as a "rigorous science" which could settle our doubts once and for all. It would be a *scientia*, not shadowy opinion or precarious speculation but true insight, with a direct access to reality, and it would be *rigorous*, that is, so articulated that its assertions would be as univocally true as the insight they express, requiring only assent, not wonder. That vision involves an assumption about the nature of reality for which Husserl argues strenuously—that being is intrinsically meaningful being, not mere being on which meaning must first be imposed. It involves, however, a second assumption about the nature of language which, except for a few scattered passages, Husserl leaves largely unexamined—that language is a wholly transparent, nondistorting medium through which reality is present with the same clarity and immediacy as in lived experience itself.

Husserl's first assumption, about the nature of reality, is admittedly crucial and worthy of being argued. In it, Husserl confronts the basic fear of *skepsis* through the ages, that *there is no truth.* It is the fear that reality is either so utterly One that any finite affirmation about it is a distortion simply by virtue of its finitude—the night vision of *poiēsis*—or that it is so incurably Many that any universal affirmation about it is a speculative construct—the daytime vision of *technē*. Husserl's confidence in the possibility of philosophy as true sight and insight, as *scientia*, is based on the unshakable recognition that the eidetic structure of being, which we have been calling its moral sense, *is there* to be seen. Being is not Schrödinger's One,[15] an infinite presence defying finite comprehension. There is the "intermediate" level of reality between fact and wonder, the level of meaningful being.

Throughout his life's work, Husserl never wavered in his conviction that precisely that intermediate level is reality in its most primordial sense.[16] A discrete fact is an abstraction from it, a universal construct an elaboration of it. The basic datum, though, in the strict etymological sense of a pure experiential given, that which presents itself in experience, is the intermediate level of meaningful being. *Meaningful being*, not pure meaning or sheer being, is reality. More than any other discipline, philosophy can aspire to be a *scientia* because, without having to posit special regional criteria of relevance, it has presented to it, in lived experience, an intrinsically intelligible subject matter. The special sciences are special in the sense that, in order to carry out their work, they must impose upon experience or isolate within it a special perspective, choosing to see reality from the viewpoint of, say, chemical composition or of patterns of behavior and nothing else. The sense of being they seek is a special sense. Philosophy can claim to be the *scientia generalis* because it seeks to see and articulate the sense of being as it presents itself primordially, prior to the imposition of any special perspective or purpose. While Husserl's self-identification as a "positivist" may be misleading in the context of our terminological conventions, it is not arbitrary:[17] though not a positivist of putative "brute facts," Husserl is genuinely a positivist of meaningful being.

The encounter with nature in the radical brackets of solitude at dusk powerfully confirms Husserl's first assumption. Freed from the categories of our collective monad, nature and our life therein do present themselves as ordered and meaningful. There is an order, there is a moral and a vital law, there is a place and a task for humans therein. Abandoned by its human maker, our urban world may appear absurd. The forest, abandoned by humans, lives on in its ageless rhythm. The order, the sense, which stands out at dusk is what makes philosophy as the intermediate vision of meaningful being, between *technē* and *poiēsis*, possible in the first place.

It is Husserl's second assumption, left largely unexamined in his works, which is deeply troublesome—that the verbal articulation of the intermediate level of reality is nonproblematic, so that philosophy, like chemistry, can establish a terminology and a body of true propositions capable of claiming an autonomous validity that is independent of the lived experience they articulate. Husserl even posits that as the hallmark of science and bids philosophy strive for it.[18] In that injunction, he focuses the second assumption underlying his project: that in a *faithful* verbal articulation nothing is added to and nothing subtracted from the experience so articulated. Though seeing and speaking may be modally distinct, their content can, in principle and with sufficient care, be identical.

That confidence is hard to sustain today. Its foundation, through the centuries, was a conviction of the adequacy of the analogy of proportionality as a means of extending the scope of language from an ostensive, mundane use to a philosophic one. Though, as Aristotle tells us, "being is said in many ways," on that assumption those ways are not wholly equivocal. As a man can be said to be one, good, or true, so can being—though in the latter case the sense of those terms is extended in the same proportion as that obtaining between the finitude of humans and the infinity of being. Conversely, those attributes can be predicated of both a man and a raccoon, though in the latter case their sense is decreased in proportion once more, this time the proportion of a personal and a solely vital being. The analogy of being here assures an analogy of meaning.

Humans who see themselves and the nature around them as God's creation, lovingly crafted in His image, have little difficulty with the analogy of being. Once, however, we see the world around ourselves as the arbitrary product of a cosmic accident, we have no guarantee of an analogy of being. With that confidence waning, little ground is left for a confidence in the analogy of meaning. The ever more vehement announcements of the demise of metaphysics—Kant's, Nietzsche's, Heidegger's, most recently Derrida's and Rorty's—may well reflect less a conviction that nothing is than the all-corroding fear that nothing can be said—that, though language retains an internal sense, it is incapable of a referential meaning extending beyond merely factual or merely formal reference. All that seems to remain for humans is to speak of fact in the sciences and of language in philosophy.[19]

We need not, to be sure, accept the extreme linguistic preoccupation of our time. Like the idealist assumption that seeing can only be a seeing of seeing, the linguistic assumption that speaking can only speak of speaking, though capable of making significant contributions to our understanding of language, seems a transient fashion. It may well be based on a misapprehension not uncommon in the history of philosophy, the confusion of the medium with the message. Even so did the materialists of a century ago note that all finite being is incarnate in and as matter—that matter is its universal medium—and conclude that therefore matter is also the message. Noting that, say, love is embodied in a series of behavioral manifestations and a wheelbarrow in planks and hardware, they assumed that therefore love *is* a series of behaviors and a wheelbarrow *is* planks and hardware. They overlooked Melville's Queequeg, who had the planks and the hardware all assembled but, lacking the idea, did not have a wheelbarrow: he placed his sea-chest in it, hoisted it on his shoulder, and carried it down to the harbor. The researches predicted on the materialist assumption did make a significant contribution to our awareness of radical in-carnation. The way in which nineteenth-century thought and policy breezily ignored material factors seems naïve and unacceptable today. Where, however, the materialist confusion of the medium with the message became the basis of thought and practice, the results proved disastrous. Analogously, we could say that in our time, with its vast increase in communication, we, rather like the Greeks with the expansion of their seaborne commerce, have been made forcibly aware that all meaning is embodied in language and have assumed that here, too, the medium is the message—that *die Sprache spricht,* that it is the language itself that speaks.[20] Since a philosophy reduced to a study of speech acts can be far more easily presented as a *technē,* such a conception is understandably appealing to a technological age, and can significantly increase our understanding of the medium—so that we would not confuse it with the message. Those very contributions, finally, reveal rather than conceal the inherent vacuity of language stripped of its referential function and of the intent to communicate.[21]

Still, even if we reject the extreme assumptions of the philosophy of language, it is hard to recapture Husserl's unproblematic confidence in the intrinsic neutrality of language and the possibility of "faithful articulation." While speaking is surely far more closely linked to experiencing than conventionalist philosophers of language would have us believe, it is also more distinct from it than the nineteenth century assumed.

The radical brackets of solitude at dusk bring out both the continuity and the divergence of speaking and being. In a forest clearing, the word is not an intruder upon experience. Nor is its function restricted to naming, whether as objectification or as a passive conceptual mirroring of discrete entities. For that is not how reality presents itself. The reality of the pole bean or of the porcupine is never their momentary presence. It is the *sense* of the cycle which is the life of the bean, from planting to bearing, or of the porcupine through all the stages of his life. Words do not merely mirror—they reach beneath the transient surface to grasp the enduring reality it manifests. So, too, with the sense of a human life. Words are the way in which that sense, the very reality of that life, emerges through the manifold doings of the seasons.

I have become keenly aware that I live my life in words. Through the days of work in the forest, the long evenings before the house, and the poetry of the nights, the experiences I live never take the form of a speechless wonder. I speak out my life as I live it. It is not the case that I first live, then verbalize. It would even be inaccurate to claim that I am "simultaneously" living on one level and verbalizing another. The two modes, living and speaking, are indistinguishable. Even when I took to writing out what I was living, introducing a temporal lapse, I was never aware of a gap or an incommensurability of the two modes. What I was writing *was,* indistinguishably, the experience, not a set of statements *about* it. More than anything else, it was that awareness of convertibility, constantly and powerfully present, that convinced me of the fundamental truth of Husserl's conviction that there is no inherent contradiction but rather a continuity and a congruence between word and experience, meaning and being.

When, however, I first started translating my notes into English and focusing on the text simply as a text, a code to be processed, edited, and recoded, I became aware of something else as well. It was not the putative impossibility of translation. Even though I could not detach the experience from *a* language, living or reliving it nonverbally, there was yet an experience, with its own distinct sense, constant through several languages and not reducible to a particular linguistic expression.

The difference between the text and the experience was of a different order. The experience I lived was fundamentally and profoundly an experience of the *sense* of life, the *sense* of nature. That intermediate level of meaningful being is what I saw and put into the text. That, too, is what I encountered in the text when I was rereading and reliving it as a reader. It was when I approached the text as a translator, a technician, that I found none of the intermediate dimension of sense in the words themselves. There were pages upon pages of minute descriptions of the world around me. There were the sixty pages describing the way the snow thaws and disappears at the end of the winter—the imperceptible receding of the snow level as droplets of water seep from the surface into the snow on sunny days, letting each layer of dust particles sink down on the earlier layer, now revealed anew, the reemergence of stumps and boulders long hidden, an inch at a time, as when water recedes, the unexpected patches of ground in the morning, bared by the warm wind, the snow-eater of March nights. Those were the notes of the first winter, with the house barely enclosed and firewood short, when spring came as a miracle, no longer expected. I put into those notes the anguish and the wonder of a hard winter and the equally hard-won insight into the invisible renewal that takes place in the thawing of the snow: the *sense,* even the *moral sense* of thawing. It was indeed there, in the text. The response of two widely different audiences, one Czech, the other American, to a few pages I published in the two languages,[22] confirmed it. My readers responded powerfully to a philosophic vision of sense. Yet the text, simply as a text, a code, contained on the one hand only factual statements which any accession librarian would unhestitatingly catalogue under "Nature, descriptions of," and, on the other hand, reflections so abstract that the same librarian might be torn between "Mysticism" and "Platitudes."

That is the crux of the divergence between discourse and a text. Discourse is a subject's intentional act, inseparable from the intentionality of communication. Its components function as meaningful in the context of communications, as pointers evoking the intermediate level of sense. Seen as the components of a code, however, no words are intermediate.[23] Separated from the intentionality of communication, words are capable of ostensive definition as designators, labels attached to objects: a "rose" means this ⟶. Alternatively, they are capable of a formal definition in the context: as here used, "beauty" shall mean *X*. The level of sense remains suspended between the subject and the word.

In discourse, articulating lived experience, words function typically not by designating but by evoking the lived sense of experience. Cataloguing fact content or speculating about it is secondary. The discourse of personal communication is of a different order. It depends on the evocation of *sense*—not simply Goodman's "system of associated commonplaces," but on a reference to being as meaningful. For here words function no longer as designators, linked to a clearly identifiable referent. They now evoke not the content but the sense of an experience, speaking by indirection to bring it out.

Here it is hard not to wonder whether the conception of language which Cassirer labels "primitive" or "mythical"—words embodying experience, participating in it and representing it *pars pro toto*—may not in truth be far more basic than the factual, ostensive usage we tend to take for normative.[24] The detachment of the word from the lived reality it presents, while crucial for a whole range of tasks on the level of *technē,* may represent not an advance but a degeneration of linguistic usage for the purposes of a philosophy which seeks to grasp and evoke the sense of being. "Nominalism," in its original sense of regarding words as conventional labels, is a powerful and legitimate tool for special purposes, but highly questionable as an interpretation of significant human discourse. For here words do not mean autonomously, with reference to a conventionally defined special region. Rather, they mean as ciphers in Karl Jaspers's sense of that term: like the parables of the Gospels, they evoke an insight and so depend on the hearer's willingness and ability to see himself, to sense and feel the sense of lived experience to which they point.[25]

Statements of chemistry and physics are not of that order. Those are special sciences whose referential matrix is not lived experience as such but a special, conventionally defined set of principles positing a special regional ontology. It is the "nothing but" principle again: a chemist, working in his field, is not concerned with water within the totality of lived experience, water as such, but only in one specific aspect of it, say, nothing but its molecular structure. That is why the statements of the special sciences can be "exact": they need not depend on the evocation of lived experience, contingent on the hearer, but can refer simply to the conventional regional matrix of their endeavor.

Philosophy, in the terminology of another age, is a general, not a special science. Its referential matrix is not the regional ontology of a science but lived experience as such, as lived, prior to all regional delimitation. Its statements, contingent on a subject's lived experience, mean as they evoke an insight, and become meaningless when they are simply memorized and recited. Their task is to call up an experience, not merely to speak of it within a formally definable matrix, since it is the sense and not merely the fact of experience which is the proper object of philosophy. Take the experience of beauty, one of the most basic elements of being human. We cannot describe it directly, in designator terms. If we speak of beauty directly, we inevitably speak of a formal construct. To speak of the experience of beauty, we can only speak of an object as red, round, fragile, hoping that, as we evoke the experience, the hearer will grasp directly the beauty which is its sense. The goal is *Eindeutung,* a sharing of the sense of an experience in empathy. The same is true of the experience of value, of the sense of nature and, inherently, of the entire "intermediate" level of reality, the meaningful being which is the ground of philosophic reflection. In a real sense, philosophy is possible only because words are capable not only of designating but of evoking—or, in contemporary terminology, because they can function *as metaphors.*

That assertion ceases to be startling once we break free of our Aristotelian conception of the metaphor as a displaced use of a word, deviating from a putative "literal" meaning and capable of being replaced by words literally used with perhaps a loss of elegance but none of content. Even were we to admit a "literal" level of meaning, a metaphor still would not be mere deviant use. A metaphor does not describe a fact—it seeks to evoke a sense. To speak of the rosy-fingered dawn, as Homer does, is not an indirect way of conveying information about the hue of early morning clouds but a way of evoking the sense of the coming dawn. Or again, to speak of the agony of a falling tree is not to describe, however poetically, the facts of the case. Since it lacks a nervous system, there is at present very little evidence for positing sensations in a tree, nor is that the intent of the metaphor. Its task is, rather, to evoke the sense of the event, of the resistance of life to its inevitable demise. So, too, when we speak of God's mercy or engage in any nontrivial discourse: we are not describing indirectly a set of facts susceptible to a "literal" description. Our usage is not even analogically literal. We are speaking in metaphors, evoking the sense rather than the mere fact of being.

It is because of its dependence on metaphor that philosophy cannot be a *rigorous* science. The meaning of metaphoric usage is nonfactual and nonformal. Its effectiveness and accuracy remain contingent on the subject's ability to respond. Factual usage might be defined independently of any reference to a subject, in terms of the relation of words and the objects they designate. Formal usage can likewise be defined autonomously, in terms of the place of a term within a formal matrix. Metaphoric usage, however, remains as intrinsically subject-related as experience itself. Though we are heir to the texts of those who preceded us, we need to rediscover, relive their meaning. A text, once true but repeated without comprehension and no longer lived, loses its truth.

Still, though philosophy because of its dependence on metaphor cannot become a *technē*, it need not become solely *poiēsis*. It is capable of being genuinely a *scientia*, not speculation about but a clear, direct grasp of the truth of being. Metaphoric usage is appropriate to it because *reality is itself metaphoric*. It is the *sense*, not merely the fact or the theory, of being which constitutes its reality.

Nothing, finally, is as fleeting, as ultimately unreal as a "fact." The thousand daily tasks that act out, say, a marriage are imbedded in the order of time. In themselves, individually and collectively, they are trivial, capable of being replaced by a wholly different set. Nor is the reality of marriage simply the idea thereof, a set of obligations and privileges which could be itemized in a contract. All those are incidentals. The reality of a marriage is its sense, ingressing in time and giving meaning to fact and substance to idea. So, too, with the raccoon and the porcupine, no less than with my table or with the man that I am. Their reality is always their sense, intrinsically yet contingently embodied in this or that factual instantiation, in this act or this object at this time. We recognize that when we replace one table with another yet speak of it as the "same" table or when we darn away a silk stocking in worsted and still think it the same stocking. No less so when we treasure a gift not for its factual value but as a token: the "fact"—the concrete particular present in space and time—is a metaphor, evoking the living reality whose bearer it is. For philosophy, whose task is to speak of reality rather than of the contingent modes of appearance, metaphor is a "literal" usage and the most appropriate mode of speaking, best corresponding to the nature of its subject.

It is a great gift of the radical brackets that they enable philosophy to recognize in fact the metaphor of reality. The starry heavens so immensely high above the glowing embers in the fire ring are a metaphor. When the Psalmist writes, "the heavens declare the glory of God," he is not making a factual assertion about the stars appearing on the evening sky conjoined with a speculative theological one. He is, quite literally, evoking the reality of the presence of the heavens.

Philosophy at its most primordial, as the vision of the moral sense of being, can not only see but also speak precisely because a fact is a metaphor of meaning as much as a word. Its statements will, superficially, take on now the form of factual assertions, then again that of speculative abstractions, each with criteria and a validity of its own. Their true significance, however, remains suspended between those two levels, as an awareness of the moral sense of life which it does not teach but evokes in its hearers. When Robert Czerny entitled his translation of Paul Ricoeur's monumental work *The Rule of Metaphor,* the title he chose may not have been a mechanically faithful rendition of the original *La métaphore vive,* yet it was most apt. Metaphor is the rule of philosophic discourse and the condition of the possibility of speaking of the intermediate realm of the sense of lived experience, perennially suspended between the fact and the idea.

The moon is a metaphor, suspended between heaven and earth. It is a metaphor that, through the millennia, has been central to humankind. The diurnal cycle is too short to set life's rhythm; the cycle of the seasons in turn much too long. Though amid the crystal-pure austere black and white world of a January snowscape a human may theorize about the green profusion of the summer, he cannot evoke the lived reality of it. It is the lunar cycle, transforming the night after each day, which sets the rhythm of life. It is also the cycle most obscured by the lights of the city. An urban winter does still differ from the summer, an urban day differs from the night, yet all urban nights appear the same.

Beyond the powerline, the moon transforms each night with its phases. There are the nights of the new moon when the forest is swallowed up in deep darkness. Those nights belong to the stars, so high above, so bright in the dark night, immutable in their order, their grandeur evoking the moral law suspended between the sky and the human heart. I feel sure that it was on a night of the new moon that Immanuel Kant wrote his famous line and the Psalmist sang of the heavens declaring God's glory.

The nights of the full moon are different. They are no less dark, but by moonlight the darkness becomes visible. The moonrise first announces itself at the rim of the sky. At dusk, the sky grows dark as on a moonless night, merging with the rim of trees around the clearing, letting the stars shine forth. Then, imperceptibly, the stars near the horizon seem to pale as the sky changes color. It is not a light which could be reflected in the treetops—those remain in deep darkness. Only the sky turns from black to a deep blue and then a light greenish hue, almost yellow, not lighted, as by the sun, but becoming visible until the stars have faded and the stage is set.

The rising full moon does not "shine," it does not illuminate the forest. Even to say that it "glows" would not be accurate. All our words for lighting seem inappropriate. They are active verbs, suggesting doing, while the moon does not do. It lets itself be seen, not crowding out the darkness but rendering it visible. The sun transforms the world in its image, the moon evokes it in its primordial presence. It is by moonlight that I have seen, with a searing clarity, that Being is not convertible with nothing.

The distance between the lived reality of the glowing darkness on the nights of the full moon and the scholastic abstraction of the dictum, "Being is not convertible with nothing," measures the full span of the rule of metaphor. Both are metaphors, the latter a conceptual one, the former a "radical metaphor" in the sense which Ernst Cassirer understood so well, presenting reality *pars pro toto*.[26] The reality itself, however, is more than either, just as the sense of the two poles is more than either.

Pause, for a moment, over the notion of convertibility. The Scholastics used that term to designate those predicates of being which, though presenting Being in different modes, can yet be used interchangeably or "convertibly." Thus we can say that Being is one, true, good. Each predicate describes being from a different perspective, yet does not designate different "parts" of being—only, in Duns Scotus's term, its "formalities."[27] Being is equally and entirely one, it is true, it is good. Its oneness, its truth, its goodness can be predicated of it in its entirety, "convertibly," with equal truth.

To claim that Being is convertible with nothing would, similarly, mean that whenever Being is said, nothing can equally well be said, that the difference between Being and nonbeing is "formal" only. The claim is a time-honored one in the history of human thought. The very concept of Being as distinct from a plurality of beings suggests it. To speak of Being as such calls first of all for a negation or a bracketing of all particularity. Being as such is *not this,* it is *not this* and *not this.* Being is what emerges when all particularity has been bracketed, not a predicate common to all beings but rather what is basic to them all and not restricted to any or to the sum of them. But when we have negated all particularity, what is there to distinguish Being from nothing? Formally, at least, Being and nothing would then seem indistinguishable. The Holy of Holies is empty. The mystics testify that the closer they approach God, the more all particularity disappears as God comes to appear as all—and no thing. That is the vision of *poiēsis:* that of ultimate reality which can be described, convertibly, as Being or as nothing and whose unity renders the multiplicity of the many illusory.

Philosophically, however, that claim has some consequences which we normally fail to associate with it. For one, if Being were an undifferentiated sameness, then all distinctions would be less primordial than Being itself, arising and fading in the *history* of Being and relative to it. The notion of the convertibility of Being and nothing is intimately linked to all moral relativism and historicism, entailing it and being entailed by it. Most specifically, if the primordial reality is indifferently Being *and* nothing, then moral categories can claim no ultimate ontological grounding. The distinction of right and wrong, of good and evil, could then reflect no fundamental distinction in the structure of being itself but only a preference which emerges at a particular stage of history and, possibly, fades again in its time. Such a relativism, certainly, need not be at all trivial. It can even affirm the validity of certain norms for a particular period and situation, but it cannot affirm the ultimate validity of the fundamental distinction of right and wrong, of good and evil. If ultimate reality were, indifferently, Being and nothing, then moral distinctions would become ontologically relative. The profound relativism of the mystical vision of the unity of life and death would find a paradoxic counterpart in the vicious relativism of the mighty who use the interchangeability of life and death as a justification for murder.

There is, however, an equally ancient tradition which speaks of a fundamental asymmetry between Being and nothing. Saint Augustine is perhaps its most familiar spokesman. To him, nothing is not equiprimordial with Being. It is intrinsically secondary, contingent and parasitic on Being. *Ab initio,* Being *is.* Nothing occurs as a negation, as a disintegration or as a lack of Being. Moral categories, the distinction between right and wrong, good and evil, thus have a basic ontological grounding in the asymmetry between Being and nonbeing. Being is convertibly one, good, true; contradiction, evil, falsehood are negations, defects. Though the specific formulations of moral categories may change from age to age, their sense remains constant, reflecting its ontological ground. Even when we speak of those moral strictures which are admittedly valid only relative to a highly particular situation—say, sharing water in arid climates—they are *absolutely,* not only "relatively," valid where they obtain. Even though Lazarus will die again, it is absolutely good that he is raised from the dead. Even though a flower will fade or a word of truth will be forgotten, it is absolutely good that it is spoken, that it blooms. The affirmation of value has an absolute, not only a relative, worth, since the distinction of good and evil is not rooted only in history but in Being itself. To speak of the torturer and his victim as indifferently caught up in the same mystery of pain is not sophistication but blasphemy.

The difference between the two claims, that Being is or is not convertible with nothing, is absolutely crucial for all thought and practice. In the former reading, all distinctions, including philosophic ones, would appear as no more than cunningly devised fables of humans—and so susceptible to being overruled by human convenience, passion, or history. The sense of being human would be exhausted by its history. In Heidegger's terms, *Sein,* or at least *Dasein,* would be *Zeit:* the being of humans, even if not Being itself, would be wholly exhausted by acts and events in the order of time. By contrast, in the latter reading, morality and humanity would not be reducible to temporality. The line of value, the dimension of eternal validity, would intersect time in each of its moments, ingressing into time and opening it up to eternity.

The crucial choice between these two fundamental alternatives, however, cannot be made simply on conceptual grounds. It is a gift of the full moon, and must be so, since it is an experiential difference, not between the ways Being and nothing are thought but between the ways they present themselves. Considered strictly conceptually, Being might well appear formally indistinguishable from nothing, yet in lived experience the two are utterly, irreducibly different. Here philosophy needs not to speculate but to see.

The experience of Being is all around us, just below the fleeting particularity of what is. It is there in the trees that merge into a forest. At a first glance, the forest in the noonday sun presents a solid curtain of greenery latticed by the vertical lines of the trunks and the horizontals of branches. As you sit still, your eyes gradually begin to penetrate that curtain. The light patch that seemed a part of the laced front recedes—there is a shaft of sunlight deep among the trees. As you walk toward it, it recedes before you and the dense green profusion surrounds you. All about you there is the curtain of the forest, but as you look it parts and recedes. There is a nearness and a depth, drawing you in. You stand still in the stillness and realize it is full of minute life. First the insects, then the birds, then, in the thicket, you distinguish the movement of an animal. A snake, perhaps—the woodchucks and the porcupines are seldom abroad at this hour. Then you break a twig and startle at the noise. You, too, are a part of that green, living stillness of a summer noon. That stillness penetrates you: distinctions merge, the living stillness becomes a unity. It is all around you and in you. The hoary assertion, the Absolute is One, becomes an observation statement: you feel and see the unity of Being.

Darkness, too, can penetrate the soul, fusing the trees, the rocks, and the wandering human in a unity. In the forest it is seldom completely dark. Even on the starlit nights of the new moon there is light between the trees. As your eyes grow accustomed to it, the shapes of the trees and the rocks emerge out of what at first seemed undifferentiated darkness. You learn to see not straight ahead but circumspectly, out of the corner of your eye. It is there that the things obscured in thematic focus appear to you. The world of the starlit forest is soft and receptive. Its shapes blend, welcoming the wanderer who treads softly, who does not insist on being the center and the focus of the night. Then the forest enfolds you in a profound peace and there is the same feeling, the sense of the unity and fullness of life. It is not the experience of the darkened forest, the boulders, the path, or the solitary walker. All that has receded and a different reality has moved into its place, that of the fullness of Being. In such moments you sense it is always there just beneath the surface of the insistent individuality of subjects and objects, ready to rise up when their clamor subsides. You must not insist, you must not impose yourself upon it.

But if you are willing to listen, it is there, the fullness and the unity of life, the presence of Being—and it is one and good.

There are the opposite experiences as well. It was early in the year, when the hard freeze sets in after the January thaw. By the third night of the full moon after Epiphany the iced crust on the snowdrifts grew strong enough to support a man without snowshoes. I could range all across the land, even the corners that grow inaccessible with underbrush in the summer, across the two-dimensional moonlit world. The January landscape does appear two-dimensional by moonlight. The crusted snow evens out the ground, the blackened tree trunks and their dark shadows become undistinguishable. The trees, frozen through, ring out as their branches clash in the wind. It is winter, and freezing hard: in the forest only an occasional whiff of wind-borne smoke from my chimney disrupts the austerity of a January night.

On such nights the stove acquires a special significance. It is an old cast-iron Franklin with ill-fitting panels: the fire glows and breathes through the cracks. It takes three armloads of seasoned hardwood but the house remains warm through the day and the long night. Over the table a white gas lamp casts a cone of bright light on an island of books, drafts, page proofs, and scribbles. So I sit on winter evenings, warm between the glow of the stove and the light.

So I sat on the third night of the January full moon. The evening comes early: it could have been no more than a single stroke past seven when the full moon swung past the uncurtained window in the peak and cast a cone of cold white light into the room. Preoccupied with my doings, warm between the stove and the lamp, I hardly noticed it at first. Only gradually I grew aware of the immense, intergalactic emptiness bearing down on my house, leaning against the shakes, leaning into the windows, pressing down on the frozen forest and deep into the snow. The familiar things of my daily work disappeared, swallowed up in the vast emptiness. Only the moon remained, and the vast, cold emptiness of the space, the deep all-devouring cold, freezing all life, pressing down on me and demanding its own.

Something like a panic seized me. I sat, paralyzed, blinded by that vast emptiness. The warmth of my stove, the warmth of my body suddenly seemed utterly anomalous: the eternal emptiness of the cosmos, freezing all life, seemed the dominant presence. There was nothing. Somewhere in some inaccessible corner of my mind I was not unaware that deep under the snow were the humble denizens of the forest, the woodchucks, the beavers, the gentle brown mice; that in their season they would reemerge, the sun would melt the snow and the green world of summer spring forth once more. But that was theory. The present reality was the vast cold emptiness, leaning hard on the frozen world from the infinitely distant stars, demanding its own.

Suddenly it seemed an immense effort to restoke the fire. Why? I was living alone. I could not strike the spark of the divine eros, I could not renew life. Only when there are two, sleeping side by side, sharing dreams, does life renew itself. I could only live it down as a fire burns down, stick by stick, burning up a scant supply of dreams until there are no more and the cosmic cold reclaims its own. A man alone is a waste of good firewood, unable to resist the cosmic cold. It would be so much easier to stop the clock, douse the fire, and open the doors and windows wide, letting in the immense cosmic cold. There was nothing. Let there be nothing, let nothing be.

The moon passed by my window and the experience passed on with it, as suddenly as it had come. The familiar objects of my world reappeared, the cup with the flower design, the embroidered pillow, the blue snail of happiness, the old clock and my stove. I got up, selected a length of fragrant cherry and put it on the fire. There were once again things to look after, page proofs to finish, lentils to soak for the morrow, a wick to trim and a fire to tend. I walked out into the moonlit night. Even the moon was the familiar brother moon once more, lighting up my path to the orchard, outlining tiny tracks by the wood pile with sharp shadows: a wood mouse had been there before me. I walked slowly along the path, pausing occasionally to hear and to remember, giving thanks for the miracle of warmth, the miracle of life, for the fullness of Being. For what I had seen in the light of the cold January moon was the terror of sheer nothing—and it is not convertible with Being.

Gorgias was mistaken. There is truth. It may become obscured among artifacts which have no truth of their own, but it stands out clearly and unmistakably in the light of the full moon upon the silent forest, in the fullness of Being and in the terrifying emptiness of nothing. Those may seem convertible as concepts, since both represent a suspension of particularity. As experience, though, they are utterly different, and their difference categorizes all experience. One is the experience of life-sustaining fullness, the other of a life-withering emptiness. Neither is a *thing*, some thing or no thing. They are the double sense of Being which philosophical metaphors evoke in lived experience.

Can we, though, legitimately speak of the awareness of Being and of the confrontation with nothing as experience? If it is experience at all, is it not a rather "mystical" one? I should feel more confident of the answer if I knew just what is being asserted about an experience when it is qualified as "mystical." If "mystical experience" were to mean, as it often seems to, an inward certitude concerning a particular set of conceptual constructs, then it would indeed be suspect. But the awareness of Being and the confrontation with nothing are not at all like that. Both are far more closely analogous to the experience of seeing at its most ordinary, not the bestowal of some esoteric *gnōsis* but a recognition of something which simply is there, to be seen, to be grasped in a direct encounter, something overt, not hidden.

Neither of the experiences I have cited is, actually, very uncommon. Though our solipsistic age may prefer to register them simply in terms of their subjective impact—as, say, a "feeling" of overwhelming joy or of a withering dread—they are still common enough and freely accessible to all observers. They require no special apparatus or conceptual equipment or, for that matter, a consciousness "altered" in any esoteric sense. The shift in the level of awareness which they involve is not qualitatively different from the change of focus which we carry out routinely in ordinary experience and in the sciences alike. Thus, for instance, there is a difference in focus between observing a triangle as this particular figure, drawn in chalk on slate, and seeing the same triangle as an instance of an eidetic relationship among angles and opposed sides—or, for that matter, between seeing two Baldwins and two Jonathans as four apples and seeing that, in principle, two and two make four.

In that change of focus, our insight does not become "mystical," nor does it shift from some "outer" to an "inner" perception. We are still seeing the same lived reality, though now in a different focus or at a different depth. Nor is the shift from seeing the number of board feet in a mast pine to seeing its beauty essentially different. The beauty is no more in the eye of the beholder than the board feet of lumber. Both are there, waiting to be acknowledged—to be *seen.* So, too, is the fullness of Being, the one, the good, the beautiful, as well as the corrosive emptiness of nothing. In encountering them, we are not looking past reality or away from the "world": we are shifting our vision from the appearance to the reality of what is, from the fact to the metaphor. If that be "mystical," then so is the lumberjack's practiced grasp of the number of board feet in a butt log, an essential survival skill for all who work the woods. For *there is* Being, and it is not nothing. Experience, even at this primordial level, is not inchoate: there is a fundamental truth to it, and, as our reflection on the metaphor as a tool of philosophic discourse sought to show, humans can not only know that truth but communicate it as well. Humans have done so for millennia. Their discourse has never consisted solely or largely of factual observation statements. It has always included statements of insight of essential necessity, of beauty and ugliness, of right and wrong. The radical bracketing of the forest clearing powerfully confirms the validity of such usage.

The question that remains is of a different order. Why does the Georgian skepsis, refuted by argument and experience, still persist? What in experience lends it its plausibility? It is not plausible as the question of whether the truth can be spoken. It may, however, be plausible as the question of whether the truth can be *put into words*, captured by them and presented in them independently of the act of discoursing. Poets have always spoken the truth, and philosophers with them. The question now is whether, independently of them, philosophers can put truth *into* words.

Putting the truth into words is not the *intentio* of discourse. Discourse seeks to communicate by evoking an experience shared. It does, however, become a possibility when humans learn to transform discourse into a text—and far more so when they conceive of the text not as indirect discourse addressed to "you, gentle reader," but as a mechanism for the storage and processing of data.

What is at stake here are two fundamentally different models of communication. In the communication between two humans who share the fundamental experience of being moral subjects, the intentional thrust of the act of communication is the evocation of understanding and the basic technique one of evoking an analogous experience. The hearer can be said to have understood when he can, albeit vicariously, "relive" the experience. Thus the purpose of an exclamation such as "See the green table!" is not to have the hearer repeat correctly the counters, see, green, and table, but to have him look in the same direction and to duplicate the experience of seeing a green table, whether in fact or in imagination. The truth is not in the statement but in the experience to which it directs us. The hearer has grasped the truth when he is in turn able to say, "I see it, too," not when he can repeat it correctly.

The example need not be trivial. A lifetime ago, when my children were small, a tiny friend of theirs, rain-soaked and scared, knocked unannounced on our door on a stormy night. She drew a well-worn doll from under her coat and begged us anxiously, "Please save my dolly. Mummy wants to burn her." She disappeared as quickly as she had come. Only a year later, hiding behind a stack of canned soup in a supermarket, she whispered to me, "Mr. Kohák, how is my dolly?"

When last I saw that house, the dolly was safe, tucked away with my own daughters' old toys and a liberal sprinkling of naphthaline under the time-darkened rafters in the attic. That girl was an American. She will never have to live through the fate of central Europe a generation ago. But she will understand, as few of her compatriots can, the desperate love of women going to their deaths who could save their children only by giving them away. Human understanding is possible because human experiences, no matter how factually divergent, are yet eidetically analogous. In human communication, the purpose of words is not to contain experiences but to point to them and to evoke them.

The case, however, is quite different in the transfer of information between two computers. Computers have no understanding, having no lived experience which words could evoke. The information conveyed to a computer or transferred between one computer and another must be wholly contained in the words themselves. The experience must be literally encoded in bytes which point to nothing so that it can be decoded and reconstructed in a perfect duplicate at the other terminal. The process engenders no understanding, no vicarious reliving of an experience. It is not communication in the human sense of engendering shared understanding, only a transfer of a code which might do so when received by a human.

In human communication, there are innumerable occasions on which the transfer of accurately encoded information immensely facilitates the evocation of understanding. Anyone who has ever had the experience of having a poet try to convey, over a badly functioning telephone, instructions for setting up a 750 cc NSU engine can appreciate that. Zen is a desperately inefficient vehicle for communicating the art of motorcycle maintenance. This is a situation which calls for the accurate encoding of information.

The basis of Gorgian skepsis is not simply the fact that humans have developed, as a subcategory of meaningful communication, the skill of reducing knowledge to data which can be adequately encoded in a set of binary electronic signals, but that they have taken it as normative for all communication. Were it so, then philosophic discourse, using metaphor to evoke a lived truth, would indeed be defective and philosophy would have no task more pressing than that of devising ways of encoding data accurate enough to match the art of the programmer.

The point, though, is that it is not so. The inversion of what is normative and what is special is here a special instance of the more general inversion of recent thought which comes to think of conceiving of reality as matter-in-motion but as a special theory for special purpose, legitimate within the framework of reality encountered as meaningful, but as the norm of what is to be judged real. On that assumption, Gorgian skepsis seems irrefutable. The great gift of silent evenings in a forest clearing is that they dispel that illusion. Reality encounters us as a meaningful *kosmos*, only contingently reducible to a mathematical schema. The intent of discourse by which its adequacy must be measured is that of communication: the encoding of data in words but one of the tools, highly useful for some specific purposes, but by no means the norm of all valid discourse.

Humans, as Husserl points out, can know the truth because the truth, the sense of being, even the moral sense of life, is not a construct but a given of lived experience. They can speak about it because, as Jaspers and Ricoeur point out, words are not only designators but also metaphors capable of evoking experience and its sense. Husserl's call for faithful articulation, finally, is not vain, though faithful articulation in philosophy must take the form of an evocation of sense rather than of an encoding of data.[28]

As the sky grows light in anticipation of dawn, the trees once again stand out as black lace against it and the clearing opens up once more in the dissolving darkness. Then the Gorgian skepsis has little force. There still is night and the promise of a new day, and a truth which stands out in the transition. Humans can see it and speak of it, they can communicate it not in words that claim to contain the truth but in metaphors which evoke it. That truth is not the veridical factual assertion of *technē* or the mute wonder of *poiēsis.* It is more basic, as basic as the distinction between good and evil and the recognition of the moral sense of life.

The Gift of the Moral Law

There still is night, star-bright and all-reconciling. As it gathers softly beneath the hemlocks, muting the harshness of the day, there is also a truth that stands out in the dusk. It is not simply the truth of the great green peace of the forest. Though in the shipwrecks of our civilization we may seek refuge therein, resigning the distinctive task with which humans are charged and seeking renewal by sinking back into nature's green peace, the truth that stands out at dusk is a reaffirmation of our humanity, not an alternative to it. We can encounter that humanity, at times obscured and grotesquely distorted, yet still present, wherever humans dwell. It is there in the great city, in the love and labor of its dwellers, in their hope and fatigue, in the rhythm of their lives. The forest at dusk teaches no esoteric *gnōsis.* It only lets the universal truth of life stand out clearly, out of the darkness of forgetting.

That truth is never wholly separable from the experience in which it is incarnate. It is the truth *of* being human, not a truth about it. To speak of it authentically, philosophy must resist the temptation of posing as a *technē* and must not fear to invoke the metaphors which call up the primordial experience whose truth it is, as Plato did not fear to tell myths, provoking Aristotle's censure. Without metaphor, philosophy's assertions could not but ring hollow, true and trivial as abstract formalism which, at best, can claim to be a truth about, not the truth *of,* being human.

Yet neither can philosophy be only *poiēsis,* a wordless sigh of wonder. Faithful articulation of the truth clearly seen requires also the "mediate conclusions and idealizing procedures" whose legitimacy Husserl grudgingly admitted.[29] It must also attempt to generate intermediate categories, or better, to let them emerge, slowly, in the work of seeing, reflecting, and speaking, constrained by the double discipline of the reality it confronts and the demands of those to whom it would speak.

The moral sense of nature—that is such a category, and the words seem so fitting, so obvious when the nature is as near as a summer rain all about. Before I enclosed my house, my living space on rainy days was marked out by a tarpaulin stretched over the fire-ring and the stump that served as my desk. It was a radically open space, the sheets of rain forming its walls. The rain-fresh air flowed freely through it, mingling with the scent of my fire. It was then that the words came alive—the moral sense of nature.

In the autonomy of the text, those same words seem cold and distant. Once upon a time, the word *moral* seemed important enough for philanthropists to endow chairs of Moral Philosophy—though even then the intent of that designation was to distinguish the chair from one of Natural Philosophy. As for the word *sense,* in English it has never functioned as a philosophical category at all.

Surrounded on all sides by the living wonder of a summer rain, I needed that word. Perhaps it was because, thinking in Czech, I relied on the category of *smysl,* the meaningful presence of a reality, which in that use has no exact English counterpart. English philosophical usage has traditionally relied on the term *essence* to designate the incoercible, intangible something that makes a being the kind of being it is. Etymologically, that is not inappropriate. Derived from the word to be, *esse,* it indicates the distinctive mode in which a being *bes*—or, in our usage, its *sense,* the way it both acts out its role and presents its meaning in the economy of the cosmos.

In actual usage, though, the cluster of commonplaces associated with that word is all wrong. It suggests a mysterious component, distinct from the being itself, which that being is yet supposed somehow to bear within it and which might presumably be isolated, either conceptually or, as in the case of the essence of vanilla, chemically. Certainly no self-respecting philosopher would so define the term. Language, though, has its autonomy. Even were we to specify that we do indeed wish to use the term "essence" to indicate the integrity of a total meaningful presence of a reality, the living reality of a pine tree, a boulder, or a lumberman who stops by to borrow my chainsaw when a leaning hemlock had pinched his own, the word would betray us, evoking connotations of its own.

The term we need is one which would convey the integrity of the nature that surrounds the wall-less space of a tarpaulin on a rainy summer's day. Its being is not that of the material furniture of a region constituted by a subject's conscious presence. Nature is not simply there, as an aggregate of physical properties, not even if we think of them as bound together by a Berkleyan "I know not what." It has its own intrinsic sense, much as we can speak of the sense of a person's gesture or of the sense of a text. When Ricoeur speaks of reading the text of experience, the metaphor is apt.[30] In meaningful interaction with our world, we are reading the text of nature: encountering in it its meaningful presence. Its meaning is not an "essence" in our usual naïve sense, a mysterious internal component. Nor is it merely an idea in our minds, picked at random and applied arbitrarily, by trial and error. It is an intermediate reality: the text has or is endowed with a meaning of its own. The cluster of letters to which we reduce a spoken sentence is alive with a sense. So, too, the series of movements which constitutes behavior: we can select out certain movements as relevant and as constituting a behavior because they are endowed with a sense. Husserl, in such contexts, uses the term *Wesen,* which can be translated both as "essence" and as a mode of being, as in the term *animalisches Wesen,* animate being. In Husserl's usage, it is also closely associated with *Sinn,* usually translated as "meaning."[31] The meaningful presence of nature around us is all of that. That is why I have chosen to speak of the *sense* of life, the *sense* of nature, to evoke the recognition that nature does have a sense of its own, an integral mode of meaningful being.

The growing awareness of the sense of nature is intertwined with the rediscovery of nature as a living presence, beneath our conventional nature construct. But there is something more that I have sought to evoke by speaking of the sense of nature as *moral.* Today that predication may well seem wholly inappropriate. In our ordinary usage the word *moral* has been reduced to triviality. For most speakers it indicates little more than a conformity to a set of social conventions or mores. It is the people who conceive of themselves as conforming to conventions violated by what they perceive as the immoral minority who describe themselves as "moral." Hegel himself can be said to have sanctioned the usage by using the term *Sittengesetz,* convention, or, literally, the law of custom, as a synonym for Kant's *morales Gesetz,* the moral law. Our age has seized on that reduction with a vengeance, effectively emptying the term "moral" of all but its most trivial meaning.

Eighteenth-century thinkers used the word differently. They bequeathed to us the idea of the moral sciences, including moral philosophy. The Germans translated that term as *Geisteswissenschaften,* the sciences of the spirit. That is the term which we in our time have sought to retranslate, somewhat clumsily, as the "humane sciences"—in turn leading at least some contemporary German authors to speak of *humanistische Wissenschaften.* So used, the thrust of the term moral was to separate the distinctively human works of human freedom from the putatively merely mechanical and causal processes of nature. The century which coined and shaped the concept of "moral" was also the century which first exploited the possibility of conceiving of nature as radically amoral and inhuman, a set of physical entities exhibiting lawlike regularities in their behavior yet devoid of all sense.[32] The term moral was needed to distinguish a free act, governed by the vision of an ideal, from a natural event wholly integrated in the causal sequence of necessity and utility. So used, the term moral pointed to the ingression of the eternal sense of being, of the good, the true, the beautiful, into the order of time.

I have reverted to that obsolete usage in speaking of the moral sense of nature. That is the crucial recognition: the sense of nature which stands out in the radical brackets of dusk is not simply a "natural" sense as the eighteenth century used that word, representing no more than the observable regularities in the order of time. The sense of nature includes also a dimension of value, not merely as utility but as intrinsic, absolute value ingressing in the order of time. The chipmunk peering out of the stone fence is not reducible simply to the role he fulfills in the economy of nature. There is not only utility but also an integrity, a rightness to his presence. When humans encounter that integrity in a trillium or a lady's slipper, they tend to acknowledge it by speaking of beauty, and it is not inappropriate. It is, though, also more—the presence of absolute value, the truth, the goodness, the beauty of being, the miracle that something is though nothing might be. With the encounter with nature in its integrity, there comes also the recognition that its presence is never free of value, acquiring its rightness only contingently in its utility. It is primordially good. The order of nature is also an order of value.

The philosophers of life almost a century ago—Emanuel Rádl among them[33]—were wont to speak of the *vital* order of nature, meaning by that term what we might describe as "biological," though purposively conceived. That order, they would say, governs all nonhuman life, wholly instinctually, leading the bee to gather pollen, the swallow to build her nest, and the she-wolf to nurture her young. A human mother is subject to the same law in her impulse to care for her child, though in her case the same order becomes *moral:* not an instinct but a call to choose rightly, capable of being obeyed or disobeyed. Even the most basic "vital" patterns, such as feeding, become "moral" for a being who must choose whether to eat or whether, by voluntary abstention, to provide food for a needier neighbor or to protest injustice. So conceived, the moral order is, in effect, the vital order seen from the vantage point of freedom.

That is a reading of the sense of our nature as having a moral significance which I can readily understand. Still, the ingression of freedom seems to entail something more. The significance of an act changes when it is no longer governed by vital necessity or utility but by the vision of absolute value. It becomes moral in a second sense as well: through it, eternal value ingresses in the order of time. Though not alien to it, that order is not a function of time. It is the value of speaking the truth when that act has no utilitarian value, simply because it is true. It is the value of courage in situations in which courage changes nothing. It is the act of justice motivated by nothing else than that such an act is just. That is the moment of eternity ingressing into time.[34]

To thinkers who conceived of nature as mechanical, as devoid of all sense—though also to those who thought nature's sense merely vital—such moral value appeared as that which makes humans distinct from the order of nature, and understandably so. Yet when humans encounter nature in the integrity of its being, freed by radical brackets from the veil of constructs, what stands out is the recognition that nature's presence, the sense of nature, is not merely natural or vital. It is not reducible to the order of time. It is also a presence of being in its absolute worth, to be approached with infinite respect. The reason why humans ought not to devastate their world is not simply utilitarian. Nor is the reason why humans ought not to waste what they derive from it solely economic. More deeply, it is *moral:* to destroy heedlessly, to pluck and discard, to have and leave unused, is an act of profound disrespect to the eternal worth of nature. For nature in its integrity is not simply a reservoir of raw materials. In the phrase we used earlier, the sense of nature as humans encounter it in radical brackets is also moral, a presence of value.

It is in that sense that, groping for categories to match the metaphors of the forest at dusk, humans reach the recognition that the sense of nature's green peace and the sense of being human in this world which it reveals is not simply "natural," "vital," but also, profoundly and fundamentally, a *moral* order. Morality, the perception of life in terms of an order of rightness, is not a human invention, a construct imposed by reflection upon unruly passion. That assumption, symbolized for us most emphatically by the Freudian constructs of the blind force of the anonymous *es* and the arbitrarty rule of a grim *Ueberich,* reflects not the sense of being human but the order of the world of artifacts.[35] In that world, there is indeed no inherent rightness, no right time of sleeping and waking, of loving and fearing, of living and dying. A bulldozer with its unheeding operator—"I'm just doing my job, lady!"—is truly a blind, brute force, devoid of all intrinsic rightness and equally capable of visiting and containing devastation, but wholly incapable of distinguishing the two. The rules we impose upon it are dictated by the need to contain that brute force. It is not surprising that a psychology reflecting an artifact world produces no less artificial constructs of the blind force savagely disciplined by an unyielding rule—and projects them upon nature.

Superficially, that model may well appear a faithful reflection of that ordinary experience which Heidegger calls *Durchschnittlichkeit* and his translators "average everydayness."[36] The impact of Freud's speculative constructions would be incomprehensible without a flash of recognition. We have impressed our self-perception on nature to such an extent that nature now seems to conform to it. The perception, though, changes drastically when we no longer encounter nature as culture's wilderness preserve where reality remains "in the wild"—by our standards, anyway—but rather encounter it in its own being, ordered by its own sense. Accustomed to thinking in terms of an imposed, not of an intrinsic, order, a citydweller first notes the absence of such an imposed order in nature. He sees mushrooms as growing "wild," not in neat trays, animals range "wild," unrestricted by leashes and cages, the entire forest, untouched by human hands for generations, grows "wild" as a neglected garden, devoid of order and waiting to have one imposed on it. At first the newcomer to the land may even try. But the forest is too vast. It absorbs human efforts. What it offers is something else: when humans give up the effort to impose their order and accept instead their place within the forest, they begin to discover beneath the seeming chaos a deep, intrinsic order.

That is perhaps the most basic realization that stands out at dusk—that there is an order, there is a sense to it all, a rhythm, a rhyme and a reason, in the symbiosis of mushrooms with the hairline roots of trees, in the patterns of animal life, in the cycle in which the forest renews itself. There is a *rightness* from which beings can deviate, but there is yet a *rightness*. When the word was fresh and unburdended with connotations, we might have said that there is *logos*. The dusk is a time of bracketing, when an experiential *epochē* covers human striving. It is a time of letting be. The world, seen by daylight, is a world of activity, structured by the human's intentional presence. Even in the deep solitude of the forest, as I go about my daily rounds, I recognize around me the world which Heidegger described in *Sein und Zeit* as my *Spielraum*,[37] a sphere of my activity structured by my purposes, ready at hand to be ordered, manipulated, used. Just walking down the path, preoccupied with other matters, I yet note a tree that needs to be culled, make a mental note of the type of wood, refer it to its possible uses. My intentional presence transforms even nature around me into an artifact. The world of my daily doings is a world structured by my active presence, unintelligible, it seems, without it. For all its rhetorical overkill, I can appreciate Sartre's description of the human as the "creator" of his life-world.

That is all too familiar, yet the most powerful realization that stands out in the dusk is that *all this is not so.* Were the cosmos indeed a senseless aggregate of tools, devoid of life or meaning of their own as the world of artifacts is, then dusk, suspending the subject's purposive presence, ought to be a time of infinite nausea. There is much to suggest that in the urban world it is in fact so: perhaps that is why, in the global city of our civilization, we seek so desperately to stave off rest with motion, silence with mechanical sound, the darkness with mechanical images. There must be doing, perhaps, because if there were not, there would be nothing.

But that is not so in the intimate green peace of the forest clearing. Here, as the dusk suspends human activity, the nature which throughout the day obligingly assumed the guise of an artifact does not disintegrate into meaninglessness. It stands out in the integrity of its own being. The brook cascades over the rocks like flowing silver. The trees swing gently in the breeze. An owl hovers in the treetop over the rabbit grazing unconcerned under the protective cover of broken branches that seemed so pointless by daylight. And, over it, ageless as the moral law, there is an immense starry heaven. There is a sense to it all, a rhyme and a reason. Nature in its integrity is not the senseless system which forms so fitting a counterpart for our sciences. It is not alien to our human mode of being: quite the contrary, it is radically its kin. Though perhaps a stranger in the world of his own making, the human in his humanity, in his being as a moral subject, is at home in a nature which is not yet his, subdued by him and depersonalized in its subjugation. Our products may be senseless; the world of nature is not. There is sense in its life as there is sense in the lives of humans. There is *logos.*

From the distance of reflection, the recognition that *there is logos,* that there is a rhyme and a rightness to the being of nature, stands out as the trait of the world at dusk which most transforms our understanding of the natural world—or, more precisely, makes it possible at all. Were there no *logos* intrinsic to nature, were the human the source of all meaning and the nonhuman world around him devoid of all intelligible structure, then the world could not be *understood* at all. Understanding, as distinct from explanation, is fundamentally and basically an *Eindeutung,*[38] the empathetic grasp of the intrinsic sense, of the rhyme and reason of its object. A senseless world could only be explained, accounted for in terms of constructs within which we subsume it and which are wholly our own, not reflections of a truth seen but mental artifacts, conceptual tools for manipulating our world. That is how my urban visitors frequently explain my world, categorizing it without giving themselves a chance to see it, to understand it. Yet that world can be understood, because there is *logos,* a sense in which humans can share, recognizing in the rhythm and rightness of the cosmos something kin to those of their own lives. It is to the extent to which humans can understand that they can feel at home in their world, at ease with it, sensing what is appropriate to it and integrating their lives with it rather than crashing through their world like a bulldozer in an herb garden.

That, to be sure, is already reflection, an "idealizing procedure," as Husserl would call it.[39] The primordial given is far more direct, the recognition of the radical continuity between the meaningful being of humans and of their world. At dusk, the full moon was muted last night by a high and filmy overcast, its edges blurred by a corona of shining clouds. Occasionally a scattering of darker clouds would drift over it. The silver light in the clearing is soft, unobtrusive. The family of porcupines that makes its home under the old dam across the stream brings out its youngster for the evening grazing. The two adults lumber solicitously around him, communicating their care and concern. Once, when he could have been but a few days old, he froze high on a young hemlock, too timid to attempt the descent. The adults coaxed and reassured him, finally easing him down gently. As long as I make no light, they pay me no mind. They share my world, but they have their own lives to lead. So does the woodchuck who comes to graze occasionally on the bright young leaves after I have mown the meadow and raked the hay. So do the snakes, muted on the top, bright and beautiful on the hidden part of their bodies. Much maligned throughout history, the snakes seem most at peace with their God of all the creatures around me. I am not a stranger in that world. There is so much life around me, so kin to my life. Though I, too, have my own ways, the creatures around me are much like I in their purposeful rhythm. Minimally, their *Sein,* like mine, is *Zeit:* their being, too, is projected into temporality.

Recent philosophy, seeking in historicity a substitute for the spirituality it has lost, has been loath to recognize the temporality of animal life. With reason: if we do not recognize the dimension of spirituality, the vision of eternity—or, with Husserl, "transcendental subjectivity"—as that which makes humans distinct, we might well have to insist that their temporality is distinctive.[40] Thus the dividing line in recent thought tends to run between the temporal being of humans and the being of all else, porcupines as much as boulders. Still, only from a very great conceptual distance could one mistake a porcupine for a boulder and lump them both together under the common label of *l'être-en-soi,* the being whose being is not projected as temporality but is wholly enclosed in itself.[41] Perhaps only the boulders, the ageless, lichen-covered boulders, could be said simply to be, *en soi,* complete, not projecting their being as temporality.

Even that, though, may be no more than an illusion, a product of our myopia. My geologist friends, thinking in terms of epochs rather than years, do speak of the life of rocks, reading out their history from their composition. There have been moments when I did sense a kinship with them. Digging my well, I had a distinct sense that the rocks that for centuries had lain deep beneath the earth—deep, at least, as a pick and shovel measure depth in rocky soil—welcome being brought to the surface to which so many of them press their way even in climates where there is no frost to push them. It seemed to me that they are pleased, and most at ease in the shallow stream, washed by the river and warmed by the sun. Those, to be sure, were no more than fleeting moments to which I attribute no cognitive significance. As Teilhard de Chardin points out, on the level of inanimate being, purely causal explanation is quite possible.[42] I can equally well confront the boulders simply as being-in-itself, not being in time.

That, though, I simply cannot do even with the young plants that rise from seed buried a week or more ago, reaching toward the sun, groping for strings and grasping them with their tendrils. They so clearly reach out to a future, spanning time. Even less can I do it with insects. There is the gypsy moth caterpillar, raising its head, looking about him, taking stock of his situation and taking evasive action as my hand approaches him. If, in defense of my trees, I kill him, I know I am snuffing out a life spanning time. So, too, with the ant struggling with his burden, hailing a passing fellow ant, communicating with him and securing his collaboration. I am grateful that I need not kill ants: they are such miracles of miniaturization with a complex sense of purpose guiding a no less complex set of vital organs, a heart beating, lungs, a digestive system, a nervous system. They are the miracle of life. Nor can I, even in strained imagination, conceive of the porcupines, the beavers, the occasional woodchuck around me as atemporal being contained in itself. The lives they live are so clearly purposive, leaving their tracks on a past and projecting into a future.

The being of nature in its intrinsic cyclicity is intensely temporal, bearing a past within it as it projects a future. When you split the butt log of a red oak, you will often find preserved within it the original sapling, dark and distinct from the layers of wood that envelope it. Each blow of the axe uncovers knots, memories of branches long since outgrown. The tree bears its past within it as its swelling buds reach out to a future. It is even more evident in the animals. In their habits and their purposeful doing, they live ever in a transition between a past and a future, guided by memory and anticipation. They bear them within, yet the difference between them and those animals who record their memories and anticipations externally, in words and texts, seems no more than quantitative. It is, certainly, not the radical difference which Sartre posits between the being *en-soi* of nature and the *pour-soi* of humans. The human, as the being whose being is acted out in time, is therein not distinct from but precisely radically kin to nature, though, to be sure, not to our mechanistic nature-construct which Sartre seems to take for nature itself.

There is, to be sure, a difference, but it is not the putative difference between human historicity and the *en-soi* atemporality of nature, but between the natural temporality of all living beings, including humans, and the illusory mechanical temporality of the man-made world. I have experienced that difference keenly in my transitions between the two worlds. In the world in which I wake, it is no "o'clock." It is dawn, the time of waking. There is light in the clearing, the trees stand out of the nighttime forest. As I go about my tasks, I sense the cycle of the day from dusk to dusk, each moment distinctive. The early dawning, when the first rays of the sun stream through the fog rising among the trees, is wholly different from the time when the sun is high and the forest alive with the buzzing of insects, or from the time of the late afternoon when the intensity of the day begins to soften with the declining sun. The plants know and honor the seasons of the day. So do the creatures of the forest, and so, too, do humans when they break free of forgetting.

All that I leave behind when I go into the city. In the uniformly lit, uniformly heated cubicles there is no season. Only the clock—and my tiring body, an intruder in that mechancal world—mark the passage of time. I am not aware of the changing seasons behind the drawn blinds of the seminar room. It is ten, twelve, two, four, six *of the clock*. Except for their numerical designations, all those times are uniform and arbitrary in their identity. Anything might be done at any of them with equal appropriateness or inappropriateness. There is no rightness, there are no seasons. Such pattern as life might have might well appear as no more than a convention, to be observed or violated at whim.

When I leave the building, the world has changed. I can sense darkness waiting for me beyond the neon screen. The headlights coming against me grow fewer as the pavement grows more ragged and finally disappear as I feel the cool of the evening forest around me. I turn into an unpaved road, then a few minutes more and I can shut off the engine and douse my headlights. The exhaust fumes dissipate rapidly. The house stands dark in the clearing. It is no longer "o'clock," it is again a season. It is the time of the rising moon and the stilling forest, the time of evening chores and prayers, a time to sit beneath the stars or to kindle a lamp that does not blind the night. My body, constrained by clocks through the long day, settles into the rhythm of the world around me. It is time to rest, time to sleep—and there will be a time of waking.

Bodies remember what humans forget when they mistake the artifact temporality of clocks for the authentic human temporality. The temporality of clocks is not, to be sure, an arbitrary invention of idle minds. It is a formalization of life's rhythm, essential for the coordination of human activities and highly useful as such. I should not wish to do without it. I love the ticking and striking of the old Lipizzaner clock with its Vienna regulator in the silent house as I fall asleep. Still, the temporality of clocks is inherently absurd, meaningless, if taken as a reality in itself. "Six of the clock," taken as no more than a halfway point between "five" and "seven," is absurd. It is meaningful only when we remain aware of it as a symbolization of the season of lengthening shadows, the time of gathering tools, the time of the glowing maples. Artifacts and constructs, like clocks, can be authentically human only as the distinctive human way of articulating a more basic truth, the rhythm, the seasons of life. If we lose sight of the sense of life they articulate, they become absurd.

So it is with all the works of humans. All the artifacts of social coexistence which appear as arbitrary conventions, to be obeyed or broken at will and to be manipulated no less at will by social engineering, acquire a new meaning when we recognize in them the distinctive human expression of something far more fundamental, of the intrinsic rightness of all creation. What stands out at dusk, with the recognition of the *logos* of being, the living sense of things, is that for some three centuries we have fundamentally misconstrued the basic question of ethics. We have approached ethics as in a vacuum, as if, in a value-free context of arbitrary possible acts, our task were to designate some as good and right while labeling others evil or wrong, with no intrinsic rightness to guide us. We have assumed that our task is not so much one of recognizing what is good and right but one of deciding what we shall so label.

We have paid a high price for that willed ignorance. Yet it is less ignorance than a willed forgetting. Humans through the millennia have known the difference between good and evil, between right and wrong. Nor have they simply sensed it intuitively. With a remarkable degree of agreement amid cultural differences, they have articulated their basic moral awareness in codes which, for all the variation in wording, express the same basic sense of being and of being human. As our social world disintegrates around us, we need not some new and fanciful doctrine of the right and the good, but a rediscovery of the lost clarity of insight that the rules in which humanity for centuries has expressed its moral sense of life are no arbitrary conventions relative to this or that epoch of history but expressions of the perennial rightness of being. What the dusk reveals is not some new morality but rather the deep truth of the ageless moral insight of humanity.[43]

The words are so familiar that we hardly hear them at all. "Thou shalt not covet." "Thou shalt not bear false witness." "Thou shalt not steal." "Thou shalt not commit adultery." "Thou shalt do no murder." "Honor thy father and thy mother." "Remember the Sabbath day, to keep it holy." We know the words, but in the arbitrary world we have built up around us, they have come to seem arbitrary, no more than one possible set of rules favored by a particular sect. Still, those commandments are not uniquely Jewish or distinctively Christian. They represent the moral consensus of humankind, rooted in the very nature of our being and tested through the centuries, in obedience as much as in the breach.

Where the world is not yet an arbitrary "man's" world, those commandments stand out again in their ontological significance. Here the rhythm of the seasons fits organically with the moral rhythm of human life they reflect. What they are, more than anything else, is an expression of a posture of respect for the order, the *logos* of the creation. Their violation does not do violence simply to the victim but to the whole rightness of being, casting out the doer from its order.

"Thou shalt not covet." This is not an injuction against the rightful striving of all beings whose being is projected into temporality. It is an urgent warning against turning the world from the place of our dwelling into an object of possession, rendered dead and soulless by greed. Of all the commandments governing the relationship of finite beings to each other, it is, perhaps, the most basic. No force is more destructive than greed, no drive more elemental. Greed is not an extension of need, since a need can be satisfied. It is the desperate attempt to fill with possessions the emptiness which humans create when they ignore the first four commandments, turning their world into a meaningless wasteland in which they are utterly alone. The rediscovery of the presence which fills that emptiness, setting humans free from greed and envy, is the greatest gift of the forest peace.

"Thou shalt not bear false witness." Amid the green peace, amid the rightness of nature, the violence of a lie stands out. It is so utterly wrong, a violation of the rightness of the *logos*. A lie is at the root of all mental distress, the discord between what humans know and what they say, or more deeply, between what humans know and what they dare to admit to themselves. A century ago, Borden Parker Bowne listed the need for truth as one of the most elementary human needs.[44] Today, that may seem quaint. We have become accustomed to living in a world of make-believe, of artifacts masquerading as physical objects—the paper flowers pretending to be living plants, the plastic furniture pretending to be wood, the robots pretending to be humans—and humans pretending to be robots. Yet through the ages humans have known that there is no condition more basic to authentic humanity than *to live in truth.*[45]

"Thou shalt not steal," for in taking from the other that with which he mingled his love and labor, you take away from his very being yet gain nothing, not having made it your own in labor or love. Theft depersonalizes not only the thief, but the world as well. The object stolen becomes dead possession. "Thou shalt not commit adultery," because that, too, is theft—taking away another's love but gaining no more than dead gratification. To be at peace with himself and his world, a human must be at one in himself, in his commitments, in his conscience. Adultery splits humans in twain. It is not only a theft, but also a lie which embodies the essence of human coveting.

"Thou shalt do no murder." Wanton killing, be it of a person, of an animal, a plant—or of a love or an idea—is an act of profound disrespect, of dehumanization so radical that it makes its perpetrator an outcast and shatters the peace of the land. Yes, there is a food chain. There are, too, the bitter works of love. Killing a wounded animal swiftly—the frog impaled on my scythe, the baby rabbit disemboweled by a cat—can be the most agonizing act of love, letting it suffer an act of moral cowardice. All that is true: there can be even a moral duty to kill. That is why I think the Bishops' Bible translation, "Thou shalt do no murder," more faithful not only to the Hebrew text, but also to the moral sense of the commandment than the familiar "Thou shalt not kill." Still, an act of killing remains an act of deep horror. Perhaps we have learned to objectify our world so that we could kill without remorse. Unquestionably, having objectified it, we do so kill, and easily. Like Cain, we find ourselves outcasts, taking what is not our own.

"Honor thy father and thy mother," since life in truth is not your own but a gift you receive at their hands. Not theirs only—every moment of life is a gift of the world around us and of the God of that world. To honor, the ability to honor—is both a distinctive human trait and the crucial component of humanity at peace. We are the beings able to cherish and give thanks. Hence "Remember the Sabbath day, to keep it holy": it is not a day of rest only. Far more, it is a day of thanksgiving. Not the absence of activity but the act of honoring, of giving thanks, is what restores the human soul and puts it at peace.

None of that, to be sure, is new. The radical brackets of the forest clearing teach no new doctrine. They do, however, give the dweller a new awareness of the age-old moral code as no convention but as a faithful expression of the rightness of the cosmos. In honoring that order, the human can be at home in his world—and vice versa, in dwelling at peace, a human learns to honor the moral code. Its precepts may come to seem as arbitrary constraints when we assume the posture of masters, proudly conquering the world. That posture, though, is our crushing burden, condemning us to loneliness in a world reduced to meaninglessness. The great gift of solitude at dusk is the surrender of that posture, the grateful acceptance of the place of a dweller in God's world. Once we dare encounter the world, the nature around us in its integrity, in respect, the traditional commandments cease to appear arbitrary or constraining. They become, instead, in the words of Jan Milič Lochman, the "signposts to freedom."

In the stillness of dusk, a double order emerges. There is the order of time, the all-reconciling rhythm of love and labor, of day and night, of the full moon and the starry skies of the new moon, the cycle of the seasons and the cycle of life, blossoming, renewing itself, and perishing. The great liberating discovery is that the human is not a stranger to it, that he has his integral place therein. The order which governs the life of the forest, the seasons of the trees, and the care of the porcupines for their young, the snakes at peace on their boulders and the human in his clearing, is both vital and moral. It gives a rhythm and a rightness to human life as well, expressed in the moral codes of human society and the deep, often obscured sense of the seemingly arbitrary works of humans. Its seasons give meaning to clocks, its dialectic of love and labor gives meaning to the devices of the cities. Even amid their man-made environments, humans need not feel strangers if they recognize in their works the rhythm of the nature whose part they, too, are—and let that vision guide them in their understanding and their use of technology.

That vision of an order of nature, finally, is the profound truth of any "naturalism" restored to validity by recognizing nature as *physis*[46] and as a creation, not a mechanistic nature-construct, as its starting point. Humans cannot live at peace with themselves and their God if they are not at peace with nature. Yet in the stillness at dusk, a double order emerges—not only the order of time but the order of eternity. That recognition comes far more slowly than the recognition of the order of time, the rhythm of the seasons. To a human grown brittle and broken in the alienation of the world of artifacts, the discovery of a living nature whose rhythm finds an echo in his own being is all-absorbing. The diaries of solitary dwellers often reflect it. They speak of the grateful peace of assuming a place in the vital order of nature, embraced by the all-reconciling night, living the rhythm of the day. But there is the full moon, the searing moon of January nights and the comforting August moon of harvest nights. It evokes a second recognition—that though we may accept both the life and the death of the chipmunk as at peace in the rhythm of nature, we cannot but rejoice in the one and grieve the other. Our moral codes testify to it. We are beings who are able to see the world in the order of its time, not solely in the sterile atemporality of our man-made world. Yet we can see it also from the perspective of a perennial order of right and wrong which stands in judgment above the order of it, ingressing in it though not a part of it. The human is a dweller in time, though not in time alone. He dwells at the intersection of time and eternity.

The term "eternity" will call for an explanation each time we use it. It is a hopelessly misleading one, though perhaps the series of metaphors we have before us might help specify its meaning. We might, for instance, speak of the order of value, though that, too, can be misleading. Even temporality has its values, the values of utility relating the present to the past whence it stems and the future toward which it is projected. The experience of which I speak as the vision of eternity is a vision of an order of value in a different sense. It is the experience of value as intersecting with time and of the human as standing out of time in going out to it, seeing the present not in its relation to what preceded and what will follow it, but in its absolute being—in its relation to what, clumsily, we describe as eternity.

Eternity, so understood, is not an extension of time, not even an infinite time. It is, rather, a vertical dimension cutting through time at each of its moments. It is the confrontation with the full moon through the trees dark with the day's rain. It is the goodness of an act or the truth of a witness which avail nothing in the order of time, yet are still irreducibly good. It is the awareness of the intensity of the blue sky on a summer day. Though it is only July, the days have been cool, almost autumnal. The cedar shakes of the house in the clearing are sun-drenched, a light wind sways the trees. The forest world is deep green all about and, high above, the sky is incredibly blue. The blue of that sky is not a function of the gray dawn which preceded it nor of the greenish-yellow which will follow it at dusk. It simply is, blue with a perennial validity unaffected by the passing of time. It is blue as, in Whitehead's term, an *eternal* object, ingressing in this moment of time.[47]

The pain of the grief suffered by a loved one has a similar quality. It once was, and it is no more. There were events which led up to it, and events which followed it, and, for practical purposes, it makes every kind of sense to think of it in those terms, in the order of time. Yet there is another perspective that will not be denied: recognizing that grief in its purity, in its eternal validity before God. So, too, the beauty of the trillium or the goodness of a moral act which changed nothing and yet, for all eternity, stands out in its nobility. Humans are beings capable of perceiving all that. They are capable of perceiving the creation not only in the order of time but in the order of eternity, lifting up its moments out of time's passage into eternity in the eternal validity of truth, goodness, and beauty of their joy and sorrow.

That is the recognition which stands out in crystalline clarity in the moments of grief and the moments of joy at dusk. Sartre and the existentialists denied that dimension of being human. Having committed himself to a militant atheism in his indignation at the Church, Sartre had to deny the dimension of the eternal in humans which Max Scheler had recognized so clearly.[48] Then, having denied what makes humans distinct, he had to make temporality their exclusive property—and, in effect, lie about raccoons and porcupines. Once, however, we recognize the shared temporality of all animate beings, we need to recognize the distinctively human task in the cosmos as of a different order. A human is the being capable in each moment of reaching out beyond the order of time to eternity. It is the human, in the recognition of the goodness, truth, beauty, and holiness of being, caught up in its temporality, who brings out its absolute validity, its dimension of eternity.

The dimension of eternity, the rightness of the green peace, sanctifies the order of time. Sir Charles Sherrington,[49] in his way no less careful an observer of nature than Joseph Wood Krutch, concluded that no life is sacred until humans recognize it as such. There is an insight in that assertion about the distinctive role of humans. Still, the green peace of the forest teaches me a different lesson—that though it may take humans to recognize it, all life is sacred quite independently of that recognition, and not life only but all being, the boulders, the leaves of grass, the infinitely distant star.

Yes, there is a food chain. The chipmunk searching for seeds among the boulders of the stone fence, companion of my days, is the food of the great owl, the majestic companion of my nights. The order of time is an order of passing and perishing—and celebrating it as the creator of novelty does not alter that fact. Certainly birth is as much a part of the process as death. For psychohygienic reasons, even if for no other, a philosophy whose vision reached no further than the order of time might well prefer to regard the birth rather than the death as definitive.[50] Yet the emergence of novelty is hardly a cause for rejoicing if what emerges is no less doomed to perish than what made room for it by its passing. The moral sense of life cannot be wholly contained in the order of time. It must be anchored in the eternity of the good, the true, the beautiful, the holy.

That is the double order, the rhythm, and the rightness. There is a food chain, a rhythm of life's seasons. It is not simply that life "exhibits a lawlike regularity," though it does that. That metaphor, so useful for the purposes of natural scientific research, becomes misleading in the search for the sense of life. It obscures the deeper recognition that there is an order, a rightness as well as a rhythm of time. The generations of the porcupines, the phases of the forest, even the death of the chipmunk, all attest to a rightness of time. The glory of being human is the ability to recognize the pattern of rightness and to honor it as a moral law. The horror of being human is the ability to violate that rightness, living out of season—doing violence to the other, perverting the most sacred human relationships, devastating the world in greed, overriding its rhythm, not in the name of necessity and charity, but in the compulsion of coveting.

What Judaism and its spiritual daughter, Christianity, sought to express in their commandments is the age-old, precious discovery of the rightness of life. Still, were those commandments no more than that, their significance to the quest for the moral sense of life would remain marginal. It is not, because they are sanctified by the moral sense of nature in a second, deeper sense, not merely its rhythm but its rightness in eternity. Their common motif is the law of respect for the sacredness of being. The ageless boulders of the long-abandoned dam, the maple and the great birch by twilight, the chipmunk in the busyness of his days and his dying, even I, making my dwelling place among them, are not only right in our season. We have also our value in eternity, as witnesses to the audacious miracle of being rather than nothing. Ultimately, that is the moral sense of nature, infinitely to be cherished: that there is something. That is the eternal wonder articulated in the rightness and rhythm of time which humans honor in their commandments, the wonder of being.

The blue sky, the moral act, the moment of grief have their absolute validity, independent of the before and the after. The trillium, in its passing moment of glory, is the locus of a beauty that ingresses in time but is not a part of it, reducible to it. That, too, is part of the truth of the radical bracketing at dusk: being stands out in its absolute, its *ab-solo,* validity—and the human in his role as the being who can reach out of his preoccupation with time to see the truth, the beauty, the goodness ingressing in it is called to testify to it. Though a dweller in time, he can see the wonder of the starry heaven. The truth that stands out at dusk is not only the truth of the order of nature and of the place of the human therein. It is also the truth of eternity.

Certainly, humans can become wholly absorbed in the preoccupations of time. As there are humans who are color-blind, so there can be humans who become blind to goodness, to truth and beauty, who drink wine without pausing to cherish it, who pluck flowers without pausing to give thanks, who accept joy and grief as all in a day's work, to be enjoyed or managed, without ever seeing the presence of eternity in them. But that is not the point. What is crucial is that humans, whether they do so or not, are capable of encountering a moment not simply as a transition between a before and an after but as the miracle of eternity ingressing into time. That, rather than the ability to fashion tools, stands out as the distinctive human calling. Were it not for humans who are able to see it, to grieve for it and to cherish it, the goodness, beauty, and truth of creation would remain wholly absorbed in the passage of time and pass with it. It is our calling to inscribe it into eternity.

3. Humanitas

A Human's Place in Nature

There still is dawn, beneath the old dam, where the bright new growth heals the scars left by the loggers, and the dweller awakens into it, a stranger no longer.

At dawn this morning I watched the old porcupine cross the river on the log footbridge I had laid, meandering, boulder to boulder, across the stream. Porcupines, like most forest creatures, can swim. I have seen one tumble into the water when the stream was in flood and regain the shore a few yards downstream with purposeful strokes. Still, they prefer to avoid it if they can. I have never seen any of the land animals enter water voluntarily. Though the raccoon loves sardines passionately, even a freshly opened can of them would not induce him to swim the stream. Now he and the porcupine make use of my footbridge, a part of my human world. An artifact of my thought and labor has become a part of their natural world, much as the lake backed up by the beaver dam is a part of mine. They come to dig in my compost pile, as I in turn have bucked and burned the butts of oaks felled and left by beavers after they had limbed the tops to build their dam and lodge. I have come to belong in this world, not because I have become less human but because this world is far more human than I once realized. When humans surrender the arrogance of domination, they can reclaim the confidence of their humanity. Nature, freed from the constraint of mechanical nature-constructs, can accept the human as also a part of its moral order.

That recognition, to be sure, comes slowly. When humans first begin to rediscover the world of nature, they do so, for the most part, in a mode of self-negation, as if they sensed a basic disjunction between their humanity and the order of nature around them. Much of the writing that seeks to rediscover the natural world, whether conservationist or romantic, is tinged with an undertone of hostility to humans and all their works. It is as if the "world of nature" meant a world freed of human presence, and respect for nature a withdrawal from it. That is the obverse of the arrogance of our humanity and leads to the conclusion that the moral duty of humans is one of minimizing their presence until such time as the human species will finally disappear from the face of this earth, letting nature reclaim it. Just as nature appears nonhuman to human arrogance, so humans themselves appear unnatural to human diffidence.

That conclusion is understandable enough as long as the basic metaphor of human presence is the bulldozer—and in our time that metaphor may well be appropriate. Still, it is not a particularly helpful conclusion, offering as it does no guidance for our being in nature. If being human were in itself an unnatural, unjustifiable intrusion into nature, the sole course of action—short of the demise of the human species at one extreme and the total displacement of nature by an artificial environment at the other—would be one of apartheid, dividing the globe between artifact areas reserved for humans and natural areas from which humans would be rigorously excluded. The polarization between Manhattan minus its parks and wilderness preserves minus hikers foreshadows that approach. Were culture a negation of nature, no integration of humans and nature would be possible.

That is not a happy conclusion, but neither is it a necessary one. The opposition of nature and culture which we take for granted is itself a cultural product, the result of a skewed perspective which identifies "culture" with that branch of the entertainment industry [*sic*] which caters to the tastes of the educated and the affluent urbanite, specifically in the area of the arts.[1] The term and the concept of culture, however, have very different roots. Culture is a matter of cultivation, echoing the Latin *cultus*, the yielding of respect, honoring the sacredness of all that is. The man of culture is one who cultivates, who honors the nobility of being. The husbandman is a man of culture, as words like agriculture and silviculture remind us, cultivating the field and the forest. The *homo humanus* of ancient Rome, the man of culture, is one who cultivates his life, not leaving it at the mercy of his momentary whims and their gratification but ordering it according to its moral sense. His task, like that of the husbandman and of all men of culture, is not an arbitrary one, displacing nature. Nature is his guide in the task of cultivation. That is *cultus*—and, in that sense, culture is not the contradiction of nature but rather the task of humans within it.[2]

If, in the course of the last three centuries, we have become increasingly marauders on the face of the earth rather than dwellers therein, it is not because we have become more distinctively human, more distinctively cultured, but rather because we have become less so. What is distinctively human about us is our ability to perceive the moral law in the vital order of nature, subordinating greed to love. In the last three centuries, however, we have guided our dealings with the world less and less by moral considerations and more and more by considerations of short-term utility—gratification of greed. In the process, we have become less human, less cultured, more "bestial" in the commonsense acceptation of that term. If we are to recover the confidence of our intrinsic place in nature, we need to do so by reclaiming, not by rejecting, our distinctive moral humanity, our task of cultivating the earth as faithful stewards. For humans, it is precisely culture, in its most basic sense of cultivation, of care and respect, not bestiality, that can be the way to reclaiming our place in nature. It is as beings capable of seeing our place in nature from a moral point of view that we can cease being marauders and can become dwellers in the earth.

Placing the question of our being in nature within the perspective of a moral law, however, raises a more fundamental question still, one which we could ignore within a solely utilitarian perspective. It is the question of the ultimate justification of being human as such. A reaffirmation of the moral sense of nature and of the moral sense of being human resolves the alienation between humans and nature, but it obliges us to ask what justifies our presence on this earth at all, since that presence is no longer merely a fact but also a moral problem.[3]

It is an expensive presence by any account, and would be so even if we broke free of our all-devouring greed and contented ourselves with the satisfaction of need.[4] Given my scant fur, I must consume nearly four tight cords of good seasoned hardwood to keep warm through a New Hampshire winter—and that is only the beginning. Though I went about it in a circumspect, cellophane-wrapped fashion, I was a predator, feeding on the flesh of my fellow creatures. Even once I opted for a vegetarian diet—after all, I do have molars as well as canines—I was still competing for food with my fellow creatures. Nor is the cost of my sustenance restricted to the modest use of the fruits of this earth with which the native American was content. I am by far the most expensive member of the community of nature. What is it that justifies the expense?

For some three centuries, we have had a ready answer—we are a "higher" species, the only intelligent beings in a world of dead matter. That arrogance, though, is today devastating us as much as we have devastated the world in its name. That is what brings us, literally or metaphorically, to the forest clearing, to seek a new beginning. Once, however, we give up that arrogance, then the answer to the question, What justifies the expense? is no longer obvious.

Are we a "higher" species? A disinterested observer, coolly examining the evidence and assessing humanity's impact upon the globe, would not be likely to come to that conclusion. The works of humans have left a trail of devastation across the face of the earth. Nor have we served our own kind well. Even without invoking mushroom clouds, the daily inhumanity of humans to each other makes any claim to superiority suspect. Porcupines do not covet, they bear no false witness, they do not commit adultery and they do no murder. How can we claim superiority? At best, we are one species among others. But then, what justifies the totally disproportionate cost of our presence?

Ask it for once without presupposing the answer of the egotism of our species, as God might ask it about his creatures: Why should a dog or a guinea pig die an agonizing death in a laboratory experiment so that some human need not suffer just that fate? Would not any answer you give justify experimentation on carefully selected classes of humans—convicts were occasionally used, Watson used foundling children—as well? Why, in the perspective of eternity, should the life of a human be more precious than that of a dog? Why should the dog's suffering weigh any less in the moral balance of the cosmos? Why should a woodchuck die, wasted by the side of the highway, just so that a human should not be inconvenienced in his headless rush to nowhere? As long as we inflict suffering only on our own kind whom we exploit for pleasure or profit, we can obscure the issue with the specious doctrine of "consenting adults," though even that is problematic. Have the wretched of this earth really consented to penury so that the privileged segment of humanity can choke on idle affluence? With animals, caught up in our works and wars, tortured in our experiments, that is not even a question. Animals cannot consent. They suffer mutely, trusting those who can speak and decide for them.

As step by step I found my way gratefully into the peace of the forest, feeling it healing my wounds and offering me a place of belonging, I became ever more painfully aware of that question: What justifies my presence in this peaceful world, what justifies the cost of my upkeep, so disproportionately higher than that of the other animals? That question is inseparable from the gift of the moral sense of nature. It is all around me, not as an accusation but as an unspoken query: How are humans justified?

For, irrational though it may seem, unwarranted and unmerited, we *are* justified. That is a fundamental experience. In a world where a layer of artifacts obscures the living sense of nature, the issue may seem moot. To Sartre, the intensely moral observer of an amoral world, a negative answer seemed evidently true. In his literary metaphors, even more than in his philosophical ones, Sartre powerfully articulated the corrosive sense of being always *in the way*, unjustified and unjustifiable.[5] His is surely a faithful reflection of the position of a moral subject in a mechanical world. Within the brackets of the forest clearing, however, just the opposite truth stands out. In the stillness of the evening, amid the sun-drenched hum of the noonday forest, in the grandeur of the lightning, there comes the overwhelming, agonizing, and reconciling recognition of being accepted, being justified. Here the dweller is an alien no longer. Nature envelops and accepts him. There is no reason, no merit, only the basic reality: we are justified, we are accepted. It is not because of what we do: given the devastation we have wrought among our fellow creatures, it can only be in spite of it. It is a free gift, agonizing for being so painfully undeserved. Nature accepts freely, as the dog who licks the hand of the experimenter who had subjected it to inhuman torture forgives freely, as a gift. Though again and again we wound the world around us, nature heals and accepts. Though we merit only condemnation, and cannot presume to claim the gifts of life, trusting in our own righteousness, we are yet justified, we belong.[6]

It is not easy to describe the sense of being forgiven. The sense of the utter violence of my presence haunted me for many years. For several months, while I shaped the beams for my house, I lived in the clearing quietly, unobtrusively. I came to know its moods, the wonder of the early morning, when I came out of my tent while the dew was still on the grass, watching the first yellow and orange flames in my fire ring. The wood I culled did not bother me—it was a part of the life of the forest whose trees do live and die. Digging the cellar was different. The backhoe ripped the earth, violated its centuries-old contours and left a scar of dead sand all around my future house. Building the house was again good—I sensed my kinship with the creatures who make their homes around me. The scar, the scar of dead sand, harsh and unhealing, remained to reproach me, a metaphor of violence. I could have done little else, yet I came to regret the decision to build. Only slowly the foregiveness came. Perhaps it began the day a great old turtle climbed up on the scar. She poked here and there, testing the sand with her flippers. Then slowly, deliberately, she dug herself into the sun-soaked sand bank. She paid me no mind for an hour or more while she laid her eggs. At last she was finished, covered over the hole and crawled, exhausted, into the shade of a bush where she rested until the cool of the evening. Then she disappeared into the river. There was forgiveness in her coming.

Next spring, after tracks leading down to the river told me that the eggs had hatched, I finally covered up the scar, digging up rich loam from the long-ago lake bed, setting up hemlock stumps for walks and enriching the new soil with oak leaves and chicken manure. By the fall, clover and rye grass had healed the scar. The clearing blended back into the forest. The grass worked a work of forgiving. The grass here is no less a metaphor than the forgiving, and the sense it presents is unambiguous. It would be folly were we to trust in our own righteousness. We are not worthy, our presence is too costly. But there is manifold and great mercy. The grass testifies to it no less than the rainbow. Irrational though it may seem, we are justified. The realization is as painful as it is reconciling: it is always easier to be damned and done with it. Still, it is inescapable. We are accepted.

Granted, that deep, self-certifying awareness is not yet an answer. It is a poetic gift of the all-reconciling night, at best only marginally legitimate in philosophic reflection. The work of thought is yet to come: the primordial awareness in a forest clearing is no more than a token. Still, it is not irrelevant. It is the warrant of reality, the assurance that our reflection is indeed an articulation of a deep truth, not merely a cunningly devised fable in which humans seek to rationalize their being. We reflect and speculate, as surely we must. In the peace of the evening, though, we are also ourselves eyewitnesses. The audacious recognition that we belong, that we are accepted, justified, is not the conclusion. It is the starting point, the primordial given. Though so much more needs be said, that initial recognition assures us that more *can* be said—and will not be idle speculation.

Reflection begins when the awareness turns into a question: How is it that human presence on this earth is justified? Then the answer can come, first on the most elementary level: humans are justified in the order of being. Humans are—and to be is to be good. That is the deep, difficult insight of Saint Augustine, *esse qua esse bonum est,* being is good simply because it is. Saint Augustine's words of long ago have faded into a formula, a conceptual counter in the game of metaphysics, no longer evoking a lived experience. We have seen too much of the grievous harm that beings cause one another in the order of time to retain a clear awareness of their intrinsic goodness simply in the order of being. Both in the order of time and in the conceptual game of speculation, Saint Augustine's claim might well appear false.

The stillness of the evening, suspending the preoccupations of the order of time, brings forth once more the long-obscured goodness of the order of being, not as a speculative conclusion but as a lived experience. There is the ageless, lichen-covered boulder at the foot of the dam. I had long taken it for granted, unheeding. Only slowly did I begin to realize how intensely, fundamentally good it is that the boulder *is,* that there is something when there could so easily be only the vast emptiness of nothing. The boulder does not *do.* Its presence in the order of being is unobscured by the preoccupations of doing in the order of time. Humans do obscure it. When, though, the dusk suspends human doing and solitude brackets chatter, when the pain of loss reminds us how easy it is not to be, then the lichen-covered boulder stands out in its deep goodness. It is good that it is. In the same vein, William Carlos Williams wrote in his haiku, "so much depends / upon / a red wheel / barrow. . . ."[7] That is the goodness whereof Saint Augustine spoke.

Snakes, too, help recall the goodness of being. They have had a bad press, yet of all the creatures of the field, stream, and forest they are perhaps the most peaceful—and most shy. Only when most fortunate do I come across one, as it reposes motionless on the sun-warmed boulders in the stream or in the old stone fence. My ancestors once believed that a snake under the threshold guarded the welfare of a dwelling, and I can empathize. The snakes of New England are, for the most part, considered common. The colors of their scales are muted, matching the tint of their habitat. Humans rarely see the brightly colored underside of their lithe bodies. The snakes, I know, have their place in the order of time. Still, watching a snake resting in the sun, motionless as he lest I startle him, I am little aware of that role. Something else impresses itself on me—how infinitely good it is that there is a snake, how utterly good in the order of being it is that this snake *is*. The idea of a "value-free" reality is a hopeless fiction, constructed by beings who think themselves the source of all value. The lived reality is different. It is good, deeply good, not in terms of its function but simply in terms of its being.

It is good that humans are, too. They are so absorbed in the order of time, obscured by the good or ill of what they do, that it is hard to grasp the goodness of their being. Still, there are glimpses. Late last night I heard the sound of a motor overhead, a slow, rhythmic throbbing. Then the red and green running lights of a small plane appeared over the tree line and moved slowly overhead. I could imagine the pilot in the darkened cabin, isolated by the throbbing of his engine, in the eerie green glow of his dials. The rim of the clearing, dark against the sky, bracketed him: though theoretically I knew that he had taken off somewhere, perhaps after dinner, and would land somewhere else, where others were waiting for him, in that moment he had for me neither a past nor a future. He simply was, suspended for the moment between my clearing and the vastness of space, and I sensed keenly how precious, how good it is that a person *is*.

So I, too, *am*, still before the house, beneath the stars, watching the dying embers of the fire, justified, like the boulder and the snake, simply by the fact of my being. When Hegel declared that whatever is real is rational, he had, I am sure, something else in mind—perhaps that there is sufficient reason for whatever comes to pass in the order of time. His words, though, can be used to point to something in the order of being as well: that the sheer givenness of being is good. In the order of being, the fact that something *is* justifies its being.

That is the level of justification which humans can reclaim when they become aware of their being simply as a fact, a sheer psychophysical presence. That is the kernel of truth even in all that we have come to think of as "materialism," in spite of the inherent contradiction in the formal conception of a meaningful idea of a merely material reality. It is the truth of the lived realization of our sheer "material" presence—or, in another idiom, our presence simply in the order of being. Like the growing and living beings around us, we are also in the order of time, projecting our being as temporality, spanning a duration from hope to fulfillment, in memory and anticipation. Then, in our ability to encounter the good, the true, and the beautiful, we are also beings who transcend temporality in a vision of the order of the eternal.[8]

The fact of being, the flow of time, the vision of eternity—those are the three orders. Whenever in its long history philosophy confounded them, it ended up in a dilemma, just as when it sought to isolate one of them as alone real. The recognition of the goodness of being is crucial, yet not sufficient. As humans, we are—but we also do, and our acts do not simply happen. We need to envision alternatives and choose among them—and our choice can make the difference between a forest culled, clear-cut, or bulldozed and asphalted for a parking lot. Our being is also intrinsically temporal, an act and a process as well as a fact.

Here, again, more is also true. We are not wholly enclosed in time. In the still vision of the green depth of the midday forest, in the stark confrontation with the January moon and the flash of lightning which fix the absolute value of a moral act, we are also beings who encounter the eternal in time. Still, the recognition of the temporality of animate being is crucial. It is the periodicity of being which presents us with the first awareness of its *rightness,* of the moral sense of life in which there is room for everything but not just anything, is appropriate at any given time.

In contrast with the pretemporal—broadly, the "materialistic"—perspective, the temporalistic vision is immensely appealing. When humans seek to answer the question, "Who are you?," they may begin with a statement of "fact"—the "name, rank, serial number" of a bygone era—but they must go on to tell the story of their lives, their memories, their present activities, their hopes and anticipations. The being of nature is no less intrinsically temporal: the oak bears the sapling within it, the beaver his ancestral memories, the human his history, all striving toward a future. The rediscovery of the moral sense of nature and the place of the human within it begins with the discovery of the rhyme and rhythm, the purposeful periodicity of being. Temporalistic perspectives, just as the materialistic ones, will always appear convincing because, on one level, they, too, are fundamentally *true.*

We have not yet begun to exhaust the resources of the temporalistic perspectives. They have a double contribution to make. One is the insight of romantic naturalism and vitalism, that there is indeed a rightness of the seasons and that the seeming arbitrariness and relativity of human values dissolve, revealing the *logos,* the *ratio,* of being human when humans realize that for them, as for the growing, living, and dying beings around them, there is a right time, that there is a rightness of time for everything. In its vitalistic and developmental guises, temporalism can teach us that.[9]

That is a difficult lesson, because the sheer goodness of all that is is so basic, yet it is a crucial one, because without it the sense of the intrinsic goodness of being would become paralyzing. It is the callousness of sentimentality rather than the putative rapacity of reason that brings it home most clearly. For years, the National Park Service made a practice of culling the herds of wild horses in the Grand Canyon. Perhaps a decade or so ago, the practice aroused public indignation, including mine. I can remember the pictures of the magnificent, free animals transformed by a single rifle shot into pained and bloody wreckage to be sold for dog food. I remember the pain at the thought and the immense sense of relief upon reading that the practice had been terminated. But the story did not end there. The herds, with few natural enemies, multiplied precipitously, far too fast for the fragile ecosystem of the canyon. In a few years, its vegetation was devastated, its hoof-beaten slopes eroding, starving burros dying painfully each winter. Though the devastation was far greater, this time there was no outcry of indignation.

Logging forced me to accept the same lesson. When I first came to the land, it had lain fallow ever since the last dwellers abandoned it, nearly three generations ago. The forest that reclaimed the pastures had not been planted or sowed. It grew wild, choking upon itself. There were trees dying for want of sunlight, others reaching heights of thirty feet or more on a three-inch butt, then breaking under the weight of January ice. There were few healthy trees in the tangle.

Still, for a long time, I could not undertake the task of thinning. Coming from the world of artifacts and constructs, where acres of asphalt ruthlessly stifle a soil stripped of loam and gravel, I lacked the confidence of my human presence. Bruised myself from a shipwreck, I wished only to be inconspicuous, to disturb as little as possible. The wonder of the woods was upon me, newly received, and I could understand respect in no way other than by withdrawing my presence to a minimum.

The trauma of the first night after the loggers came is still with me. I walked out by moonlight but could no longer find my familiar paths amid the tangle of wasted tops and slash. I wandered through the wounded forest, grieving my decision. Yet where only a tangled bush had been, there are now young oak saplings, growing straight and true. The starved, slender trunks are filling in and putting out healthy branches. There is a cluster of shoots around each maple stump: I no longer hesitate in pruning them back and selecting the strongest. And there are mushrooms, *hříbky* and *křemenáče*, where the sun is warming the forest floor again.

It is a difficult lesson, one which I will never learn gladly, and a dangerous one as well. Utility can so easily excuse rapacity and cruelty. A horror came over me when a neighbor concluded he would have to shoot his dog, who had become rabid—and several bystanders pressed in, eyes agleam, "Let me shoot him!" "No, let me!" Yet that scene is reenacted daily, on small scale as well as grand. Judgments of relative value can finally be legitimate only against the background of the recognition of absolute value in the order of being—the recognition that, though the culling of the herd may be necessary in the order of time, the death of a wild horse remains tragic in the order of eternity. Values of utility, finally, are just that, not values of goodness. The works of destruction can never be justified as good, only as the bitter work of love. The callousness of utility is as morally abhorrent as the paralysis of sentimentality.

Still, it is a lesson we have to learn. For better or for worse, we have become a part of the balance of nature and can no longer simply withdraw. We must bear the responsibility of stewards, daring to make decisions and learning to recognize that there is not only the absolute value of being, but also the relative value of beings in the order of time. It is easy to become rapacious marauders in the process. It is, however, not inevitable if we learn to know and respet the rightness of time, the rightness of the season.

Temporalism, understanding the relative value of utility, helps us understand that. Had we but the absolute value of the order of being and the moral command of the order of eternity to guide us, we should remain paralyzed. Choices are possible because of the relative good and evil of the order of time.

The second valuable insight of temporalism, this time in its progressivist and historicist guise, is the opposite recognition, that so much of the evil, so much of the suffering to which humankind have for generations resigned themselves, is in truth not at all inevitable, that the passage of time can actually make a difference. Here the example of empirical medicine, with its stubborn refusal to accept as inevitable all the ills to which the flesh is heir, is perhaps the least controversial. But there are also the more controversial examples of men like Henry Ford or Tomáš Baťa,[10] who refused to accept the age-old verity that the laboring classes must remain forever condemned to the poverty of producing goods which only their "betters" could purchase, and who staked their fortunes on paying a wage which would enable their workers to become the purchasers of their own products. Or conversely, even Marxism, though it has spawned so much suffering and sorrow, can still awaken hope in Latin America because of its one crucial article of faith, that grief and injustice are not inevitable, that life can be better than it is. It matters little that it is the Western working man rather than the regimented subject of the Soviet empire, nominally Marxist, who lends credibility to that faith. What is crucial is the basic temporalist conviction that time is real, that it makes a difference, and that the future can be better than the perennial present.

That, finally, is the double insight of all temporalism—the vitalistic recognition that there is not only absolute, but also relative value, inhering in what from an absolute perspective appears as no more than passing and perishing, and the historicist recognition that, within the parameters of relative value, there is hope: things can be better than they are, human effort can make a difference. Those are not simply speculative abstractions. They are appealing less because of the arguments advanced in their support than because of their immediate experiential truth. In a hundred daily actions, what redeems us from the sense of ultimate futility of the order of time with its knowledge that the house I build will decay and fall, the love I cherish will pass in time, is the vitalist recognition that in spite of its absolute futility it is all still relatively good, intensely good in its season. Similarly, it is the historicist hope that the grief of the present can and will be redeemed by a future fulfillment, that sustains us even in the tedium of everydayness. Purpose can be a substitute for absolute sense.

Within these parameters a far more significant answer to the question of the worth of being human becomes possible than the merely factual justifiction that humans in fact are, real at least as much as "real socialism" is real, and so presumably also "rational," justified. On the level of the act rather than merely the fact of being human we can say that humans are worth the cost of their sustenance because they are the *beings capable of doing good.* Humans can sustain each other and other beings in pain, sorrow, and distress. To be sure, other animals can do that as well: I have watched a hen mother orphaned ducklings or one of the dogs who live with me comfort the other when he came home with a bullet in his paw and his lip viciously torn. Yet human capacity for alleviating suffering is much greater. The miracle of verbal communication virtually abolishes all limits on the range of empathy. Humans can share joy and sorrow, they can enrich the present with memories and sustain it with hope. The twin gift and achievement, the wonder of science and the marvel of technology, give us the possibility of rendering our presence on this earth benign. We have the capability, perhaps for the first time in our history, to safeguard nature, our shared inheritance, for all its creatures, and to alleviate massively its vast surplus of pain. That in fact we have used our potential heedlessly and destructively is true enough but not ultimately to the point. What is crucial is that we have the ability to do the good and that, if we choose to use it, it is capable of justifying our presence on this earth and at the same time of giving direction to our individual lives. There is, potentially, a source of the confidence of being human in the ability to do good. The recognition that being is also time and that time—or better, acts in time—can make a difference does represent a crucial insight. Humans are justified by their ability to do good.

Still, even that is not enough. The problem is not simply that the track record of temporalistic philosophies is most ambiguous, though it is certainly that. It would not be easy to argue that human life on this earth has become unambiguously more humane because of the technological advances in which the Henry Fords and the Tomáš Baťas of this world placed such well-intended confidence—or that human presence on this globe has become more justifiable because of them. At the other end of the temporalist spectrum, Marxism, for its part, has aroused immense hopes but produced a self-perpetuating nightmare.

The problem of principle, though, is more basic than all such problems in fact. It is that *relative* value, the great positive discovery of all temporalistic perspectives, is *absolutely* absurd. The existentialists and their heirs, the "greens" of our time among them, became agonizingly aware of the vast absurdity of a life whose meaningfulness is predicated on "progress." Only in a most myopic perspective does life become meaningful by virtue of being used as a means to something whose value is in turn solely instrumental. The infinite instrumental regress which the nineteenth century regarded as progress is coming to appear increasingly as the "rat race." No less so the generation which grew up in central Europe under Soviet rule is painfully aware of the hollowness of the "triumphant march of the proletariat" toward ever greater affluence.

Here it is crucial to tread humbly. In truth, as beings whose being is projected into temporality, we humans can claim no status more special than the raccoons, the porcupines, and the woodchucks we slaughter with our motorcars. The good of which we are capable in the order of time may be quantitatively greater, but so is the evil we in fact do. If we can claim a qualitative difference for our species, it is not its role in time but its ability to stand out into eternity. Humans are the beings who can recognize, in the flux of time, the intersecting dimension of the eternal. There is beauty, beauty *ab solo,* in the fragile wonder of the first trillium—yet that beauty will dissipate and perish with the order of time unles a human pauses over it in grateful wonder. There is a truth and a goodness of being which will dissipate and perish—but for the humans who can honor it, acting in ways which are wholly irrational in the order of time but bring into that order the eternal rationality of the categorical imperative. It is the humans who are willing to suffer and to die—needlessly, as time judges need—so that the goodness, the truth and the beauty of the eternal, would not perish but would rise to eternal validity. It is Václav Benda, recently released after serving a four-year prison term because he refused to collaborate with the political police, saying simply, "There is this commandment, 'Thou shalt not bear false witness.' "[11] It is all those who choose to live in truth, Šimsa, Bonhoffer, Niemöller, Patočka, the millions of nameless, unnoted others who have suffered and died—and often far less dramatically, who have *lived*—so that the good, the true, the beautiful will not dissipate unnoted into the cosmos. They are the salt of the earth. It is they who anchor our chains of instrumental value in absolute worth. It is they, too, who remind us of the full and specific sense of our humanity and our place in the cosmos, as the beings who, living at the intersection of time and eternity, can bring the eternal into time—and raise time to eternity.

That eternity is not an "other" realm, discontinuous with the order of time, nor an infinite prologation of it. It really does ingress in time, reorienting the moment from its horizontal matrix of the before and after to a vertical one of good and evil. To me, lightning became the most vivid metaphor of that ingression. In the solitude of the rain-drenched forest, it is an awesome phenomenon. I would sit in the doorway, staring into the darkness. The clearing, usually starlit, would be immersed in darkness under the heavy overcast: I could not even distinguish the edge of the tree line. Then suddenly, without warning, the whole clearing would be illuminated in a pale violet light, every detail clear, cut off sharply from the invisible "before" and "after," frozen in an absolute presence, utterly still. I don't think I have ever seen movement by lightning. That may seem possible in an urban context where the moment of illumination, though far brighter, is continuous with the neon-lit flow of time, not cut off by intense darkness from the before and the after. Here the thunderclouds and the heavy rain extinguish all residual glow. The darkness is total, masking all continuity. The flash of lightning presents a moment of the world's being taken out of the context of its temporality, present *ab solo*. The metaphor has its limitations, but the experience is a powerful one. It is the overwhelming recognition that being cannot be contained in time.

The categories of the "temporal" and the "eternal," though barely philosophically intelligible today, remain indispensible. The temporal perspective of a sequence of events, the preceding determining that which comes after, does create the illusion of being as wholly contained in time, merely natural in the reductive sense of that term. Drifting with the flow of time, humans can perceive their acts as "perfectly understandable" quite independently of their moral worth. So, presumably, can animals, though they may not articulate that awareness conceptually. By contrast, the recognition that something may be perfectly understandable and yet be *wrong* is a distinctively human recognition, cutting across the flow of temporal reasoning with the vertical slash of moral insight. Here eternity, the perennial, atemporal vision of the ideal, enters temporality so that we can, legitimately, speak of the human as the being who lives at the intersection of two dimensions, the temporal dimension of nature and the value dimension of eternity.

It is as dwellers in time that humans find their place in nature; it is as bearers of eternity that they find their justification. So stated, though, though properly inspirational, that insight remains so distant from the lived reality of it, from the tangible goodness of white birches and of drawing water at dusk to water the caraway, the dill, and the peas that are just putting out first blossoms. The miracle of incarnation is not abstract; it is as tangible as the labor in which love becomes embodied and comes to belong, from eternity to earth, but not just earth in general, but to this spread of land, to these boulders, to these trees, to this river.

The mystery of incarnation, enacted in every stroke of the hoe which makes this land mine and which makes me no less its own husbandman, may be a stumbling block because it is acted out in such earthy ways, in belonging, and belonging is so perilously difficult to distinguish from having—and having can so easily become a substitute for being.[12]

When humans attempt to leave the lockstep of greed and gratification and reach out for a different dimension of being human, they, like Saint Francis before them, inevitably know the longing to leave all thought of having behind. As it is tempting in the order of time to avoid the guilt of doing by abstaining from acting, so in the order of being it is tempting to avoid the burden of having by abstaining from it. Greed, the twin brother of pride, has ever been the driving force of the most destructive and self-destructive human acts. The logic is familiar enough: in their pride, humans seek to dominate their world, to possess it, free to use or abuse, destroy and alienate it as they see fit. Again and again, they have in fact succeeded in alienating it, though not in the sense intended by the old Austrian civil code which so defined ownership. Whatever I come to possess, to dominate, be it a tool, an animal, or a fellow human being, can no longer be a companion. It becomes alien. The world humans master, though they may claim to own it, does not become their own, belonging to them in the intimate sense in which a father belongs to a son or a husband to a wife. The possessed world becomes a dead world in our hands, lifeless and meaningless.

In a sense, the utter absurdity of having, conceived as a task and a goal of being, may be one of the most valuable lessons which successful consumerism has to teach a humankind conditioned by millennia of want to consider possession the fulfillment of life. The accumulation of artifacts that never become our own is evident in our garage sales: an incredible clutter of gewgaws, each representing an investment of life and labor never repaid in use, is laid out as unwanted burden. It is seldom the small, cherished possessions, companions of a lifetime, that appear on the tables. Typically, it is high-cost items, a rusty LP grill, seen on a television, bought on an impulse, used once, then stored away; alpine skis with rigid plastic boots, built to peak competition standards, then bought by someone who thought it might be fun to try skiing. From the latest electronic gadgets to fourth husbands, they are items bought in the illusion that possession can mean fulfillment—and unceremoniously discarded when the illusion bursts. We are hopelessly burdened by excess possessions, closets of once-worn clothes, and yet we build more closets to fill, afraid that if our lives lost the purpose of acquisition they would have no purpose at all.

It is not surprising that the rebelling children of affluence can be so easily persuaded that private property is the root of all evil and led to project as their vision of the Kingdom a condition they think "natural"—one in which the world would belong only to God or to an anonymous "all," while each human, unburdened by possessions, would contribute his all to a common store while drawing from it what he thinks he needs. They will not be dissuaded by the recognition that animals in fact have their cherished belongings and defend them fiercely, nor by the nightmare of alienation which that vision has wrought among humans. A different truth presses in on them—the depersonalization of humans and nature alike by the quest for possession.[13]

The conflict they are experiencing is once more the intrinsic conflict between love and instrumentality, though on a deeper level—the conflict of being and having to which neither the solution of poverty nor that of affluence can be consistently applied. We are incarnate beings: for us, having and being are inseparable. To be at all means to have a body and a place in the world which are my own. The slave who cannot call even his body his own is not more free for having been "freed from the burden of possession" any more than the farmer reduced to an employee of a state farm in latter-day feudalism. As the slave's body is alienated from him, to be used, traded, or destroyed independently of him, his very humanity is being denied. The body I have and am is my most intimate point of entry into the world. It serves me, at times it sustains my flagging spirit with its vitality, at other times it reminds me of my finitude with its limitations. Had I no body, I would not be present at all: Husserl points out that we can imagine even a ghost only as present as a ghostly body.[14] Saint Paul tells us that, even in glory, we shall receive spiritual bodies, while Saint Thomas observes that the so-called natural immortality of the soul would be little to be desired were it not for the promise of the resurrection of the body which breaks the isolation of consciousness and leads it into the world. The respect with which we treat the body left behind by one departed this life reflects a recognition of the intimate union between a person and the body which belonged to him.

In an order of decreasing intensity, we show a similar respect to other things which belonged to the deceased. Though we no longer bury a person's cherished belongings with him, we do not bury his body naked, as it came into the world. For the body is not a monad. All that a person cherishes and cares for through a lifetime becomes its intimate extension. My old coat, the blue glass snail, the hammer which was long my companion, the land I loved, and the beams of the old house that sheltered my children, all that may not be *me*, as Hegel thought it was, just as my body is not simply *me*, yet all of it is intimately mine, my dwelling place, my presence. A person to whom nothing belonged would himself have no way of belonging. *Der Mann ohne Eigenschaften*—the human devoid of properties—is always a fiction and usually a lie, as in the case of the affluent monastic orders which honored their oath of poverty by having their estates owned nominally by the Church, or of the superrich of the "real socialist" societies, who own nothing but enjoy the total domination and exclusive use of a state limousine, apartment, country cottage, and expense account. For an incarnate being in a finite world, being is indissoluably bound up with having.

Therein, though, lies the rub. It is not simply the problem of the order of time, the senseless accumulation and misuse of possessions, easily perceived as destructive and resolved in the recognition of human role as grateful stewards of God's creation. It is a problem of being as well, the intrinsic contradiction between being, whose justification is love and respect, the posture of a person in a person-al world, and the posture of having which, no matter how lovingly, makes the other mine, using him as a means of my presence, not as an end, whether the other be my body, my land, or the community of humans I call mine.[15]

Here a glimmer of a hard answer emerges slowly, like the cool silver disk of a night light glowing in the forest. It begins with the recognition that two postures which we habitually treat as synonymous with having and with each other, that of possessing and that of belonging, are not only distinct but, in truth, are diametrically opposed. What I would claim to possess can never belong to me—and whatever belongs to me I can never treat as a possession.

It was the land that taught me the difference. When I came to live in the clearing, I could claim a legal possession of the land. The papers had been signed and notarized, the bounds surveyed and staked. It was "my" land. Still, in truth, the land did not belong to me, nor I to the land. It belonged far more tangibly to my long-ago predecessors whose memory lingers in the cellar holes, the paths, the old orchard and currant bushes. It belonged to the occasional fishermen who knew the hidden pools of its river, and the hunters familiar with its deer tracks, even to the deer, the chipmunks, and the porcupines. Though I held the papers in my hand, I was an alien, claiming possession as a conqueror might claim his spoils, but what I so possessed was not yet my own and no legal act could make it so. Only life and love have that power.

Through the long seasons, my relation to the land changed, gradually but fundamentally. As I walked the paths, cleared the brush, pruned the old trees, and pondered over the cellar holes, I came to belong to the land—and the land came to belong to me in turn. It would be wholly misleading to claim, with Locke, that mingling my labor with it, though I did so in prodigious amounts, gave me a claim to possession. The more the land and I belonged to each other, the less did I possess it. The very concept of possessing belongs to a different order. It is a formal claim, not a lived bond. It represents a unidirectional claim to mastery—the "right" to "use or abuse, destroy or alienate"—

rather than the experience of mutual belonging. The claim to possess cannot grow out of a lived experience: it is an abstract, legal claim, a construct established by social convention to order the life of a world of artifacts. It may well be necessary in a crowded, complex society, assigning responsibilities and rights. It may even be legitimate, as a formalization of a lived experience. But the truth, the reality itself, is of a different order, the personal experience of a bond between a person and the land he tills, the worker and the familiar tool which is the companion of his labor, the person and his body. Those are not experiences of possession and domination but of being at ease, at home with each other, of belonging together.

The bond of belonging that grows up over years of life, love, and labor is the most basic truth of being human in a world. Here the claims about the "sacredness of private property," trite and blasphemous when used to justify abstract possession, become meaningful. They reflect not possession but the utterly basic relationship of belonging between a human and his world. It may well be within the prerogatives of the society which established those conventions to modify or disestablish them as it sees fit for the common good. To sever the bond of belonging that love, life, and labor shared have forged between two humans or between a human and the segment of the natural world in which he is incarnate is always a crime and a sacrilege, no less heinous than depriving a person of his body. That is a bond no human imposed and no human may cut asunder. As the land and I came to belong together, I ceased to possess it: I could no longer "alienate" it as if it were a possession, sell it or carve it into subdivisions. The old peasant in Konstantin Rasputin's novel,[16] who knows she must stay with the trees that bore her fruit and the graves of her ancestors on the land about to be flooded by a dam, knew well the sense of belonging. I belong to the land, as it to me—we belong together. When I have left it, as one day I must, it shall belong to those whom I loved and who are prepared to love it. Perhaps it will be the creatures of the forest and the solitary fishermen to whom it belonged before me, perhaps others will come to dwell thereon. Though someone, perhaps the Society for the Protection of New Hampshire Forests, shall technically "possess" it, the land will belong to those who belong to it. The land must belong: as belonging, it lives; as possessed, it becomes dead.

The distinction between possessing and belonging is crucial. Though humans may need to formalize having as possessing, the living truth of having is belonging, the bond of love and respect which grows between one being and another in the course of the seasons. The claim to having is as strong as all the love and care a person gives, and only that strong. It is crucial to have no more than we can love, for without love the claim to having becomes void. Loveless having, possessing in the purest sense, remains illegitimate, a theft. The coat that hangs in the closet, unused and unloved, does indeed belong to the needy person who has none. The point of that ancient adage, however, is not simply the obvious, half-true and half-false one, that the person who claims to possess a coat but never makes it his own by love, care, and use "does not deserve" it, or that the needy somehow deserve it by virtue of their need. Claims of entitlement are beside the point. The basic point, strange-sounding in a world of artifacts, is of a different order—that *things need to be loved,* used, and cared for.[17]

That, I am convinced, is the inmost meaning of having. Humans are justified by the power of their love to bring the world alive, to give things the love, care, and use they need for their fulfillment. Thus they act out the incarnation. That is not a matter of taking possession of the world but of making it our own in a bond of mutual belonging, of taking the world with us from the flow of temporality into eternity. That is the task, at once the privilege and the obligation of humans as beings who dwell at the intersection of time and eternity. In being loved, in becoming *own,* a part of the world acquires an eternal significance. Even an artifact: the countless toy panda bears, mass-produced, mass-distributed, and mass-destroyed as unsold merchandise, disappear in the dark stream of time. The Pandy Bear once loved by a little girl, worn smooth and misshapen by many nights of hugging, stands out of time into eternity. Though in the order of time it will disappear in its turn, as she will herself, in the love she shared with it it will remain, in eternity. The tree cherished as the marvel of tinsel and light becomes eternal in the love, joy, and pain of the humans gathered around it. Not that it will be long remembered—in all likelihood, it will not. Yet though it were forgotten before the twelve days of Christmas are spent, it would still have stood out into eternity in the moment of its glory. So will the land I have loved, as I have loved it. Though it, too, will disappear in the order of time, as I shall in my turn, the love I bore it and the peace we shared in joy and pain stand out into eternity before God. That, finally, is the meaning of incarnation: humans can raise the world of nature to eternity. That is the great power of love, pain, and joy—opening eternity to time.

It is, no less, an awesome responsibility, for humans can also drag the world with which they belong with them to eternal damnation as they close themselves to eternity. The dog who loves his alcoholic master is dragged down with him to destruction; the land, the forest, the things possessed become depersonalized together with their possessors. That may well be the sense of the dark line of Scripture, that "through man sin came into the world." Humans, in the having in which their lives are inscribed in the temporality of the natural world, take the world with them: as they corrupt and destroy themselves, they can do no less with the world with which they belong. By the same token, humans also have the great power of letting the world they love share in the healing bestowed upon them when eternity intersects the temporality of their lives. It is up to us.

When the silence of dusk replaces the day's speaking, the wonder still remains: we are justified. We are justified in the order of being, together with our kin, the trees, the boulders, the creatures, as bearers of the miracle of the creation: that there is something, not nothing. We are justified in the order of time as we take up the task to which we are called therein, to be faithful stewards of the earth. We are, finally, justified by grace in the order of eternity, as we raise the creation above the passing and perishing of the order of time in an act of love.

Or perhaps not we, specifically, for we fail, too much, too often. It is the idea of humanity, our humanity, that is justified. Thus it is not by rejecting our humanity, but quite the contrary, by reclaiming it, that we find our place in nature.

Of Humans and Persons

It is much easier to decry our dehumanization than to reclaim our humanity. "Dehumanization" has become a code word for all the ills of our age. By an easy extension, "humanism" has become a code word for all that is sweet, lovely, and of good repute. It would take a brave man to question it, as Heidegger did.[18]

Yet "humanism," precisely as a code word, has become eminently questionable. Its dictionary definition—or at least one of them—as "a way of life centered on human interests" does not exactly inspire confidence. It smacks of the heedless egotism of our species which is at the root of the dehumanization of our lives. Yet it is not an arbitrary definition. It has its warrant in the dictum of Protagoras so beloved by the Renaissance, that "man [*sic*] is the measure of all things"—no less than in the nineteenth-century *hubris* of a "religion of Man rather than god."

To be sure, humanism can have positive connotations as well. There is a noble tradition of moral humanism, both of the ethical fervor of Unitarianism, which invokes the biblical injunction about "whatsoever ye have done for one of these" as well as the unambiguous assertion that "the Sabbath was made for man, not man for the Sabbath." To a Czech, the word evokes the moral humanism of T. G. Masaryk which runs through the entire Czech philosophical tradition, from the Hussite reformation and Jan Amos Komenský down to Jan Patočka in our own time.[19] There is nothing facile, nothing superficial about that tradition whose core is an insistence on the ontological and ethical primacy of moral categories. What "humanism" will mean, if anything, will depend very directly on the way we define our *humanitas.* Its meaning will be quite different if we take, as definitive of our humanity, our ability to grasp the eternal moral law in time than if we define ourselves in terms of our *allzu menschlich* pettiness of greed and gratification.

Historically, the conception of *humanitas* has its antecedents in the self-experienced cultural superiority of the Hellenes over the barbarians. The term, *homo humanus,* is Roman: for the ancient Romans, the "humane" person was first of all a person of civility and culture in contrast to the crudity of the rustic and the barbarian alike. Though the term is an anachronism, the *homo humanus* was essentially the human as a moral rather than merely biological, instinctual subject.

To be sure, in its actual content the Roman definition of *humanitas* included a great deal of cultural parochialism as well. The moral traits of the *homo humanus* were not only moral but also emphatically Roman, embodying the mores and prejudices of the well-to-do and well-educated citizens. Yet for all its implicit parochialism, the conception of *humanitas* does contain a fundamental insight—that the human in the fullness of his humanity is not simply a product of "natural" drives and needs, accultured in the course of history to accommodate the demands of a reality principle imposed by social coexistence. That was all that most Romans were willing, whether fairly or not, to allow to the barbarian, whom they regarded less as a specific person than as a type, a being whose being is shaped entirely and directly by a quest for gratification of need and desire, unmodified by any but hedonistic utilitarian considerations. The point of affirming the *humanitas* of humans—or, at this stage, at least of some humans—

was to identify the *homo humanus* as the being not simply driven by stimuli but also capable of responding to ideal motivations.

To be sure, the Romans held the barbarian in disdain as unredeemably crude, and that need not be accurate. A life wholly contained within natural needs and their satisfaction need not be at all crude, as John Stuart Mill pointed out. The conventions of hedonism and of utility can, in fact, be extremely elaborate. Its motives, however, though perhaps wholly free of greed, remain strictly those of need. Goodness remains reducible to utility, rightness to prudence, beauty to aesthetic enjoyment. The point of reference is individual preference, not the generically human vision of a moral sense of life. What is missing is the recognition of intrinsic beauty, rightness, goodness. The barbarian, as the ideal type which that word suggested to the Romans, is a being locked in temporality, marked by the innocent egocentrism of a healthy animal. The mark of *humanitas,* by contrast, is *cultus,* the recognition of the moral sense of life and of the intrinsic value of the other. However parochially the Roman mind may have formulated it, the *homo humanus* is a being who no longer simply asks, "Do I like it?" but "Is it beautiful?," not simply "Is it useful?" but rather "Is it good?," no longer simply "How do I feel about it?" but rather, "Is it right?" The perspective focused on the sole question, "How do I feel about it?" is the essence of barbarism.

To the Enlightenment, which for several generations knew the Romans only as the Romans knew themselves, the Roman perspective appeared quite evidently accurate. As we gradually gain a less biased view of antiquity, the equation of "humane" with "Roman" becomes difficult to sustain. The barbarians, for all the crudity of their life, were not nearly the uncomplicated products of the clash between drive and reality principle which the Romans took them to be. Nor was Roman *humanitas* in practice as noble as the Romans described it. The distinction between the *homo humanus* and the barbarian simply does not coincide with that between the Roman and the Goth or the Celt. Freed from that historic identification, however, the distinction of humane and barbaric remains as a fundamental one between two modes of being human, one locked in the lock-step of need and gratification, the other opening out in *cultus.*

Given our predilection for psychology, we in our turn are likely to give the distinction a psychological rather than a cultural content and read it as a distinction between "immature" and "mature" developmental stages. One writer at least—Lawrence Kohlberg[20]—has even attempted to superimpose the cultural and developmental projection and to speak of mature and immature societies, much as Hegel's nineteenth-century followers were wont to do, whether to justify revolution or colonialism. It seems likely, though, that we shall have to abandon this identification no less than the cultural one. Nor is the equation with "natural" and "artificial" any more persuasive. The distinction between a moral and a barbaric sense of our humanity defies easy equations. Still, it is a real difference, though between two modes of being human rather than between two instances. *Humanitas* is the quality of living at the intersection of time and eternity.

That remains the valid moment in what has often been parochial, the ideal of *homo humanus* and of our *humanitas*—more recently "humanism"—not simply as a natural or a historical fact but as a moral ideal by which the human can orient his life. That, in fact, is the aspect of Roman *humanitas* to which the great Stoic thinkers pointed in less naïve though still inevitably culture-specific terms. In the Stoic metaphor, the distinction between the humane and barbarian modes of being came to coincide with the distinction between reason and emotion. To modern readers of Stoic texts, used to equating reason with reasoning and nature with the physical system described within the framework of the natural sciences, those texts often appear confusing. The Stoics seem to be advocating an "unfeeling intellectualism."[21] For the Stoics, though, reason was not reasoning. It was the moral order of the cosmos, the *logos* in which humans may participate as bearers of the spark of reason. Nature here was the autonomous rhyme and reason of reality. The privilege and the distinguishing mark of humans is not our reasoning ability but rather our Reason, the divine spark which enables us to break free of the blind tyranny of drives and gratification and to grasp the moral sense of life. Unlike the slave of passion, a wise man is one capable of living in harmony with the moral order of the cosmos.

When we read the Stoics anachronistically, endowing the terms "reason" and "emotion" with their contemporary psychological significance, it is easy to make light of Stoic teachings. If anything, it becomes quite difficult to see how reasonably intelligent humans could have thought that human life can be transformed into such a cold, intellectual abstraction. Then it becomes equally easy to point out that the Stoics could not possibly live up to their own teachings. The driving force of the humanitarianism so prominent in the Roman Stoa—the Stoics, after all, built bridges, staffed hospitals, reformed the courts, and administered an empire—was obviously not reason but the *love of* reason.

Such an obvious criticism, though, misses an important point. The basic contrast which the Stoics sought to express by their opposition of reason and the passions was not an exercise in faculty psychology as much as a reflection of the experiential difference between a moral and a mundane, temporal sense of life. The categories they chose may have become unfortunate with the shift of meaning of their terms in modern psychology. Or perhaps they were unfortunate from the start. Certainly, it becomes rather awkward when we need to speak of a rational emotion—as the love of justice—and of emotional reason, as in the case of calculating egotism. Any set of categories, though, will become unfortunate if we fail to grasp the central insight which they seek to articulate. Conversely, the failings of any categorical schema become unimportant when we read its terms as pointers, evoking a basic insight. The categories of reason and the emotions, for all their undeniable defects, served remarkably well, both in antiquity and in the Renaissance, to express the fundamental difference between a life conceived as merely temporal and life conceived as having a moral sense.

With the triumph of Christianity in the Middle Ages, the humanism of ancient Rome receded from prominence. To the moral zealots of the new creed, humanism became symbolic of a self-indulgent egocentrism, much as it seems to have become to Alexander Solzhenitsyn in our time. Then as now, the utter misunderstanding on all sides is as palpable as it is distressing. The Christians, far more than either they themselves or the cultured Romans of their time realized, were in their moral fervor precisely heirs of the classic *humanitas* which, a century or two earlier, carried far more the connotation of selfless service than of self-indulgence. In one of history's great ironies, the Christians regarded the cultured Romans as "barbarian" in the classical sense—as persons whose humanity was no more than a reflection of natural need and greed, conventionalized to fit the constraints of reality but devoid of a transcending moral vision. They remained blind to the radically atemporal, moral vision of humanity in Roman Stoicism. When they encountered it, as in Seneca, they frequently assumed that the author must have been a Christian, as many medievals in fact believed of Seneca. For now it was the Christians who were proclaiming a moral conception of being human.

Verbally, the categories of Christianity appeared radically different from those of old Rome and were to become even more so in time. While old Rome contrasted culture with crudity and the Stoics reason with emotion, the Christians contrasted the sacred with the mundane. Specifically, it was the contrast between the human conceived *kata sarka,* according to the flesh, with the human conceived *kata pneuma,* according to the spirit, terms quite alien to the Roman intellectual tradition.[22] Yet the basic perspective is closely analogous. *Kata sarka*—yes, the human conceived according to the flesh is still the old barbarian, the man of passions whose humanity is no more than a product of greed and gratification, no matter how refined. And *kata pneuma?* It is the human capable of responding to God's challenging and redeeming call, capable of breaking out of the bondage of utility, placing his life in the perspective of the vision of the Good. The terms have changed, but the fundamental humanistic vision persists.

If anything, Christianity augmented rather than denied the humanistic vision in attributing cosmic significance to the human drama. It is through the human, the Christians insisted, that "sin came into the world," that the basic rightness of the creation was disrupted and the human alienated from the ground of his being. In turn, it is through a human, God become man, and through the humans who hear him, that the restoring grace enters in. That is the uniqueness of the human role in the economy of the cosmos: the human is capable of operating not only on a "natural" level of need and gratification but also on a moral level of good and evil, which, through him, enters into the world. In the terms we have been using, humans mediate between temporality and eternity.

That is a Christian vision, but it is no less a humanistic one. What the Christians rejected was a degenerate humanism which attributed a moral significance to a "humanity" conceived in strictly temporal terms, making human need and gratification the measure of all things. What they reaffirmed, though rejecting the term, was the classic humanist vision of the human as a moral subject, capable of knowing truly and acting rightly, in a morally ordered world.

Christian humanism decayed in its turn as the Middle Ages progressed. The radically nontemporal, moral dimension of being human came ever more to be encoded as a substantival "immortal soul," the contrast between the natural and the moral was ever more replaced by a contrast between the natural and the "supernatural." In another one of the ironies of intellectual history, the new Renaissance humanists reaffirmed the moral dimension of being human, including its Stoic rationalist components, under the label of the "natural" against the "supernatural." It is ironic but not surprising. When the moral came to be conceived as "supernatural," it came no less to appear as an irrelevant, pale copy of the richness of concrete moral life—or of "natural" life and "natural" reason.

As the Renaissance saw it, that "natural" life was by no means one-dimensional, a lock-step of need and gratification. The Enlightenment, applying the Renaissance insight to praxis much as the Roman Stoics applied the teachings of the middle Stoa, rediscovered the Stoic conception of reason as the faculty which opens a moral dimension to human existence, not as "supernatural" but as intrinsic to it. The struggles of the Enlightenment with the ecclesiastical authorities of the time, typified by the futile clash of Austria's Joseph II with the Church, again seem a tangle of misunderstanding. Both sides of the dispute were defined in terms which, each in its own way, sought to affirm precisely the moral dimension of being human. Revelation, as the Christians conceived of it, and reason, as the Enlightenment understood it, both pointed to the distinctive dimension of being human which breaks the lock-step of need and gratification with the vision of the good, the true, the beautiful. Perhaps the conflict was doubly inevitable. The term "revelation" had lost the significance of the clear vision of the transcendental dimension of being human and had come to mean, instead, a highly mystified doctrine. Reason, too, was no longer simply Plato's clear rational vision but, with Galileo and Kepler, increasingly meant reasoning. The resulting conflict burdened modern humanism with an antireligious bias, which inevitably led the humanists to stress the "this-worldly," the "natural" character of the *humanitas* they proclaimed. When, however, we understand "natural" in the reduced sense of the merely biological and temporal, devoid of any moral sense, then such "natural" humanity can represent only the pathos of everydayness, not a moral ideal. So conceived and proclaimed as the measure of all things, "humanity" does indeed become a justification of self-indulgent greed. Then a new voice must arise, castigating humanism in the name of its own basic insight, the moral vision of life, only speaking of it in some new terms, perhaps as a moral naturalism. . . .

Yet naturalism has problematic connotations of its own, serious enough to warrant yet another attempt to recover the older term. Perhaps because the starry heaven above is so powerful a presence in a forest clearing, it was Immanuel Kant who, for me, served as a catalyst of that recovery. Kant, to be sure, is a problematic figure. It is also true that, together with Descartes, he helped steer Western thought along the solipsistic lines of the "Copernican" revolution, reducing reality in itself to unknowability and turning the task of knowledge from seeing and listening—clear vision and faithful articulation—to one of designing constructs.[23] His *Theory of the Heavens* would seem far removed from the primordial philosophic vision at dusk. Yet the opening line of the conclusion to his *Critique of Practical Reason,* "the starry heavens above and the moral law within," is a classic outcry of just that vision. Kant is radically aware of the human as a moral subject. When we reduce his profound vision of moral humanity to a "formalistic theory of ethics," we shall inevitably find it wanting. Max Scheler, in his earnest grappling with Kant, points out with evident justice the shortcomings of Kant's work, most basically Kant's dismissal of all values that present themselves in the order of time as *eo ipso* merely prudential. Kant, as Scheler reads him, saw clearly that a moral "ought" cannot be derived from a prudential "is"—and concluded that reason must supply it from without. He overlooked the moral sense of being, the radical intersection of time with eternity.

For all the justice of Scheler's criticism, though, it is still Kant who offers the challenge, sets the perspective, and provokes the insight of what, with some qualms, we have been calling "humanism." That insight is humanistic in the profound sense of seeing the moral rather than the merely factual or historical dimension of being human as definitive of our *humanitas.* Implicit in it, there is a triple recognition. One, which Scheler and Husserl were to elaborate far more adequately, is present in Kant's *Preface to the Metaphysics of Morals:* the recognition that there is a truth, there to be seen, and that humans are capable of such vision.[24] To speak of that vision as a "rational intuition" is misleading, both because of the technical connotations of "reason" in current usage and because of the irrationalistic connotations of "intuition." Husserl's and Scheler's favorite German term, *Wesensanschauung,* the ability to perceive the sense of what is, may be more to the point.[25] It is the claim which remains speculative in a world of artifacts and constructs, devoid of a sense and a truth of their own, but becomes evident in the radical bracketing of solitude at dusk: there is a sense, there is a *logos.* Humans are not condemned to speculation; they can *see.* It may be the greatness of Kant's three *Critiques* that, contrary to his apparent claim and intent, their final impact is not one of producing speculative assent but of evoking a vision of the true, the good, the beautiful.

Linked with that is the second recognition, which I think definitive of humanism, that nature and history alike are relative to the eternal, the Idea of the Good which Kant, with indifferent success, sought to formulate as the moral law. His specific formulations have been subjeted to innumerable critical examinations and, invariably, found wanting. With reason. Words do not contain the truth, they point to it and evoke it. Even the oft-noted fact that Kant's various formulations of the moral law are not convertible with each other should alert us that their unity is of a different order. Each in its way seeks to evoke a vision of the moral law. To be sure, even the term "law" has become misleading in its formal, legalistic connotations. Terms like moral structure, moral order, or, in our usage, moral sense of being, its essential rightness, may serve better. But it is the reality which is the point and to which Kant's formulations point—that there is a rightness and that humans are capable of perceiving it with the same evident clarity as they perceive the starry heavens above.

There is a third aspect to the essential humanistic recognition which again we owe to Kant: the harmony of the order of the starry heavens above and the moral law within. We might, again, quibble over terms: the moral law is really not "within." The fundamental reality to be seen, however, is that there is no essential conflict between the moral sense of being human and the sense of the cosmos. It is not because humans are as impersonal as objects are reputed to be. Rather, it is because the cosmos, the starry heaven, is far more personal, essentially continuous with the moral order of being human.

That triple recognition, of the human as capable of grasping his moral place within the order of the cosmos, represents the core of the "humanistic" conception of being human. Though it is not Kant's explicit formulation, still in a very real sense we owe it to him and should bear that indebtedness in mind when, as in Rádl's case, we take Kant to task for his part in working the Copernican revolution in philosophy. Precisely by his clear, uncompromising recognition that moral judgments are radically "nonfactual," nontemporal, reflecting not the vicissitudes of the temporal process but a vision of the moral law alone, Kant stands as witness that the unique place of humans and their task in the cosmos need not entail a dehumanization of nature and an explosion of the arrogant human will to power—in spite of his own demeaning view of nonhuman nature.

That, to be sure, remains a perennial danger—and the fortunes of positivistic humanism in the nineteenth century testify no less to that. In fairness to positivism, we should recognize that its impulse, wholly forgotten in our time, was fundamentally and quite explicitly moral. The utilitarians were almost compulsive reformers and general benefactors of humanity. Though it would be difficult to derive Bentham's or Mill's reforming fervor from the overt contents of their doctrines, it is still impossible to overlook it. Similarly, Auguste Comte's "cult of humanity," no matter how flawed and quaint in retrospect, had a clear moral thrust. Perhaps no one formulated that thrust as clearly and explicitly as the grand old man of ethical naturalism, John Dewey. His *Experience and Nature* stands as a grand monument to the attempt to combine a postivistic sense of nature with a moral sense of experience.[26]

It is not the failings but the greatness of Mill, Comte, or Dewey that shows most clearly the limitations of their approach. Theirs is a humanism wholly contained in temporality. What is absent from it is precisely the recognition of the transtemporal reference which anchors utility in a vision of the Good. Dewey comes closest to that recognition. His conception of joy, of enjoyment as true fulfillment, making being whole, is really nonutilitarian. It is the intrinsic joy of being that it invokes. In Dewey's work, to be sure, it remains marginal. The operative value concept here is "growth," reflecting the vitalist and historicist attempt to find the eternal in time, value in the process itself. For all the noble attempts, a humanism which sees in our *humanitas* no more than the factual and temporal reality of our lives stands in a perennial danger of slipping into a narcissism of our species which perceives our humanity no longer as a moral obligation but simply as a rationalization of our rapacity or an excuse for our flabbiness. Humanism becomes tenable only when it recognizes that the human is *not* the measure of all things, his moral *humanitas* is. Humanism becomes defensible when what we take as definitive of our humanity is the ability to transcend the narcissism of our species and to see ourselves and our place in the cosmos in the mirror of the moral law.

Or so I thought, through evenings of reflection. Not long before, I had received a new Czech translation of Vergil's *Bucolica*, in resplendent hexameters. I memorized it, and the mood was on me.

> O Tityre, rozvalený tam kde stín, kde vánek a tráva,
> píšťalou rákosovou pěstíš si náklonnost mùz.[27]

Had it not been for the cellar holes, I might well have rested content with some such modified religious humanism. It is intellectually satisfying and most respectable, with its two millennia of philosophical tradition. It can provide an adequate accounting of the place of humans in the cosmos, and can even generate categories capable of subsuming our ordinary dealings with our fellow humans, in the street, the store, the office, giving it a touch of class.

It cannot, though, subsume the cellar holes, still and vine-covered in the noontime sun, where humans had once lived, loved, labored. The presence of my predecessors on this land, gone long before my time, is of a different order. It is so ethereal and yet so utterly tangible in the small traces of their works. Now there is only the forest, yet human hands once planted those vines and cared for the apple trees, human hands had raised the boulders of the old dam and wedged them with small stones. I can subsume the people passing me in the street or the people whose doings the newspapers report within humanist categories. My predecessors on this land defy those categories: they are so eternal and yet so concrete in their presence.

There have been others who dwelled on this land. As I go about my tasks, I come upon the fading traces of their presence. Amid the wild growth by the low stone wall, some currant bushes have gone wild, both red and white. Once upon a time, a woman raised a garden there. When I first came to the land, I decided to dig a ditch to drain a swampy patch. Sighting along the lie of the land, I chose the likeliest route and set to digging. After a few yards, I realized that I was clearing a long-forgotten drainage ditch, filled over the years with twigs, leaves, and branches. That land, though, had been under water while the dam stood, and no one lived there after the dam gave way. It must have been one of the earliest settlers, living there before the dam flooded the land, who, as I did, sighted along the lie of the land and, choosing the likeliest route, set to digging. I came as a stranger to a wilderness and yet even here the verse of Scripture spoke to me—"we shall dig again the wells of our fathers."

I have not literally dug those wells again. When the dam burst, the groundwater level receded some three fathoms. To follow it down would take long and dangerous labor in cramped quarters. There are springs nearby, close to the surface. But I have found three wells. The land on which I live, today a part of a forest extending for miles around, once sustained enough families to fill a schoolhouse with some two dozen children each year. Families were larger then, but each child attended school for only four years. It would have taken some twenty to thirty families to keep the school filled. For such a concentration, there would need to be jobs. There were, in fact, two mills, the sawmill and cooperage on my land, boasting the four-foot circular saw which gave it its name, and a gristmill downstream, each employing several men. Their presence slowly emerges from the silent forest. Each winter's frost brings up a horseshoe or some farm implement. This spring I found a drop-forged ax-head which had lost none of its temper over the years. The old-timers believe that a man's strength—his *virtu,* though they would not use that word—is vested in his ax. When I found this one, I sensed it as a gift from the generations of my predecessors, their acceptance of me among the cellar holes that mark the dwelling sites of a century ago.

There is a well-preserved, carefully built cellar across the road. The house that once stood there had two chimneys and two stories, covered with yellow clapboards. Doctor Ryan lived there, early in the nineteenth century, and his son, Colonel Ryan, after him. The fragments of their lives preserved by the Historical Society include samplers and paper dolls made by Colonel Ryan's daughter: once they had been cherished. Then there was John Preston, whose descendants still live on the other side of the mountain. He had bought the mill from Colonel Ryan and operated it with his partner, the enterprising Derastus P. Emory, who was born a laborer's son and died a millionaire at a time when a dollar was a day's wage. There were, I have heard, also the Smiths, humble folk who left no record, but whom the oldest inhabitants of the town remember living here in a large rambling farmhouse at the time when the mill burned down when a new owner sought to dispose by fire of a pile of tailings on a day not quite rainy enough for the job.

The cellar hole of the Smiths' farmhouse brought home to me most clearly the reality of the others on the land. One of its buckling walls gave way under me as I was clearing what once had been an orchard. As the stones shifted, they revealed a flat file in what had been a crack between the threshstone and the cellar wall. I held it in my hand for a long time, imagining its long-gone user who must have searched for it, so certain that he had it in his hand just the other day, so certain it must be here somewhere, turning to his wife, as men will. . . . Suddenly, holding that lost and found file in my hand, I found myself wishing desperately that he may not have grown angry and shouted at his wife about that lost file. Humans grow angry so easily, so heedlessly venting their anger at those nearest and most vulnerable, needlessly, wantonly injuring what is most precious and most fragile. That, too, was ever so, through the millennia. Holding the file, I realized with all the powerful immediacy of direct insight how superficial are the spectacular changes in constructs and artifacts which fascinate us so. What is most real is also what is most perennial, the basic counterpoint of good and evil, of love and hurt, of labor and devotion, of hope and sorrow. I thought of Helen's spinning basket with its cunning casters, as Homer describes it. The woman of this house might well have had a sewing basket just like it and taken the same gentle, familiar pleasure in it. I hoped intesely that the farmer did not grow angry and hurt his wife in the small tenderness of daily life because of the lost file I had found. At the same time I realized what is wanting about philosophical humanism, even a moral humanism. Humans are not only humans, moral subjects and vital organisms.

They are also *Persons,* capable of fusing eternity and time in the precious, anguished reality of a love that would be eternal amid the concreteness of time.

A person is a being through whom eternity enters time. Perhaps the man whose file I found amid the crumbling foundations of his house once said to his wife, "I will love you for ever." That is an incredibly audacious statement for a being who dwells in ever-flowing time. Yet he said it. It was an intensely personal statement. A person is a being who can cherish—and bear the pain of losing.

A person is a being whose being has an integrity of its own. It encloses a past within itself, as the oak encloses the sapling, and opens up a future within, as the mother porcupine bearing her young within her. A person is a being who is not just an aggregate but an integral whole, as tangible as the currants planted by a woman long ago, yet transcending time as her memory.

A person is a being who meets you as a Thou, not just a "you," opening himself to you, both offering and claiming respect. In the encounter of persons, categories of respect—*moral* categories—are in order. Not simply categories of purpose: purpose can also be mechanical and pointless. Nor categories of causality. Rather, it is the categories of respect, of good and evil, of right and wrong, that govern the encounters of persons.

Humans are beings capable of being persons. The category of Person, though, is both higher and deeper—and broader. My predecessors, whose presence I feel so keenly on this land, are no longer humans, yet they remain persons, their presence personal—and I know I owe them the respect due persons. God, too, though once he was also a man, cannot be said to be "human." Yet he can be said to be Person, most eminently so, a personal, not an impersonal presence. His creatures, too: they are not humans, yet neither are they impersonal, biomechanisms. Their life has an integrity, they command respect as bearers of value in time. They, too, are persons, each after its own kind. Nor could we speak of the universe as human: in defining ourselves as distinctively human, we stress our isolation within it. Yet it is not inappropriate to speak of the *kosmos* as personal, the locus of eternal value embodied in time, marked by an integrity that demands respect. As humans, we may feel strangers within it, yet as Persons, we are radically kin.

I would not apologize for my distinctiveness: I cherish the millennia of *humanitas* whose heir I am. There are, though, the cellar holes;

there are the raccoons and the birches, there is the moon and the spirit of God, ever present amid the hum of the sun-warm forest and the ageless boulders. A philosophy of humanism, for all its value, must remain a special case theory. More is needed—a philosophy of personalism.

A Philosophy of Personalism

There still is night, many-splendored, all-reconciling, and there is the new day that rises up in the gray autumn dawn. There is a promise of snow in the graying sky. The forest, its summer profusion muted by the heavy blanket of damp leaves, awaits its coming. The trees, bare against the sky, are ready for it. Even the boulders take on their autumnal mood. Whatever may seem true in the simplified human environment of the cities, here the ultimate metaphysical question stands out in a profound simplicity. Shall we conceive of the world around us and of ourselves in it as *personal,* a meaningful whole, honoring its order as continuous with the moral law of our own being and its being as continuous with ours, bearing its goodness—or shall we conceive of it and treat it, together with ourselves, as *impersonal,* a chance aggregate of matter propelled by a blind force and exhibiting at most the ontologically random lawlike regularities of a causal order? Is the Person or is matter in motion the root metaphor of thought and practice? That answered, all else follows.

Nor is it a question of reflection alone. Given the awesome power with which our technology endows us, not only our fate and the quality of our lives, but the fate of our planet may well depend on the answer. Yet it is a difficult question to reach with our familiar cognitive apparatus. It is not a question of fact or theory which could be settled on empirical ground. Nature lends itself willingly to either interpretation. The forest around me, my community of kin, obligingly assumes the mask of board feet of lumber, the living beings around me, my fellow humans included, no less obligingly conform to a model of stimulus and response, susceptible to behavioral conditioning.[28] Only the ego, the irreducible *I* who is the subject of moral acts and the author of textbooks of behavioral psychology, seems to resist the reduction. In truth, philosophers have ever been driven by doubt back to the certainty of the ego—Saint Augustine with his "Si falor, sum," Descartes with the "Cogito, ergo, sum," Commenius with his "ráj srdce," the paradise of the heart, or Husserl with the "transcendence in immanence" of *Ideen I* § 57.

Solitude convinced me of the futility of such a retreat. The *ego cogito* so clearly does accompany all my apperception, as real as the strength of love and labor. It shrinks, though, to a paltry thing, brittle and ephemeral, whenever I seek to retreat into it. A person alone, locked into the solitude of his reflection, cannot even guarantee his own reality. He must open himself out to the world—and be filled with whatever he conceives of the world as being. Whatever a person perceives around him will seep within as well. Humans cannot conceive of the world as an absurd play of blind forces, yet retain the confidence of their own humanity. Descartes's ego can be a starting point but not a retreat. If it is, it will go the way of the world. The crude reductionism of J. B. Watson may be intrinsically unbelievable, his own missionary fervor testifying against it. But there are other models, believable if we choose to lend them credence. There is the historicist model, reducing even the reality of good and evil to the vicissitudes of history, or the psychoanalytic model, reducing the reality of the subject to a product of subhuman drives and superhuman constraints. No empirical datum can prevent us from adopting them. A metaphysical model is in principle compatible with any state of the universe, since it is not an attempt to catalog its facts but rather an attempt at reading its sense. The fundamental metaphysical question calls for a choice.

It is a metaphysical question, and the option is a binary one: shall we opt for the model and posture of a meaningful cosmos ordered by a moral law, or shall we opt for the model and stance of a chance aggregate of matter? Is the Person or is matter in motion the ultimate metaphysical category? There really is no third. Vitalism, proposing *life,* the vital principle, as a third option, is really not an alternative, though it is tempting in its intuitive appeal. At the turn of the century, it did seem an attractive option. To vitalistic thinkers from Bergson to Teilhard de Chardin, life, *élan vital,* seemed to accommodate the best of both possible worlds. It appeared to account for the purposiveness of human life, yet lend itself to the needs of the sciences, compatible, in its teleological determinism, with their categories. Though the natural sciences for the most part discarded vitalism in their turn to mechanism, vitalism, minus its name and mystique, became deeply rooted in psychology. The attempt to explain conscious comportment in terms of putative needs, from "tissue" needs to "higher" needs, provided a paradigm which combined determinism with teleology and was essentially vitalistic.[29]

Still, in retrospect, vitalism seems more to combine the failings of both alternatives. As Ricoeur pointed out with devastating effect, the purposiveness of needs cannot account for the teleology of behavior in beings for whom hunger can be the motive of theft, labor, or a hunger strike. Here the conception of life is intelligible as an expression of spirit, not as an autonomous explanatory principle. Conversely, for the purposes of chemistry, the concept of life or *élan vital* is too purposive, too teleological. Here the parameters of causality and extension will serve far better, and quite legitimately, as long as we attach no ontological validity to them. For all the utility of the concept of life for describing the doings of animate beings in the order of time, the ultimate metaphysical question remains a bipolar one: shall we conceive of the order of the cosmos as primordially and ultimately causal or moral?

Personalism in philosophy—for personalism is a perspective in philosophy far more than a particular philosophical system[30]—is the decision to treat the Person, the Person-al mode of being, as the ultimate metaphysical category. It is less a speculative conclusion than an act of trust that the harmony of the embers that glow with the warmth of the human heart and the stars that proclaim the glory of God, the primordial vision of the cosmos as a society of persons[31] governed by a moral law, is not only the naïve first impression of a primitive mind but also the ultimate conclusion of deep thought. Between the primordial and the ultimate vision, there stands the fruits of *skepsis,* rejecting the moral sense of nature as an illusion and probing for other, impersonal models of explanation. Personalism in philosophy is the recovery of the primordial insight, the vision of a *kosmos,* on the other side of skepsis.

Or so it may be in principle, though as a matter of historical fact that is not how personalism in truth emerged on the American philosophical scene. To Czechoslovakia's Emanuel Rádl, heir of Hans Driesch's vitalism and of the moral humanism of Czech thought over the centuries, the link between the moral sense of nature and the personal view of the cosmos may have seemed obvious. The man who introduced the designation *personalism* to the American scene, however, Borden Parker Bowne, was a student of Hermann Lotze's and an heir to Immanuel Kant.[32] The result is a contrast: Bowne's immense sensitivity to the presence of God in all His creation on the one hand, the harsh Kantian contrast between the Person, the sole bearer of intrinsic value, and things, mere things, purely phenomenal, devoid of ultimate ontological dignity, to be used and expended to serve human ends.[33] Perhaps, too, Bowne was a child of his age, the ebullient age of "progress" and technological "conquest of nature." Whatever the reason, his personalism often seems more closely akin to existentialism than to the personalism we have been presenting, a vigorous affirmation of the irreducibility and reality of the Person, the moral subject, amid a world which Bowne is content to regard as impersonal, value-free, and ultimately unreal.

The contrast is jarring: Bowne's delimitation of personal reality is perceptive and valuable. His analysis of personhood as the model capable of subsuming unity-in-plurality, being-in-becoming, is philosophically invaluable and seems to cry out for a wider application, not simply as a description of the being of God and humans, but as a fundamental metaphysical principle. Bowne's pupils, Edgar Sheffield Brightman the best known among them, put the tools he bequeathed to them to excellent use. The personalism they represented provided the philosophical foundation for Martin Luther King's transformation of the American consciousness, and not by chance. The personalist insistence on the metaphysical and moral irreducibility of the person provides the one secure bulwark against all arguments of expediency and tradition. Injustice can always find utilitarian justification. It must be challenged on moral grounds, and those personalism provided, no less in Czechoslovakia than in America.

Still, even in Brightman's thought, there persists the bifurcation of reality between the dignity of the personal and the putative instrumentality of the nonpersonal. Brightman, to be sure, is willing to extend the category of the personal, at least in lesser degrees, even to much of the nonhuman world, speaking, in one passage, of the "mind of the grasshopper."[34] He insists on the personal as the ultimate metaphysical category and on the perception of reality as a society of persons. Still, he treats personhood not as coextensive with individual reality but as contingent on the presence of certain characteristics. The world as a society of persons, in Brightman's writings, does not refer in the first place to the nature of the cosmic order and the relationship among beings but to an alleged characteristic of certain of those beings, their personhood. One of Brightman's most perceptive, sympathetic critics, Frederick Ferré,[35] attributes that hesitation to a fear of panpsychism: if we extended the Kantian command, "as an end, not as a means merely," to all beings, would we not have to attribute a mind to all beings, as, on Ferré's reading, Whitehead seems to do?

No, I do not think so. I do not believe that Whitehead's recognition of the "subjective aim" of all beings constitutes a pan-psychism, the attribution of a psyche to all material entities. Perhaps it is because, in the radical brackets of the forest clearing, nature does not present itself as "material," waiting to be endowed with a psyche to merit ontological dignity. Here the dignity of the world of nature, of the lichen-covered boulders no less than of the old badger and the young oak trees, is the primordial starting point. It is not contingent on the attribution of any set of traits. Nor is the overwhelming sense of the clearing as a "society of persons," as structured by personal relations, a function of any alleged personality traits of boulders and trees. It is, far more, an acknowledgment of the truth, goodness, and unity of all beings, simply because they are, as they are, each in his own way. That is the fundamental sense of speaking of reality as personal: recognizing it as Thou, and our relation to it as profoundly and fundamentally a moral relation, governed by the rule of respect.

It is in that sense that any consistent ethic must needs be personalistic, and doubly so—according to all beings the respect due to persons and recognizing the model of a community of persons which Kant described as the "kingdom of ends" as the root metaphor for understanding the moral sense of reality. For a person, ultimately, is not just a being who possesses a psyche or manifests certain personality traits as much as a being who stands in a moral relation to us, a being we encounter as a Thou.[36]

That is a metaphysical option, and the reason for choosing it cannot be theoretical or empirical, the conclusion of arguments faultlessly, futilely constructed in an impeccable British manner, valuable as such arguments can be. There can be arguments, surely—and the report of the Club of Rome presents a compelling one: an ethic of universal respect is essential to our survival. The true reasons, though, are of a different order, the product of a vision rather than of speculation. They are the product of the philosophic wonder with its open-eyed recognition of the evident moral sense of being—and of the far more difficult decision to trust that wonder in spite of the corrosive suspicion of skepsis.

Fechner's time-worn terms, *Nachtansicht* and *Tagesansicht*, if we translate them with a bit of poetic license as the shadowy perspective of suspicion and the clear vision of trust, might serve well. More than aught else, the personalism of the radical brackets is a reaffirmation of the reality and veridicality of what humans encounter in ageless philosophic wonder. To an age conditioned by habits of suspicion to rejecting the evident as naïve and to searching out tortured speculative explanation, such act of trust must appear as naïveté—and so it is. It is, though, a second-order naïveté, a willed, conscious reaffirmation of the reality of meaningful lived experience, motivated by the chastened admission of the futility of cunningly devised fables.

The shadowy perspective of suspicion has conditioned our thought for three centuries and more. We have made a cult of sophistication, dismissing the clearly present moral sense of life, of true and false, of good and evil, of right and wrong, in favor of cunningly devised fables. The personal reality of our being and the moral sense of nature, our primordial givens, appear to us as something to be explained away by the prepersonal realm of dark drives or the suprapersonal realm of History. The great personalist inversion is a reaffirmation of the primacy of meaningful being, the primacy of personal categories in a morally ordered cosmos. Within such a framework, there is room for categories of vitality and utility, of need and satisfaction, as describing ways in which the order of value is acted out in time and animate nature. In turn, within it, we can recognize the order of efficient causality as the way in which the order of value is acted out in space and material nature. Without the framework of an order of value, utility would reduce to futility—and causality, as Hume recognized, to constant connection. Within such a framework they become useful concepts. The chemistry and the biology which to initial naïveté may appear a deadly threat to our humanity, appear to the second naïveté as legitimate ways of describing the way in which it acts itself out in life and matter. While the claim to the primacy of the material denies the legitimacy of the vital and the moral, the recognition of the ontological primacy of the personal establishes the validity of the vital and the material.

That is the gift of the radical brackets, the gift of the forest, of the porcupines, and of the wayfarer with whom God comes into the house. It is the reaffirmation of the validity of being human in the cosmos, the great personalist inversion. It is an act of trust, and, as all acts of trust, a gift.

4. Skepsis

The Shadow of Doubt

The affirmation of the ontological primacy of meaningful being for which, with some trepidation, I would revive the designation "personalism" calls for nothing less than an act of confidence in the ultimate reality of persons and the ultimate veridicality of individual consciousness. It is the affirmation that persons, as moral subjects, are real in the order of eternity, not merely actual in the order of time, and that they are the subjects of their lives, not the transient products of some allegedly more fundamental prehuman or transhuman force. It is no less the affirmation that human consciousness is fundamentally not illusory: though, admittedly, it is accidentally capable of error, it remains essentially *capax veritatis,* capable of grasping truth. That audacious confidence is the gift of the radical brackets.

It is a fragile gift. To the Renaissance, that confidence may have appeared evidently justified—yet even the Renaissance conviction of the lucidity of consciousness and the rationality of the cosmos had its dark obverse of doubt. The "age of reason" was also an age in which witchcraft flourished no less than astrology. The age of science that succeeded it reaffirmed the personalist confidence on the far more problematic grounds of a faith in "progress." It, too, had its obverse, the suspicion that the unfolding of history is not a purposive progression but an eruption of a blind and ultimately self-destructive force. Schopenhauer and Nietzsche were, after all, also a part of that century. Our own time has inverted the Renaissance perspective: though our acts remain predicated on the personalistic affirmation, the theory to which we increasingly look for guidance treats impersonal doubt as the evident datum. In the radical brackets of the forest clearing, the personalistic confidence stands out as the true sense of the cosmos and of our place therein. Beyond its confines, in the world in which, willy-nilly, we live, breathe, and have our being, doubt presses in and will not be ignored.

In one of its personae, that doubt is one which arises from within. The apostle Paul testifies to it in his anguished outcry, in Romans 7:19: "The good that I would I do not, the ill that I would not, that I do." It is a universal experience. Paul articulated it in terms of the bondage of sin; a later age spoke of demonic possession and, later still, of "alienation" requiring the attentions of an "alienist." In recent decades, depth psychology expressed that doubt forcefully with the conception of a dynamic unconscious. Though its theorists may differ, they share a common suspicion that our overt acts and thoughts are not the free acts of moral subjects but involuntary manifestations of a deeper, hidden reality beyond our ken. The criticism of their theories, no matter how telling, cannot dispel the doubt those theories articulate. The force of the cognitive claims of psychoanalysis is a moment of recognition. We experience our bondage long before anyone formulates a theory of determinism.

There is a second persona as well, the doubt that comes from without, acknowledged by Sophocles as fate. It, too, has received a powerful recent articulation, in this case in historicism, whether in the Hegelian conception of a purposive history or in the Marxian conception of a material historical determinism. Together with their many variations, both of those conceptions give expression to the deep suspicion that the logic of events is not that of individual moral acts but of a transpersonal History and that persons, though actual, are not ultimately real but derivative from it. That suspicion, again, will not be laid to rest with counterarguments. It is as old as the ancient conception of fate and as deep as the experience of human longing brought to naught by the vicissitudes of events. Once again we experience our bondage long before historicism gives it an overt expression.

Any reaffirmation of the reality and the veridicality of moral subjects must come to terms not just with psychoanalysis and historicism, but with the experiences from which they arise. Radical brackets can suspend the ontological claims of psychoanalytic and historicist theory easily enough. What such theories present, after all, is not a faithful articulation of a clearly perceived experience, but rather highly speculative constructs which claim to interpret and explain that experience. What those brackets cannot suspend is the experience which lends credibility to the fanciful theoretical constructs of psychoanalysis and historicism—the suspicion that things are not what they seem, that the actual is not the real, that our consciousness is illusory and the lives we live and know themselves but an impoverished reflection of true reality. It is a fear far deeper than the fear that we may be mistaken in this or that belief. It is, rather, the fear that not just our beliefs but our reality itself, the world we know and our lives therein, are an inauthentic, deceptive distortion—and our true belief no more than true reflections of a false actuality.

In the history of Western thought, that suspicion has been articulated most clearly in a category which, in our passion for compartmentalization, we would be likely to label "theological" rather than philosophic, that of *the fall.*[1] That category acknowledges what may be an assumption or a recognition—or perhaps simply a vague sense—that the world of our experience, the world *pro statu isto*[2]—is fundamentally distorted and radically alienated from its true being. It is not primarily a historical category, refering to an alleged mythical event of long ago, even though in our historicist passion we tend so to read it. Rather, it is a systematic category, describing the actual as not fully real and perhaps as not even a reliable clue to true reality. It is an expression of the fear, the suspicion, or the conviction that this is indeed a "fallen" world whose present being is not a manifestation of its true being but only of the vast distance between what happens to be and what truly is.

It would be a mistake to write off that perception as no more than a product of idle theological speculation. For one, it is grounded directly in lived experience, reflecting the aching recognition of the gap between the profound *goodness* of being and the painful imperfection of what is. Being is so utterly good, it is so deeply good *to be.* Then why do we make such a sorry mess of it? Humans have such an immense capacity for good—and, really, such a vast store of good will. Then why, why do we visit so much destruction on our world and our lives in it? Or, less dramatically, there is such a gap between what an apple could be—healthy, ripe, moist with dew—and the sorry, crabby specimen from my old orchard. Quite apart from all theological injunctions, there is, in lived experience, much ground for experiencing this world as a fallen one.

Nor is that putatively theological recognition absent from pure philosophy. Parmenides describes this world as the realm of seeming, Plato as a cave of shadows, or, in the *Statesman,* as a topsy-turvy one, a "world running backwards."[3] In philosophy, however, we encounter discriminations, not simply the aching unease of lived experience. In them, three ways of conceptualizing the fall emerge as ideal possibilities. One of them, which might or might not have been dominant in Plato's thought, treats the fall radical and absolute. It reflects not only a doubt but a despair over this world, not simply as a distorted image of true being but as wholly, irretrievably alienated from it. The truth, then, not only is not *of* this world: it is not even *in* it. This world is but an illusion and a perversion—and the strategy of the enlightened, who have seen through the deception, can only be to reject it, to leave it behind, escaping to a better realm. That can be the driving impulse of piety or of activity, seeking to destroy this flawed world utterly and to create a whole new reality, as in the case of secular radicalism, or asking God to do so. Less dramatically, it is also the perception expressed by the conviction that the reality accessible to us is wholly phenomenal and not indicative of the nature of the noumenal reality in itself.[4] In their various ways, all such views express the conviction that the fall is radical and total.

It is that suspicion that is the root of true *skepsis.* In the confident age just past, bouyed as it was by a faith in "progress," the word "skepticism" acquired a much milder, methodological sense. Still in the early decades of our century, writers dealing with the methodology of the sciences recommended a "skeptical" attitude, meaning by it nothing more drastic than an ordinary caution in accepting belief, asking for reasons and suspending judgments until they are offered. Though priding themselves on their "skeptical" attitude, those investigators did not for a moment doubt the intrinsic ability of humans to know the truth. Masaryk wrote in good faith when he proposed a probability calculus as a response to Humean skepsis:[5] to his age, skepsis meant no more than a functional doubt with respect to the truth claim of individual assertions.

Were skepsis really no more than that, probability could be an answer. If, to Nietzsche's heirs, that answer appeared trivial beyond notice, it was because skepsis runs far deeper. Its basic suspicion is not that any specific assertion does not correspond to reality, but that the reality which it describes is itself a false reality, a mask rather than a manifestation of the real. Or, reverting to the theological metaphor, skepsis is the expression of the suspicion that ours is a fallen world, an inauthentic one, so that even true statements about it cannot claim to be the truth.

The nineteenth century, for all its dark undertones, had little understanding for Nietzsche. Perhaps, in its closing decades, it was simply willfully naïve, insisting on preserving the illusion of a world of sweetness and light down to the shot at Sarajewo and the smoke over Auschwitz. Yet even Matthew Arnold, the author of that phrase,[6] knew better. The nineteenth century did not simply willfully refuse to acknowledge the reality of evil. It assumed a different, no less time-honored conception of the fall as essentially contingent and episodic, no more than a collective name for a set of specific and specifically remediable lapses in a fundamentally sound creation. As the conception of the fall as radical can be associated with Plato, so the conception of the fall as superficial might be associated with Aristotle. It is such a conception which would justify us in regarding the mean as "golden" rather than simply mean. The assumption here is that, by and large, the actuality of humankind and their world runs true to its reality so that, again by and large, it presents us with its faithful image. There are, to be sure, deviations, but the point is that they are indeed deviations, individual departures from the norm, occasioned by ignorance, ill will, or accident, and as such can be dealt with case by case. If, however—or so the scenario runs—we are careful to isolate the deviations and take the "normal" as the norm, whether qualitatively as in Aristotle or statistically as in much of contemporary social science,[7] we can depend on actuality to provide us with a reasonably reliable image of reality and an adequate standard for correcting its distortion.

It was not so much willful naïveté as this conception of the fall which underlay the attempts to counter skepsis with a probability calculus and to answer moral questions with empirical research. If the fall were indeed superficial and episodic, then it would not be unreasonable to expect some methodologically sophisticated version of, say, a Kinsey report to provide us not only with a description of American mores in the Age of Eisenhower but with a norm of "normal" human sexuality. The age of "progress," now in its final phases, with its confidence that not only will technology grow more complex but that, in due and not too distant time, it will make a significant difference in all the woes that the world is heir to, provides another dramatic illustration of the conception of the fall as fortuitous and episodic. Less dramatically, so do the phenomenalist and naïve realist convictions that, this way or that, phenomena are in fact noumena, the thing in itself but an aggregate of its ways of appearing.

Much of the critique of traditional personalism has focused on what its critics perceive as a tendency to regard evil as contingent and episodic. The confidence in the merely episodic nature of evil may have been convincing when Victoria was on her throne, Karl Marx sitting harmlessly in the public reading room of the British Museum, and Thomas Alva Edison was busy at work in his laboratory. Yet even then the faith was suspect. Overtly, it was drastically shaken for England by the Boer War, for Germany by the war of 1914 and its aftermath, for all of Europe by the war of 1938 and the Soviet occupation, for America finally by Vietnam. Those, however, were less the causes of the shift in European consciousness than manifestations of forces which seem to defy comprehension in personalistic terms. The massive eruption of passion in the nightmare of National Socialism, the inexorable grinding of history which reduced half of Europe to a gulag, simply did not seem explicable in moral categories, as the product of the mistaken or ill-willed decisions of Adolf Hitler or Joseph Stalin and their heirs. They themselves appeared caught up in an irresistible tide of the subhuman and the transhuman, by the demons of passion and the necessity of History. Nor does our daily world seem morally comprehensible any longer. In the conceptual and technological restructuring of it, we have restructured the givens of our daily experience. The very "balance of nature" which, laudably if belatedly, we seek to respect by restricting certain technologies, has already been deeply disrupted. The social ills we try to remedy with specific, laudable measures reflect a disruption of our entire social existence. The fall in our experience is not just an isolated incident but a universal condition. It pervades all of our world and our being therein, veiling the thing in itself no less than our lives in themselves.

Even within the radical brackets of the forest clearing, it is no longer possible to recapture the innocent confidence of the personalists of a century ago that the fall is merely episodic, an unfortunate, unintended by-product of rational acts. The forces of passion and fate have proved too real. They can be ignored—as ignored they are in much of our "empirical" research in the human sciences—only at the cost of ignoring or denying our moral humanity as well. A denial of the prehuman and the transhuman cannot produce an adequate strategy of being human in the cosmos.

Neither, though, can a conception of the fall as radical and total. Were we to think of our moral humanity as illusory and of the world as offering no clue to the nature of reality, the sole strategies open to us would be those of individual escape to a heaven or a garden of Epicurus, or those of a revolutionary apocalypse which would wipe out the corruption by applying globally Mr. Kurtz's final recommendation in Conrad's *The Heart of Darkness.*[8]

I cannot accept either strategy, that of despair or that of rage, not because I am unaware of the reality of evil but because, in the brackets of the forest clearing, I have also seen the profound goodness of being, simply as being. It is not that, lulled by the peace of the forest, I could revert to the confidence of the old personalists that the flaw is accidental and remediable. The ominous forces of passion and history are too real, not merely the creatures of theory, and cannot be bracketed away. Nor can I recapture the Renaissance confidence that human persistence can break the veil of deception and distortion. I know, as Heidegger also discovered, that it cannot.[9] It is, rather, that my evenings have given me a confidence in the ability of reality, of the thing in itself, to present itself in spite of the veil—and of the possibility of the human, purged by solitude and pain of his arrogance, to receive its presence. It is a grand and startling gift, not an achievement. Humans can only receive it, not earn or deserve it. When, though, they are ready to receive it, setting aside their pride, the gift is given, the veil is drawn back. It is then that Emanuel Rádl's recognition applies—that the truth of being human is to redeem and reclaim, not to destroy.[10]

Perhaps, continuing the religious metaphor, we could say that though there is the fall, there is also epiphany. Though evil is powerful, grace is more powerful still. In our time, though, that is not a particularly transparent metaphor. Alternately, we might borrow Husserl's metaphor and say that the phenomenon is the noumenon as present, the noumenon appearing in and through—not "as"—the phenomenon. The divine *eros,* say, is distorted in the love of two human beings caught up in the care of their days, and yet it is there, not episodically, fully instantiated in some "perfect marriage," nor empirically, as the mean of all human marriages, but essentially, as the *eidos,* the sense of marriage present in and through the utter imperfection of all lives shared. It is a betrayal of our humanity to settle for an undemanding cohabitation as the best we can expect. It is folly to wait for a perfect marriage. The great gift and the glory of being human is the possibility of recognizing reality as embodied in the actual, as the sense of the actual. Amid the flawed world of time there is yet the ideal, present as its sense. The porcupine is no more exempt from the fall than I am, yet the truth and goodness of being shine through the imperfection of his embodiment.

The forest clearing, the world revealed in radical brackets, does not constitute an antelapsarian enclave, somehow preserved from the fall. In this respect, Robert Frost's bittersweet vision of the world "north of Boston" is far more honest than Thoreau's exaltation of his Walden. Nor is the world beyond the confines of the forest ever wholly stripped of the truth of being. Truth is present in the fallen world, and can shine through it. Confidence in the face of skepsis cannot be based on the denial of the fall, but it can be based on the confidence in the ability of being to shine through. So, too, the personalistic affirmation of the reality and truth of the moral subject in a meaningful cosmos cannot be based on ignoring the bondage of passion and the momentum of history. It can, though, be based on the recognition that the truth of being human shines through both the prehuman and the transhuman dimensions of our being. The strategy of personalism in the face of the ideologies of the impersonal, psychoanalysis and historicism, cannot be one of seeking to deny the reality of fate and passion, but one of recovering their Person-al dimension.

The Spell of the Demon

It is easy enough to sustain the trusting confidence of personal vision on a calm starlit night or of a humming summer afternoon, while the blade of my axe swings rhythmically against the shining white of rock maple, its rhythm at peace with that of the forest. At such times the agonized bondage of passion and the involuted constructs of psychoanalysis seem far away, no more than a cunningly devised fable of idle men. It is tempting to dismiss them as self-indulgence and to think of the tangible goodness of physical labor as an adequate cure.

There are, though, the other times, when the forest grows dark as heavy clouds close up over the clearing and the sky splits with an ominous blue light. The rain comes suddenly, sheets of water beating down vertically on the leaves. In the uncanny daytime night, flashes of lightning rend the sky and thunder rolls and reverberates across the valley as the immense power of the clouds lashes out against the earth. There is a sense of a dark, ominous force abroad, exploding from behind the clear world of the sunlit day and the placid surface of a mind seemingly at peace.

It was on a violent summer night like that that I sat, fascinated, by the front window, staring into the darkness. Anticipated yet unexpected, the flash of sheet lightning would reveal the clearing, each detail fixed in a frozen moment. Just for a flash, then the clearing would disappear once more in the darkness until the next flash would bring it back, timeless, frozen. Then, without a warning, a flash of lightning lit up the clearing and I saw, clearly, not more than three meters away, two rain-drenched men, dressed in the fashion of a century ago. One was holding the other under the arms, straining to draw him up from the watergate to the wagon road. The other hanged limp in his arms, his head dangling, heels dragging in the sand, toes pointed up, as if stunned or dead. The man who was dragging him was looking over his shoulder at me, his face contorted in a grimace of fear and horror. Behind them, where the gap in the dam is, there was darkness, as if the dam still stood, the sawmill on top of it. Just for a moment; then the clearing disappeared in darkness. The next flash of lightning came only seconds later. It revealed the clearing, empty and still, as I had so often seen it.

I fumbled for matches, lit a lantern, and ran out. The storm was receding, the rain had stopped. The clearing and the forest lay still, silent around me. There were no tracks in the rain-lashed sand before the house. I called out, looked about, then doused the lantern to avoid being blinded by its light and walked up the paths into the woods in all directions, listening and sensing shapes in the darkness. I found nothing. The night after the storm was calm and comfortably dark, the forest at peace. The vision, whatever it was, flashed through the clearing and disappeared without a trace. Only much later did I learn that, a century ago, there had been rumors of a murder at the mill and recognized, on an old daguerreotype, the face I had seen for a frozen moment outside my window.

I attach no cognitive significance to that vision. I know, on some unacknowledged level of my mind, that running outside and searching in the woods was a distraction. Outside, among the trees fresh with rain, there was nothing but the peaceful night. The vision, the moment of fear, then the exaggerated behavioral response, all that came from within. Perhaps I imagined it all, or perhaps I had read the story and stored it away, unnoted, until in an overwrought moment something within me forced it to the surface.

That, though, is the disturbing point: something within me, something hidden that I bear within as a part of me yet have no awareness of it, no control over it. The fundamental conviction of which the entire personalist turn and the personalist inversion are based is precisely that, while allowing for the possibility of contingent error, things are what they seem, that the truth is overt, not hidden. Personalism is, basically, a foundationalism of the overt: the conviction that, once stripped of the veil of artifacts and constructs, our daytime consciousness is fundamentally veridical, and that the reality it presents to us, value-laden and meaningfully ordered, is true reality, not an appearance that would have to be accounted for in terms of some putative deeper, prehuman reality. The moment we admit the reality of what Ricoeur aptly calls "the hidden," not of the contingently unknown in the world about us, but of a hidden dimension of our own being, in principle incapable of crossing the threshold of clear consciousness because of psychological hindrances, the adequacy of our personal daytime consciousness is put in doubt. What if the dark, impersonal hidden is in fact the true reality, and the peaceful daylight self but an appearance, manipulated beyond our ken by a premordial, impersonal force?

That is in fact the possibility raised by depth psychology and the challenge posed by philosophers convinced of its cognitive validity.[11] Their claim is not simply that there is more than we have hitherto taken into account, but rather that reality is *other*—and that any philosophy of the overt, be it phenomenology with its confidence in the possibility of clear vision and faithful articulation, or a personalism based on it, committed to the ontological primacy of the personal, is not simply wrong but naïve. To know truly, on that assumption, it is not enough to see clearly. If anything, clear seeing is deceptive, since the reality it presents is illusory. To know would have to mean to reconstruct the hidden prepersonal, elemental forces which, beyond our ken or will, determine the patterns of our overt behavior and the contents of our overt thought.

Were that claim theoretical only, it could be met handsomely on the level of theory. A useful first step would be simply a critical reading of Freud's classic *Traumdeutung*, somewhat interpretatively translated as *Interpretation of Dreams.* The Freudian constructs, much like the artifacts of our *technē,* have become so much a part of our mental furniture that reading *Interpretation of Dreams* today seems simply to confirm the obvious. Placed in critical brackets, though, the argument becomes anything but that. A reader who suspends the uncritical assumption that, of course, "there is" resistance and all the rest comes to the startling realization that the only bit of evidence Freud actually has to offer is that there are dreams which do not conform to the pattern of wish fulfillment. Every step Freud takes beyond that rather meager data base is predicated not on evidence but on a postulate—that *all* dreams *must* represent a wish fulfillment, whether they in fact do or not. If we were to reject that postulate, the entire theory would die aborning. Only if we choose to accept it do the subsequent steps follow. Then we can argue with Freud that since dreams, by our postulate, must represent wish fulfillment and since some of the dreams we dream clearly (only now we should have to say "apparently") do not, there must be a "censor" which disguises them so that they do not appear as wish fulfillment. We can then argue further, as Freud does, that if the "censor" needs to disguise the wishes we fulfill in our dreams, then those wishes cannot be the wishes of our waking self, which we know and could readily admit to ourselves. Thus there "must be" something within us that generates them—a prepersonal, prehuman source of dark archaic drives, sex and aggression. This source will later be labeled "libido," later still the *Es* or *Id,* the anonymous "that" which, rather than the personal I, *Ego,* will be said to be the active source of our strivings. The overt shape they will take, to be sure, will be a product of the *Es*'s conflict with our "higher I," *Ueberich,* which again will be said to be not personal but suprapersonal, an internalization of societal constraints. The waking person we are, the *Ego,* appears not as an agent but as a patient, the passive product of the struggle between two impersonal forces, one subhuman, the other suprahuman. The Person has in effect become an illusion, a mask displayed by the hidden conflict of impersonal forces.[12]

The superstructure which Freud built up on this slender foundation is so imposing that it is easy to forget how utterly slender the foundation in fact is: no more than the postulate that dreams must be wish fulfillment plus the fact that many are not—unless we postulate the entire incredible mental machinery of Freudianism. Once postulated, however, that machinery becomes self-confirming. If a patient "manifests patient recognition," that is, admits that what the analyst proposes as the "true," hidden meaning of a dream or an act, though nowhere accessible to clear insight, is in fact true, the theory is confirmed. Should he deny it, though he do so in good faith and clear conscience, he is manifesting "resistance" and so again confirming the theory: the interpretation is evidently so true that the "censor" will not let it come to consciousness. It is, in effect, the principle of *právo útrpné,* interrogation at torture. The accused can confess and be tortured to death for his crime. If he refuses to confess, he will be tortured until he does or until he dies.[13]

Already between the wars Karl Jaspers, himself a psychologist and the author of the authoritative reference, *Allgemeine Pathopsychologie,* pointed out the self-blinding folly of the argument.[14] H. Hartmann responded by seeking to reinterpret Freudianism as an experiential theory whose concepts can be operationalized, albeit with doubtful success, since Freudian concepts claim to describe not overt phenomena, accessible to empirical investigation, but rather their latent causes. Paul Riccoeur in turn pointed out that the experiential grounding of psychoanalysis could not be empirical, but would have to be hermeneutic, uncovering the hidden.[15] Yet, as Alfred Lorenzer pointed out in his turn, a phenomenological hermeneutics stripped of its cutting edge, the Husserlian *Evidenz,* is a dull tool indeed. Lorenzer proposed a criterion of validity based on a principle of coherence: psychoanalytic cognition is to be considered veridical if it conforms to Karl Marx's Sixth Thesis on Feuerbach.[16] If Karl Jaspers, by then a very old man, read his work, he might have chuckled: the circle of dogmatism which he had described in his *Reason and Anti-Reason in Our Time* had come a full turn. Reality which fails to conform to theory need no longer be resistance. It can also be false consciousness.

Were the force of psychoanalysis solely theoretical, it would be as easy as that: a rather weak theoretical claim meets a rather devastating theoretical criticism. As theories go, Freudianism does not go very far, and could, in any case, be suspended by phenomenological brackets.

In fact, however, theoretical criticism has had remarkably little effect on the appeal of Freudianism, whether as a therapeutic practice or as a philosophy of the hidden. Rather like with Marxism, believers proved willing to reinterpret the theory beyond recognition, going through veritable mental somersaults rather than give it up. For though the theory be ever so far-fetched, the experience it invokes is very close to home. Again, what Freud has to say about it may be largely autobiographical, but the very fact that he speaks of it at all evokes a powerful response. The strength and resilience of Freudianism is that it speaks, however inadequately, of something that is only too real, of an experience we all know well though we would rather not. Any personalistic philosophy must come to terms not necessarily with the theory, but with the experience it evokes, if it is to remain credible.

Even in the peace of the forest clearing, there is the experience of the hidden. It need not be turbulent: it can be as peaceful as the deep dreams that present themselves unbidden in the still of the night. They are not dreams of exotic illicit desires. Those may have plagued Freud's improper Victorians, but not the children of a permissive age who had long since seen them all acted out. More often, they are dreams of agonizingly painful beauty, of memories whose passing a person simply cannot accept and so stops remembering—during the day, at least. Or they may be memories of grievous pain a person has caused but grieved too late to make amends. My ancestors spoke of it as yellow and black melancholy, *žlutý* and *černý tesklivec,* grief and remorse. I know they are with me during the day as well, though I am careful not to remember them. Only occasionally they catch me unaware, a sudden, involuntary "ouch" that makes me double up. Those, too, are a part of what I am, an unacknowledged part which yet affects my actions. I know that for a long time I avoided some places on the land which were places of such memories, inventing excuses, often at considerable inconvenience. I could do no other. What then of my vaunted freedom?

There is a second experience as well, long attested in history—that of compulsion. Not the "demonic possession" of popular imagination: that is too self-consciously dramatic. Addiction brings home that experience at its most dreary and most shabbily desperate. I have both known it, as once a smoker, and watched in those around me, as alcoholism, amorous obsession, or a whole range of compulsions devastated their lives and left them agonized observers and unwilling agents of their own destruction. All evidence available to me suggests that it is simply not true that the addict is happy with his addiction, oblivious to the havoc it is wreaking upon all he loves. Far more typically, the addict is keenly, agonizingly aware of it, despairing over it, longing to be free—yet at the same time terrified of the possibility. It is as if his being were no longer his own, as if the focus had shifted from his lucid, daytime person to a deeper, prepersonal self represented by the addiction so that any threat to it becomes a threat to an identity more basic than the personal. The despairing suicide note left behind by a young addict in Springfield sums it up: "I love cocaine, the white lady of death. She is me and she has killed me."

If personalism is to make good on its promise of a philosophy of the overt, explaining the mechanical and the vital by the moral rather than reducing the moral to the vital and the mechanical, it must come to terms with those two kinds of experience—the experience of the hidden, of all that is I and yet is alien to me, and the experience of the pathological, of behavior experienced by the subject as if it were no longer he who acted but a prepersonal something that lives in him and compels him to act.

Over years of long evenings, I sought to do that. I sought to walk toward the demon, as I walked toward the lights that glow in the forest, and I have sat motionless before it, as in the presence of a pain too great to bear movement. The demon, though, always dissolved before me, leaving me alone as the author of my acts. Then, too, I have walked to the places of memories, and sat still in the soft night, unresisting, letting the hidden other come. Yet the memories that drifted up were always mine, a part of me. I was left with a different question: Why should they be alien?

There are, I know, times when entire dimensions of a person's being seem dark and alien, much as the night can seem. As it long has been our strategy to banish the night with lights and to fill it with familiar daytime objects, so, too, we have sought to flood the dark recesses of our minds with the light of consciousness and to furnish them with entities it could comprehend. That strategy, though, fails utterly with respect to the night. The night will not be taken by storm, conquered by lights. So treated, it retreats and remains alien, threatening just beyond the circle of light cast by the lantern, full of fearful shapes and ominous shadows. Encroaching upon it with our lights, we cannot come to know it. It retreats and becomes alien. Might it not be the same with the dark and hidden places of our minds?[17]

The fundamental personalistic inversion in coming to terms with the night is an act of trust: the decision to accept the night, not floodlit but in its own soft darkness, to be still within it and let it present itself, not peopling it with the shadows of our fears but accepting it as it comes to us. It is, to be sure, not something that happens at once—and, in places where the night is perennially violated by the glare of floodlights, it may never happen at all. There the darkness may well ever remain alien and threatening. Only where humans dare douse their lights and be still with the night can it happen.

Then the night comes softly, imperceptibly, its shadowy forms no longer terrifying, no longer compelling. Slowly, the night grows familiar. There are differences, of course. Seeing itself is different. By daylight, we see by looking, focusing directly on the object ahead, demanding to know. In the night, that object would become blurred and indistinct. It is the things we do not embarrass by staring, letting them present themselves in the corner of our vision, that let themselves be known. Perhaps it is a matter of seeing by indirection. Perhaps, too, it is a matter of seeing with respect and acceptance. What is that shadow, what is the light that appears on the old dam each summer evening at the rising of the moon? I do not know, and do not insist on knowing. I see it: it is there as I am here, each in our place. So let it be. It is a great gift to discover that I can live with so much that I do not know. Might not our hidden places, too, come to appear alien because we insist on knowing, lacking the patience to be still, to accept?

Gradually, the sense of day and night changes. They are very different, but neither is alien, impersonal. Both are the dwelling places of persons. Most Native Americans knew that. Theirs were cultures at home in the darkened forest and on the starlit plains. Blind persons know it, too. For them the night and the day are perforce equally places of dwelling. To go on living, they must learn to live with so much they cannot see and know, living by trust. The great wonder, the great gift was the discovery that even I, heir to centuries of urban civilization, can begin to sense it. The night need not be alien.

It was, actually, less a change in a mode of thinking than one in a mode of sensing, of experiencing, yet for me it transformed the entire relation of *Tagesansicht* and *Nachtansicht,* of the thematic and the hidden, of the conscious and the unconscious. When I first came to the land, there was so little I could remember. I was a survivor. Too many of my memories, too many aspects of my own self were simply unacceptable to me, the remembrance of them grievous unto me, the burden of them intolerable. Nor did the unacceptable include only or even primarily the obvious memories of guilt and shame. Far more, it included memories of sorrow which involved no guilt, only grief, and just as prominently memories of great joy turned to grief by passing.

I spent many evenings watching the dusk gather beneath the hemlocks, listening to the river and the forest. On such evenings, undisturbed by even a distant light, a distant noise, the memories against which I had long struggled came to me, one by one. In the deep solitude of the forest, the pain dissipated from them, the keen grief turned to soft sorrow, and there was peace. Nothing was undone, nothing "explained," as I had tried so hard to do earlier. Memories that once seemed alien became a part of me, the rich depth of the person I am. Increasingly, the problem for a personalistic perspective came to appear to me not one of accounting for the impersonal, alien hidden within me—there is none—but rather one of coming to understand the dynamics of alienation and reconciliation.

I think I can sense why so much of our being becomes degraded to the point of seeming alien, until the hidden reality posited by theoreticians of the unconscious comes to seem as an accurate description.

Humans can accept pain only where there is reconciliation, or, in a different idiom, can accept guilt only where there is forgiveness. Ours, though, is an unforgiving age. We lack even a clear understanding of what forgiveness would mean. Usually, we confuse it with justification, and that again not in the profound biblical sense of being made just but in the trivial sense of finding an excuse—and we are very good at that. Yet the pain remains, excused but unforgiven. Forgiveness takes more than excusing, more than a dismissal of responsibility or significance, our usual "you could not help it" or "it does not matter." It is, rather, a healing, taking up into wholeness. An injury is forgiven when it is integrated into the whole, losing the power to hurt. Thus the body "forgives" as it heals the wound, a new tissue surrounding it and making it whole. Though a scar remains, there is no more pain. So, too, the forest takes up the wounds in a wholeness, young trees healing the logging scar. Humans, too, can forgive that way, surrounding the disruptive experience with the integrity of life.

In the mundane world of our lives, though, there is so little integrity. The world of artifacts and constructs has little rhyme or reason of its own. Its *logos,* if *logos* there be, is man-made—and as flawed as its maker. The texture of that world, of that life, is too disrupted, too marred by conflict, to surround and heal the injury. The forest surrounds it, overcoming the disruption. In a human conflict, bystanders are far more likely to take sides, intensifying the conflict, than to surround it and heal. We live in the conviction that there are victors and vanquished, little noting that the conflict itself is a defeat. But in a world which cannot heal, cannot bring reconciliation, there can be little admission of guilt and pain.

The guilt and the pain are there, the harder to confront since they must needs be kept out of sight. Quite trivially, we crush no flowers as we walk the concrete of our streets, forgetting the crushing weight of the concrete itself, scarring the earth. Few of us have had the experience of slicing the throat of a rabbit as it nudges up to a familiar hand, then blowing under the skin and pulling it off entire. We buy our meat from gleaming cases, cellophane-wrapped—and seldom pause to think of the incredible, needless brutality of our slaughterhouses. Only occasionally are there glimpses—following a truck of half-frozen crated chickens, many injured, mute with horror, bound for slaughter, I must fight not to remember other freightcars. The mangled bodies of forest creatures along our highway remind us of the destructive presence we represent, not by ill will but even on our lawful occasions. Anaximander knew that pain: beings by their passing and perishing, he wrote, pay for the injury they have done each other in the order of time.[18] We refuse to know it, preferring to let an "unconscious" build up of all we would rather not confess. Where, though, there is no confession, there can be no forgiveness. And again, where there is no hope of forgiveness, there can be no confession. And how could there be forgiveness? We have insisted that there is no one to forgive, that we alone are persons in a dead world of impersonal artifacts and material objects. God? It is not easy to sense the reality of God in a world from which we have excluded him.

That, I know, is a terminology not readily comprehensible in our time. I would hesitate to speak in terms of letting God reenter his world that we may meet him there, though it may be quite accurate. Still, it is something that can be meaningful as a conclusion, not as a starting point. That needs to be more familiar: the surrender of the arrogance which admits none but ourselves to personhood, the willingness to see our world as kin which demand respect but in turn can also forgive and heal, as the trees and the porcupines can share pain, as the ageless silvery river bears it away. Then the hidden depth of our being can become not alien but ours, reconciled, enriching, and sustaining.

For the hidden, I have become convinced, is not by its very nature alien and autonomous. It is the depth of our being which can become alien when we are unwilling to respect the integrity of our being. Even the archaic motives of our dim evolutionary past are not transmitted to us unaltered, a primeval beast hiding within us. They are transformed, much as motivation can become autonomous, as a labor of necessity which becomes an avocation, reaching us in a human, personal form. Even the putative "sex drive" which so fascinates the perennial late Victorians in every age is, in humans, no autonomous biological drive. It is a privative, truncated remnant of what is authentically human, the ability to love. That, though, is the order. It is love, the love of persons sharing a life in freedom and fidelity, that is the primordial human reality. When it is broken, its components can become autonomous, degraded, and alien. That, though, is a defective state. To claim it as "normal," as if marriage were a heteronomous societal attempt at taming and canalizing "natural" carnal lusts, inverts the order of reality, even when it does describe the actuality of humans bereft of sustenance in a world of artifacts.[19]

The task of appropriating the hidden is an open-ended one, a part of the reason why times of quiet, long evenings before the house, undistorted by the glare of lights and the blare of tape-decks, are so essential to human survival. Be still, and know: for only so you will know. The experience of the hidden, to be taken up in trust, is a continuing challenge to every person. It is not, however, a challenge to the idea of personalism since the hidden, unless we ourselves mutilate it, is not impersonal.

There remains, though, the second experience, that of compulsion, of which Saint Paul writes in the anguished lines, "The good that I would do, I do not, the ill that I would not, that I do, wretched man that I am. . . ." That is no longer simply the experience of a part of myself as hidden, as alien, but rather of a force compelling, constraining me, masked in the petty psychopathologies of everyday life, breaking forth in clinical pathology.

Part of the strength of depth psychology and of Freudianism in particular, in spite of its theoretical weakness, lies in its claim of having uncovered the hidden causes of pathology and in its promise of providing relief to persons in anguish. Nor is its strategy of tracing pathological behavior to an alien, prepersonal force dwelling within us without precedent in human thought. Perhaps the earliest imagery, in shamanism as well as in the Scriptures, is that of the demon, the unclean spirit inhabiting the desert places of the earth and looking for a person in whom to lodge himself. The image may seem archaic, though if you but wander the waste places of our cities, the crumbling, boarded-up buildings, sidewalks covered with wind-driven refuse, discarded wine bottles still in their paper bags beside the sleazy, heavily fortified liquor shop, it acquires a new force. Those are the desert places where no healing is, where unclean spirits live and pervade the derelict humans living out lives laid waste.

Freudian psychoanalysis revived a different, no less time-honored image, that of the devil and the angel struggling for a soul, as a way of conceiving of those human acts which seem incapable of explanation in terms of conscious, "rational" motives. In medieval woodcuts, the subhuman and the suprahuman force assume humanoid forms, the cunning devil, goatfooted and malicious, the angel pure and good, struggling with all their might and vigor—though the devil is usually the more vigorous—for the passive and bewildered soul of the hapless believer. In the Freudian version, the devil is secularized as the primitive drives of aggression and sexuality, struggling with what evolved from an angel to a conscience and finally to internalized societal constraints. For all the change of imagery, however, the principle remains constant. The conscious I, once a soul, now a person, is not an agent but a patient—literally, from the Latin for "to suffer," "to be the passive object of." His acts are not, strictly speaking, acts at all but rather the outcome of a prehuman process. There is, though, one significant difference. For most of its history, humankind regarded demonic possession and the passivity of the soul as an exceptional state, induced by the presence of an alien force which could be cast out without destroying the subject. Freudianism, at least as received by many of Freud's philosophical readers, makes it a structural condition of being human.

As the psychotherapeutic profession increasingly cut its ties with the Church and the care of souls, building up new links with medicine, another model inevitably suggested itself, that of a physical disorder, either an injury or a disease. In fact the appeal of Freudianism may have been in part that it lent itself admirably to this approach, even adopting the terminology of physical medicine, as in the case of the "trauma." The assumption here is that the organism, physical or psychic, can equally be traumatized by an outside force, as a blow with an iron rod or an experience of shame. Sometimes the organism recovers, at other times, however, the recovery is flawed—the bone does not set correctly, self-confidence is not restored. Then the physician must reset the bone or reenact the experience, as appropriate. Even insurance-claim adjustors, hopelessly bewildered by William James's *Principles of Psychology,* 2 vols., can understand mental illness in those terms. A convention seems to have arisen, honored though unacknowledged, of thinking of psychotic disorders on analogy with disease, leading to heavy reliance on psychoactive pharmaceutica, while thinking of neurotic disorders on an analogy with unhealed injuries, calling for resetting the mental bone.

All three models have their virtues and their flaws. For our purposes, however, the significant point about all three ways of conceptualizing the experience of compulsion is that all treat the person as a patient and seek an external, alien agent to account for his acts. Though the term itself has long since fallen into disuse, psychotherapists continue to think of themselves as alienists, the time-honored designation of their profession: dealing with some alien factor entering the person's psychic body, not with a tragic derangement of a Person's life.

There are, in fact, powerful experiential grounds for that mode of conceptualization, even apart from all theory. The experience itself is agonizing—encountering a person you have known, someone intimately familiar, yet the familiar response is not there. You speak of memories once shared; there is no response. When there is a response, you feel as if the person were not responding to you but to someone visible only to him, somewhere behind you. Could someone change that much? Surely not: the familiar person is sitting there in front of you, in an ill-fitting institutional blouse, hair a bit dishevelled, but it is still that person. At that point it is almost impossible to resist the impulse to think, yes, it is that person, but possessed, displaced by something alien. It is almost a relief when visiting hours are over and you can return to your memories. Oddly enough, as you say good-by, using a name to which the person seems no longer to respond, you sense that he, too, is relieved to return to his world, strange and far away.

It is immensely tempting to resort to some conception of demonic possession if you are the next of kin. The whole system supports it: it justifies it in treating the patients as only that, patients, no longer agents to whom respect is due. It is emotionally easier as well: you can retain the cherished memories unaffected. It is still the same person, below the surface, only "something came over him," he is possessed, infected with an illness. Besides, it is not impossible to integrate such a conception with a personalistic perspective simply by adopting the latter as the norm "under ordinary circumstances" while allowing for a special category of humans barred from personhood by "mental illness," much as we routinely adopt normal vision as the norm while allowing for a category of humans barred from seeing by blindness.

It is easy, and tempting—except for one obstacle: the afflicted person himself. Mental patients, overwhelmingly, do not think of themselves as "patients" but as agents, and of their "illness" less as of something they suffer than something they do. Most of them by far are in fact self-committed. There is something rather disconcerting about the breezy, cheery way in which they will speak of themselves as "crazy"—and about the uncanny knack with which they single out an impostor. "You are not crazy," they will tell him with the accusing undertone of "you are not one of us," "you are . . ."—what? They will seldom use the word "sane." You are a spy. Or perhaps a state inspector, or a psychologist doing research—we are "crazy." Mental illness here in fact appears as something one does, much as one might do psychology or public service. And who should know better? I have so often been wrong when I let myself be lured into the arrogant assumption that I know a tree, a porcupine, or a dog better than he knows himself. Why not take them at their word and carry the personalist inversion even here, into the darkest recesses of the troubled mind, and assume that patients are persons, their burden not a "disease of the psyche" but a distressing disarray of their lives and a person's act in response to it?[20]

I know of one man who has done so, though I am sure there are many others: gifted clinicians, regardless of the theory to which they formally subscribe, inevitably do so in practice. He was András Angyal, a Magyar psychotherapist trained in Vienna, writing in the United States in the 1950s.[21] His book, *Neurosis and Treatment*, has long been out of print, though for the wrongest of reasons. Angyal, as many refugees will, identified wholly with the ethos of his new home and time, the whole Mom-and-apple-pie mood of the Eisenhower age of peace and prosperity. Not surprisingly, before too many years had passed, his readers came to reject his work with a patronizing wave—"I'd rather be neurotic than naïve!"

That reaction, though not without its justification, utterly misses the point. The significant aspect of Angyal's work—theoretically in the tradition of classical Gestalt theories, of Koffka, Köhler, and Wertheimer—is that it sets about describing the entire range of nervous disorders and prescribes treatment for them on the assumption that "mental illness" is in fact something persons do, a way of coping, however defective. It is fascinating to follow him, disregarding Mom-and-apple-pie much as we willingly disregard Freud's Viennese provincialisms, as he goes about the task. His basic assumption is always that each person wants to live as free, satisfactory, and full a life as possible. That, however, requires a double confidence, first that the world, whatever its flaws, is essentially manageable, not wholly unpredictable and overwhelming, and, second, that the subject, whatever his limitations, is basically capable of coping with it. Where that double confidence is wholly absent or objectively unwarranted, the subject gives up and escapes into psychosis, in effect stopping the world and getting off. Where, however, that double confidence is not wholly absent but only impaired, the subject develops strategies of coping within limits of possibility. To an outsider, they may appear contorted, constricting, in a word, neurotic, and with good reason. For the patient, though, as he perceives himself and his world, they may well be adaptive. The pattern is familiar from entirely ordinary experience: for a young man of dating age who thinks himself a painfully awkward dancer but a superb swimmer, it is highly adaptive to develop a strong allergy to cigarette smoke (and to purchase a season pass to the municipal swimming pool). Why not think of the neurotic as, in principle, doing the same? After all, to a dissident in Czechoslovakia today paranoid behavior may well appear maximally adaptive: a sober, factual description of his objective circumstance does read like something straight out of the A.P.A. *Diagnostic Manual.*

Angyal follows out that clue with brilliant success. Step by step, he analyzes the classic forms of neurosis, traditionally attributed to the workings of hidden forces, without once having to invoke them. The description and prescription are complete simply in terms of distortions of life patterns, accounting for the whole range of phenomena dealt with by Freudian psychology—as well as for some which, like the absence of guilt feelings in some forms of obsessive-compulsive neurosis, are problematic within the Freudian matrix. At no point does Angyal distort his evidence, at no point does he claim that, appearances to the contrary, theory shows the truth to be something else. His approach is purely personalistic in our sense, though he never uses that term. He treats his clients as persons, not patients, seeking to understand their behavior in meaningful, not causal terms, as we understand a person—and succeeds.

For me, the Angyal book provides the needed evidence that the personalistic inversion can in fact be carried even into the realm of compulsion. It does not, to be sure, make psychoanalysis obsolete, but it does change its philosophical significance fundamentally. It does not make it obsolete because, in the shadows, we do in fact see best by indirection. Were the sufferer able to see the reasons for his mode of acting in clear, direct insight, psychoanalysis would be unnecessary. The point is that he cannot, not because some putative "causes" are in principle invisible, but because the vision is too painful. Before he can confront that part of himself, the subject must often constitute it as something alien, distant, and so emotionally manageable. That again is familiar enough. Children will frequently have their teddy bears say what they do not quite dare say themselves. Their parents will similarly become aware of their own faults first by recognizing them in others, in literature, or in history. Even so, it might often be necessary to project the present causes of distress either on a putative mental mechanism ("not I but my libido . . .") or upon a memory, possibly fictitious, in distant childhood ("not I but my mother . . .).

That example, embodied in the concept of a childhood trauma, makes the point most clearly. To explain present behavior as the involuntary effect of an experience long ago is a standard psychoanalytic practice heartily welcomed by clients. A man whose marriage is being destroyed by his own folly will eagerly speak about his mother, though she be dead these twenty years, digging up or inventing ever new memories. To claim that it is those memories which are presently and effectively "causing" his present disastrous behavior, is simply too far-fetched. The past *is* not, and has no power to cause—unless it is recalled and endowed with force by serving as the *symbol of something present.*[22] The causes are, invariably, all too painfully present, too painfully, in fact, to be seen directly. That is the great good use of the examination of memories—not that they "cause" anything, but that the things which a client chooses to "remember" can help to identify most precisely what it is in his present, unmentioned situation that is problematic. The attempt to bring about a cure by altering memories cannot but be futile: that is not where the causes lie. As long as the present situation remains uncorrected, the client will always come up with new "memories"—a phenomenon all too familiar in therapeutic practice. The "memories," though, can be a most useful diagnostic tool and, at times, also a tactful roundabout way of approaching the present.

Mutatis mutandis, the same could be said of the elaborate mental mechanisms posited by various depth psychologies. In dealing with the admittedly difficult process of transition from youth to adulthood, especially in a society which has no conventional rites of passage, it might very well be therapeutically effective to reconceptualize the experience in, say, the familiar oedipal terms, speaking of it *as if* the young man desired not the self-confidence of manhood but rather to possess the mother and dispatch the father. It is, certainly, far easier to speak of such things than of the painful, embarrassing daily conflicts and decisions of which the transition and the crisis are in fact made up. The "as if" mode is entirely legitimate, and often helpful—until we drop the qualifier *as if* and start speaking and thinking as if we were in fact describing a reality, hidden, primeval, beyond our personal control. Then it becomes vicious—and false. The reality, after all, is that of a young man taking his place as an adult, capable of being symbolized, among other ways, also by the oedipal myth, not the other way around.

There is, incidentally, another good reason for considering the mythology of the unconscious a useful therapeutic tool in the mode of *as if* rather than a factual description. Freud himself appealed to the therapeutic effect—cessation of symptoms—as the confirmation of his conceptual schema. That therapeutic effect, however, is not unique to practitioners using Freudian imagery. Jungian, Adlerian, Eriksonian, but also Christian imagery, using the traditional conceptions of sin and absolution, produce approximately the same distribution of success and failure. To me, this strongly suggests that it is the conceptualization itself which is therapeutically effective, the particular imagery accidental. If that is the case, any therapeutic warrant for the cognitive claims of psychoanalysis disappears. The mythology of the impersonal remains legitimate only in the mode of *as if*, as a conceptual tool, not as a description. Reality is the person, acting in a situation—and needing help.

So conceived, the putative "discoveries of psychoanalysis" no longer pose an obstacle to a personalistic reading of the cosmos and of our being therein. Yes, there is a hidden; there is always more to a person than meets the I. It is not, though, an alien, impersonal reality but the rich depth of personal being. Then also, yes, there will be times when humans will be able to speak of their aching lives only by projecting them upon the screen of memory or of a putative unconscious reality. When they do so, though, they are acting in a mode of *as if*. The true agent remains the person.

What, though, can that mean on the ward? Nothing, perhaps—the hopelessness is deeply built into the bleak walls and the pale fluorescent light. Or perhaps something, though something very modest, a plea for remembering that these are not "patients," they are *persons*, agents, seeking to act as best they can, within however limited a range. What they can do for themselves, be it ever so humble, may be more important than what can be done "for them." I know, it would be a futile illusion to think of relocating our mental wards on backwood homesteads like the long-ago "lone forties," though I know of no context that can offer an equal low-demand environment combined with the optimal opportunity for rebuilding self-confidence in basic tasks as a backwoods cabin, an axe, a splitting block, and a stove to keep going. That, I know, is at best a metaphor. Still, few people can rebuild their lives and confidence by performing make-work tasks while all that matters, their living and healing alike, is done for them. Again, gifted clinicians, regardless of theory, have long known that. So does the Episcopal Order of Saint Anne, committed to treating people who otherwise would be patients as persons as much as possible. They may have hit upon something important precisely because they have generated no grand theory. Theories are *as if*. Persons are reality, persons matter.

Humans, I am convinced, can break the spell of the demon, because it is self-imposed, though not by a simple act of the will, since the imposition is not a simple act, either. It is interwoven with the pride which denies personhood to the world of nature that can heal and sustain. It is no less interwoven with the fear born of a lie, which makes it impossible for humans to be still and let what is hidden speak, lest it reveal too much. It is linked with the complex system of self-deception which we have generated in order to justify what we know to be unjustifiable.

Yet there still is night: behind that complex there remains, within us and without, a living world, a world which is God's, not man's, a world within whose moral sense there is room for humans, for persons, to be at home. As humans recover the moral sense of that world, even in their cities, among their machines, they can break the spell of the demon.

The Vertigo of History

Humans can, in an act of trust, break the spell of the demon, recognizing in the shadows the depth of their own being. That is the core of the answer to the charge frequently leveled against Husserlian phenomenology and, more broadly, against all personalistic approaches—that they cannot deal adequately with the nonconscious dimensions of being human. That charge is the counsel of a fear that dares not approach that which it fears. Then the dread and the passion can become alienated, yet they are not intrinsically alien. They are the depth, not the encircling horizon of being human.

History, too, is the depth of being human—but it is also and irreducibly its horizon. Hence the second charge is far more serious[23]—that a philosophy which would do justice to the morality of the subject cannot do justice to his historicity. Perhaps that is why National Socialism, invoking the vertigo of the passions, survived but for a generation, while Marxian socialism, invoking the vertigo of history, retains its strange fascination in spite of three generations of painful failure.

History, like passion, is the depth of our humanity, and cannot be excised from it by fiat. Though humans strive to forget, immersing themselves in a solipsism of the instant, even though they may seek to escape to the seeming timelessness of nature, *there still is* remembrance. The rings of the old hemlock remember two centuries of dry and moist seasons, the horseshoe grown into the crotch of the apple tree recalls a long-dead husbandman, the sapling ensconced within the butt log of the red oak preserves the youth of the tree. There is history in the long-abandoned cellar holes and the half-tumbled stone fences, in the overgrown wagon roads and the filled wells. There is a richness of the past in the language that shapes our thought, in words that preserve a lost past. The New Hampshire carpenter who speaks of "scribing" a measurement acknowledges, unknowingly, the heritage of the glory that was Rome.

That is a history that I, too, have brought to the forest, the richness of my solitude and the wealth of companionship through the ages, in legend, song, and story. The humane quality of our lives is a direct function of our ability to appropriate and cherish the depth of history as much as the wonder of nature. Conversely, the stifling horror of the consumer mentality is its deadening effect on our sensitivity to history as much as on our sensitivity to nature. The history whose heirs we are is the depth, the *sub-stantia,* of our humanity. As I wander the long-disused paths, pausing over the cellar holes, fragments of that history drift through my mind like Odysseus' hearth-smoke of Ithaca or the wells of our fathers in the Old Testament. I know the horror of the line from Ecclesiastes, "and the place thereof shall know it no more." Though a wayfaring sojourner on this land, lately come, I strive to appropriate its memories that I may belong to it. As Plato acknowledged in his much-abused conception of *anamnēsis,* there is self-discovery in remembrance.

Yet there is also a vertigo in the memories of the vine-covered cellar holes, in lives once lived and loves once loved, an echo of what Sophocles knew better than we—that history is not only the intimate depth but also the ominous horizon of our being. Women and men lived here once, at peace in the rhythm of their labors. The stone walls, constructed with no aids other than a team of oxen, a stone-boat, and a crow-bar, bespeak an intent of permanence. They built to stay, yet something forced them to abandon their works. They had coped effectively with nature and the seasons, but far beyond their horizon, on the far side of Temple Mountain and down the railway from Greenville to Boston and beyond, forces were gathering which would render their effort vain.

One winter the frost brought to the surface a heavy cast-iron object in what had once been a barnyard and is now just a forest clearing. When I had brushed it clean and freed it up with penetrating oil and naval jelly, it proved to be a heavy pulley. Lubricated, it spun easily on its turned shaft. The absence of wear testifies that it had seen but little use before settling, forgotten, beneath the rotting timbers and the falling leaves. As best I can determine, it seems to have been installed shortly before the sawmill ceased operating in 1903. Down to the last, the cooper was still investing in his shop. He and the workers who used that pulley had lost none of their skill. The demand for that skill, however, was not of their making. It was military service in surpressing the Southern bid for independence that introduced millions of Northerners to underwear and created a demand for knitted goods. That in turn created a need for the crates in which the knitting mills at Highbridge packed their products, to be carted down the valley to the railhead at Greenville. That railway was supposed to continue on to the mill and, through New Ipswich, past the sawmill on to Jaffrey and Peterborough. An economic downturn interrupted the construction at Greenville; there the trackage, finally abandoned in 1976, terminates at what was once the depot. The transshipment by horse and wagon represented an additional burden on waterpowered knitting mills whose power source failed regularly when the river froze in January and went dry in August. Inexpensive cardboard barrels made heavy wooden shipping crates a luxury in competition with coal-fired steam machinery and urban mills with their own sidings. The men who labored on my land, crafting those crates, probably knew little of the horizon of history closing in upon them. If they did know, they were powerless before it. They labored on—until one day the sluice gate closed for the last time, the great overshot wheel creaked to a standstill, and the forest moved in, reclaiming its own.

When I was born, half a world away, the wheel had been still for thirty years. The dam washed out in a freshet six years before my time. I knew nothing of that—neither I nor the parents who bore and raised me had the least suspicion that, half a century later, I would be clearing the land under the dam and raising a solitary dwelling in the clearing, speaking and writing in a foreign language in a strange land. Ours, too, was the intent of permanence. We took it for granted that I would live out my life as a citizen of Masaryk's Czechoslovakia, in the peace and freedom won in the war to end all wars. Yet even then the storm was gathering. In the year of my birth, Adolf Hitler, whom a German contemporary dismissed as "a charlatan with a peculiar charm for the Bavarians," launched Germany on the road to apocalypse with his national brand of socialism. To the east, an ominous force fueled by the injustices of the czars and the malignant genius of Lenin and Stalin was preparing to engulf half of Europe. Amid all that, we lived our daily lives on our island of decency in the illusion of permanence, unknowing. Those of us who knew or suspected found themselves powerless before the drift of history.

My forest clearing, too, is an island of peace. The well I have dug, the stone fence I have built with a crowbar and a come-along to do the work of oxen, the house I have framed no less than the pages I write, bespeak the intent of permanence. Yet beyond my horizon, on the far side of Temple Mountain, down the road to Boston and beyond, in Moscow, Washington, Prague, in obscure corners of the globe, forces are again at work which, within the life left me, may well once again scatter all my works before them as the autumn wind scatters the mosaic of fallen leaves. In time, it will have become History. Now it is history in the making, the ominous horizon of my life of which the latest headlines illuminate no more than obscure fragments.

That is the deep question of history: how can humans live with the awareness of the vast, dark force around them, the horizon of which the Greeks spoke as fate and which we have sought to domesticate by labeling it History with a capital "H"? In part, surely, we deal with it by willful forgetting, restricting our vision to an enclave of clear light, a microcosm within which we can sustain an illusion of control. The *New York Times* is for sale at the local stationer's; most of us, though, prefer the *Peterborough Transcript.* It is comforting, a needed escape. Such forgetting, though, can never be complete—and its price is the loss of the enriching depth of history together with the ominous horizon. Those two personae of history, as depth and as horizon, will not be separated. Nor is there escape in the selective memory of the sundial which marks only the sunny hours. It is precisely the remembrance of the sunny hours that is most painful once they are gone, swept away in the flow of history. Paradoxically, the bitter remembrance of the German occupation has a built-in comforting component: it ended, it is over. That same component, however, makes the memory of the euphoric years of our first republic immensely difficult to bear:

in retrospect, that outburst of joy seems so vain, so doomed. The ominous horizon surrounds us, there is no escape. How can humans live with what they can neither accept nor escape?

Over the millennia of human history, humankind have fallen back on a double strategy, the resignation of the prayer, "Thy will be done," and the immense, audacious hope of the Apostle that "all things work together for good for those who love Him." Though we no longer speak the language of the King James Bible, that double strategy remains our recourse in the face of the half-guessed events that threaten to overtake us, in the bluish-pale loneliness of our hospitals, the shabby dawn of our streets, and the impersonal viciousness of our divorce courts. Though we seldom acknowledge it amid the shipwrecks of life, love and hope continue to survive by clinging to an extreme confidence: *it will be all right,* whatever comes, unwanted, unacceptable, unavoidable, it will be all right, in ways we may not be able to imagine or pray for, it will somehow be all right. Life will go on, whatever happens. We could not go on living if we ceased to believe that.

It is a strange conviction, a faith that would be evidently false in the order of time if each passing moment did not, in its transience, also contain the intersecting dimension of eternity. In the order of time alone it is so often not all right. There is so desperately much death and pain, love lost, lives destroyed, hopes scattered before the wind and washed away by the flood-crest of history. Within the order of time, the very "happy end" is the ultimate mockery, being both happy—and an end. Humans can confront the anguish of finite goodness only in the recognition that it is not only caught up in the flow of time but also, in its goodness, forever inscribed in eternity. When Whitehead spoke of the "consequent nature of God,"[24] he was but noting, albeit in an unfamiliar idiom, what humans have ever known—that the intense, anguished beauty of children playing in the sun by the river, heedless of the horizon about to close in upon them, is bearable only because it is forever inscribed in eternity.[25] It is that knowledge, primordial and fundamental, that enables humans to sustain their self-conscious finitude in the faith that it will be—or perhaps eternally is—*all right,* that all things work together for good for those who love Him. In that sense, and perhaps in that sense alone, it is true. What is good, insofar as it is good, cannot perish: it is forever inscribed in eternity. Only when humans know the eternity that intersects each moment of time can they live with the knowledge of finitude, at peace with the horizon of history.

It is, I believe, the loss of that recognition that is the key to comprehending the obsessive fascination with history which has distorted Western thought in recent centuries to such an extent that the West proved ready to sacrifice human morality for the sake of accommodating human historicity. That appears to me as the reason why a perspective which extols our historicity usually appears to us as superior, even though it obscures and stifles our humanity. For, more than aught else, in recent centuries we have lost our sense of eternity. We may not speak of it in just those terms, to be sure. Rather like patients bearing a sickness unto death within them, we prefer brave euphemisms, speaking of having brought the Kingdom of God from heaven to earth—though not actually, but only as a promise to be fulfilled in an indefinite future. Such may indeed have been our intent, to make eternity accessible by bringing it down into time. The effect, though, has been quite different. Eternity brought into time loses its perennially copresent reality as a dimension of the present. The reality it gains in exchange is that of the grapes of Tantalus: that of a promise of a future which devalues the present as imperfect but itself remains forever beyond reach. The promised land of our rhetoric, be it prosperity or communism, is on the horizon—but the horizon is an imaginary line which recedes as we advance toward it. Having sought to possess eternity, we have become the prisoners of time.

It is a bootless venture, seeking to assign blame for the historicism which has so distorted Western thought that we have justified ever bloodier sacrifices of the present generation to an ever-receding better tomorrow, all in the name of "progress." Christian writers, self-professed heirs of the vision of eternity, are apt to blame Feuerbach and his Marxist heirs, even though Marx did little more than offer a fashionably "scientific" version of a conception of progress he shared with most of his contemporaries, not excluding the captains of industry who genuinely thought themselves as benefactors of humanity both in amassing and in disbursing their fortunes. Conversely, more than one Marxist writer has claimed that, in his historical determinism, he was but refurbishing the lost insight of the Judeo-Christian conception of history as *Heilsgeschichte,* a history of salvation, even though, in Christian thought, the motif of a return to the purity of the primitive church is far more common than any call for striving onward toward an ever better one. No Christian looks for a new improved model of the Messiah. Neither reading, ascribing blame to the Christians or to the Marxists, is particularly convincing or helpful in understanding the phenomenon of historicism, the conviction that both the sense and fact of time are products of and wholly enclosed within history.[26]

For the purposes of understanding, Jan Patočka's judicious assessment might prove more fruitful.[27] Patočka does not assign blame. To him, historicism does not appear as an arbitrary, willful attack on the vision of the eternal (he speaks of "absolute") sense of being. Rather, he sees it as an attempt to fill the vacuum created by the loss of that sense—the absurdity of which Nietzsche and his heirs are keenly aware—with the vision of at least a relative sense of being human as meaningful, if not absolutely with reference to eternity, then at least relative to a transient historical context.

Patočka's idiosyncratic metaphor of an absolute and a relative sense of history lends itself to translation on a number of levels. In the terms we have been using, we could say that the late medieval Church made the vision of eternity intersecting time effectively inaccessible, appropriating it as its exclusive instrument of power while substituting for it a promise of a reward in an infinite future understood as a posthumous prolongation of time—the notorious "pie in the sky." Europe first sought to wrest back that vision in the Reformation. Then it turned to seeking the Kingdom in a future after all, though this time in an earthly future to which the Church could not block access. Or, on a more concrete level, we could say that as the Church failed to make eternity real in time by addressing itself to the problems of desperate poverty, cruelty, and injustice which were the obverse of Ruskin's vision of the Middle Ages, humans turned their hopes to the future as the secular surrogate for eternity. Each reading, together with others more or less specific, has its historical justification. In all of them, however, a basic insight remains constant: in recent generations, European thought has been profoundly affected by collapsing into each other two dimensions of being human which humans had long treated as distinct: the line of temporal progression, from *before* to *after,* and the line of moral judgment, between *good* and *evil.* Whatever else may be true of it, ours is a time for which *later* has acquired a sense of *better*—while *better* has been drained of all meaning except that of *later.*

That the line of temporal progression and the line of moral valuation do indeed represent the two fundamental axes of being human belongs to the most primordial data of lived experience as well as the most basic recognition of phenomenological reflection upon it. Humans, as Heidegger insisted and our awareness confirms, do live "in" time.[28] Our lives, our being, are extended over a sequence of moments as a story that is told or an air that is sung, the dynamic of our consciousness is that of a stream, spanning a retention and a protention as well as a memory and an anticipation, fusing them into a complex now.[29] That is a primordial given, and it may even be more, a clue to a more basic reality of being human. Perhaps the basic reality is that of extension and of location as such, of a here-now located with reference to a *near* and a *far* which are indistinguishably spatial and temporal. In truth, humans can visualize temporality only in spatial terms. Time in our visualizations becomes a highway along which we travel, with the past appearing as a landscape we have traversed but which is still there behind us, while the future is said to be already there, "down the pike" before us. The converse holds as well—humans conceive of space fundamentally in temporal terms. Near is within an hour's easy walk or a few minutes' drive, far is many days' journey away. Even the physicists' construct, the light-year, is no more counterintuitive than the mariner's knot. Long ago and far away seem as intertwined as the here and now.

If that is indeed the case, it would add an experiential and hence a metaphysical significance to what hitherto seemed to be strictly a regional, metaphysically neutral construct of modern physics, the conception of a four-dimensional space-time continuum. More important in the present context, it would reveal the conception of time and temporality to which Heidegger and his contemporaries tended to attribute an absolute significance as a metaphor for a far more generic trait of *localization,* thus comprehending the human mode of being and that of the cosmos and providing the basis for a comprehensive conception of reality rather than marking off human temporality as distinct and opposed to the rest of the creation. The experiential interrelation of space and time may prove a vital phenomenological clue for further investigation: perhaps temporality is in truth but one mask of the fundamental phenomenon of extension and location. Perhaps extension, which Husserl singles out as the definitive mark of material reality,[30] is continuous with the temporality which is the distinctive mark of vital, animate reality. Then, too, there is the intriguing, ever-recurring correlation of temporal metaphors with verbalization, intrinsically extended in time, and of spatial metaphor with visualization. Perhaps the distinction of space and time reflects the distinction of sight and speech, nothing deeper.

All those are tantalizing possibilities. For the present, though, those questions must and may remain unresolved. Though intuitively, without either evidence or *Evidenz* to support it, I suspect that the temporal extension of vital reality is but one face of and a metaphor for the universal trait of the extension and location of all being, the point that needs be made remains unaffected whether this is so or whether temporality is a reality *sui generis,* as the vitalist and process philosophers down to Heidegger take it to be. That point is the recognition of the two distinct axes of being human, that of temporal progression—be it solely from *once* to *some day* or therewith also from *there* to *some place*—and that of valuation, the axis extending between good and evil, as irreducibly distinct. The way the relation between these axes is conceived may well be the most distinctive mark of any philosophy, the conflation of the two the distinctive mark of all historicism.

In much if not most human thought, these two axes have traditionally appeared not only as distinct, but even as mutually irrelevant. In all two-tier conceptions of reality, each axis defines a world of its own. The order of time may be a vale of tears, though it may also be, as the statuary in some Hindu temples reminds us, a garden of pleasure as intense and as fleeting as the tears. The point, however, is that in both modes it remains a realm of seeming, a veil of *maya,* in which no true value can be realized. A transient good, after all, is in principle a contradiction. As humans implicitly acknowledge when, in spite of life's transience, they pledge each other eternal troth, the pure good cannot be transient. In light of that deeply felt requirement, humans have repeatedly assigned the good to a realm untainted by transience, one defined by the axis of value and conceived as radically distinct from that defined by the axis of temporal progression, leaving value atemporal and time valueless.

In this respect, the spiritual outreach of the Judeo-Christian tradition represents an audacious departure. In spite of the interpretation given to the conception of *Heilsgeschichte,* the history of salvation, by the age of "progress," it is not really the case that Christianity identified the two axes. Actually, the Judeo-Christian conception could be said to have sharpened the distinction between time and eternity by stripping time of the nimbus of infinity. The axis of temporal progression here is finite, reaching from the creation to the Last Judgment, explicitly denying any claim of time to a sequential infinity. Yet while finite, the progression from the creation to the Last Judgment or from the fall to salvation is not a "progress" as we have come to understand that term, as a growth to perfection. The later here is not *eo ipso* better or worse, the end is not the cumulation of what preceded it. In the most dramatic metaphor, the fall, though subsequent to the creation, is emphatically not an improvement upon it. Though Saint Paul may, in retrospect, speak of the Law as a "schoolteacher unto Christ," the Christ is not the product of a gradual evolution of ever-better prophets. The Christ, in the Christian conception, is present in history but not its product. He enters into it, intersecting the line of temporal progression with a wholly different, vertical line of eternity in the Cross.

That intersection of time and eternity is the most adequate metaphor of the conception we have been calling Christian. The lines of temporal progression and of value here do not coincide, but neither are they parallel and unrelated. The line of value—the scale of good and evil—intersects the line of temporal progression in each moment. Time thus becomes not valueless but the locus of the realization of value, with a crucial double consequence. Value no longer appears as something abstract, constituting a separate reality. Rather, it ingresses into time, is realized in it, and bestows worth upon it. Time, in turn, no longer appears as intrinsically free of value. It is in time that eternal value—not simply the relative advantage in the order of time—is realized. History is not the story of a creative evolution, but the story of the mighty deeds and great events in which value enters time and time rises to value. Even its sequentiality is not simply irrelevant. It can prepare the conditions for the ingression of value "in the fullness of time," or it can effectively prevent its realization. It is in that sense that *Geschichte ist Heilsgeschichte,* history is the history of salvation or, in an older metaphor, the stage on which the drama of salvation is acted out.

It is, however, a far cry from such a conception to the historicist conception of an intrinsically *saving history* whose sequentiality itself determines and constitutes value. History in a Christian conception is a history of salvation, but it is emphatically not a saving history. It is God who saves, ingressing into history. History itself does not. What is later is not *eo ipso* better—nor, as in the inverse historicism of the myth of a retreat from a Golden Age, is it *eo ipso* worse. Paul is not an improvement on Jesus by virtue of being later, nor is the modern Church an improvement over the primitive one. Each moment of history has its own value which must be judged independently, against the eternal axis of good and evil, not in terms of its relation to what preceded and followed it. Progression is not, of itself, a progress: intrinsic value is a function of eternity, not of time.

By contrast, the historicist conception of a saving history—be it Henry Ford's idea of "progress," Bergson's and Teilhard de Chardin's "évolution créatrice," or Hegel's or Marx's "historical determinism"—represents a radically different conception. Here history, having been stripped of its eternal significance as the locus of realization of eternal value, is called upon to generate its own relative value. A noble act, no longer seen as intrinsically worthwhile as realizing absolute value, appears absurd unless its value is salvaged by its historical utility. It is as if Western humankind, having lost sight of the God who saves in history but still convinced of the reality of salvation, had to look to history itself to save. In effect, the historicism of Western thought since Fichte and Hegel is then an attempt to find in history a relative meaning which would fill the vacuum created by the loss of its absolute meaning. The two axes, that of temporal progression and that of moral worth, are here pivoted at their intersection until temporal progression comes to appear as simultaneously a moral advance—and moral advance loses all meaning except that of an "advance." Historicism and its age, our age, are then marked by the conviction that "later" also means "better"—and that "better" retains at least the meaning of later. The puzzling accusation that phenomenology and all philosophy which seeks to do justice to human moral personhood cannot do justice to human historicity—even though, in truth, it was the rediscovery of human morality in the Renaissance that brought about a rediscovery of history—boils down to the charge that a moral personalism cannot accommodate the conception of "progress" and of history as *l'histoire créatrice.* The putative flaw, so perceived, begins to appear as a virtue.

To be sure, to an age seeking an escape from the meaninglessness of individual lives in the spectacular drama of social wholes and historical processes, the charge of ignoring the alleged meaning of History appears serious indeed. The tense insistence with which that charge is usually leveled betrays a sense of threat—as well as the profound ambivalence of Pandora's last gift. In the usual reading of the story of Pandora's box, hope, the final gift, tends to be presented as a compensation for the untold grief and sorrow unleashed when the box was opened. There is, we assume, a promise of a happy ending. Though sorely beset, the human retains a hope to sustain him. Albert Camus's familiar "Le Mythe de Sisyphe" suggests a different reading. As Camus reads it, Sisyphus' plight is desperate only as long as Sisyphus remains in the bondage of hope—in his case, the vain hope that some day he will succeed in rolling the boulder to the top of the mountain. Though that hope may sustain him in his labors, it also turns the inevitable slipping of the boulder from his hands into a crushing disappointment. Once Sisyphus abandons hope—in terms of the verdict of the gods, he has none—his lot is drastically transformed. His task is still agonizingly hard, but no one ever said that working for a living would be easy. To earn our daily bread in the sweat of our brow is our common lot. Were Sisyphus a compulsive rock-roller who enjoyed rolling rocks for its own sake, he would foil the gods. Even short of that, there are the other times. At the end of the day's work, the boulder having yet again slipped from his hands, Sisyphus can straighten up, look down at the shimmering Mediterranean and set out, striding easily down the mountain through the warm evening. Perhaps, freed from the hope of "success" and of its inevitable disappointment, Sisyphus can even discover the pleasure of matching his muscles against the boulder's weight, discovering the beauty, joy, and goodness of the present which hope obscures in fixing our gaze on the future. For that is the price hope exacts for the consolation it offers—the surrender of the present.

The immense impact of historicism may well be that of Pandora's last gift. Brought down into a future time, the Kingdom of Heaven has certainly proved a far more powerful opium of the people than it ever was in heaven. Generations of Europeans, amid the nightmare of the Industrial Revolution, uprooted and impoverished, were able to forget the travail and torment of their lives under the spell of the shimmering promise of a better tomorrow. It mattered little whether they conceived of those better tomorrows in terms of alabaster cities gleaming or in terms of the instant magic of a workers' revolution: it was the shimmering vision that mattered. Though the parallel is not often noted, the various Marxist movements were and are far more otherworldly than Christianity ever was for the believing Christian. To the believer, after all, the "other world" is never wholly other. The Kingdom of God is among us, eternally intersecting time. The dominant trait of a life of faith is the present living, all-transforming presence of God, not the hope of a future reward. By contrast, in the Marxian vision, especially in its "revolutionary" rather than its "trade-union" form, the promised land is wholly otherworldly, a future promise rather than a present reality. Even the order of time itself appears as a prehistory, and the order of being human within it wholly flawed, a distortion of human's species essence. In this present world, the faithful are bade to bear the suffering of their lives, sustained not by some equivalent of the presence of God but *solely* by the hope of a future reward, the socialist pie in the ever-receding future.

After more than half a century of what the Soviets term "real socialism," it is superfluous to argue that the historicist "pie on the horizon" is wholly illusory, devoid of all reality. Reality, however, was never what made that vision appealing, even though early socialists may have been no less convinced of its imminence than the early Christians. Rather, the power of all historicism was and is its ability to offer a present sense of meaning. Though that meaning may be only relative, there is meaning in the temporal progression itself. When Eduard Bernstein said of the German Social Democracy that "the movement is everything, the goal is nothing," he spoke more perceptively than his comrades were willing to admit. Old communists, long disabused of all illusions, are yet loath to leave the movement, not for fear of being excluded from a glorious future but for the fear of the emptiness of the present stripped of its utilitarian justification as a stepping-stone to Utopia. Historicism in all its forms has proved by far the most powerful opiate humankind ever administered to itself—and the age devoid of a vision of eternity needs opiates badly. Might not the ultimate arguments for historicism prove to be that which nonbelievers once advanced in the defense of religion—that, though not true, it is necessary?

That argument is powerfully reinforced not only by the horror of nihilism from Nietzsche down to secular existentialists, but also by the horror of the social disintegration of our time. What Paul Tillich called the anxiety of doubt and meaninglessness is the common denominator of all the forms of that disintegration: the most basic human need, as Viktor Frankl recognizes no less clearly than Saint Augustine, is for meaning.[31] Humans can bear an incredible degree of meaningful deprivation but only very little meaningless affluence. Might not the relative meaning offered by the historicist vision be preferable to meaninglessness? After all, young nationalists, communists, or Jehovah's Witnesses, their eyes fixed on the ever-imminent, ever-receding Kingdom of Heaven in History, seldom need to look to the cruder opiates like drugs and alcohol. . . .

That argument, advanced already in defense of the young National Socialists whose dedication contrasted so sharply with the aimless decay of Germany's Weimar Republic, usually provokes a counterargument based on the horror of the apocalypse now: of the time when the shining future becomes an ordinary present and the young idealists, able to seize power but unable to realize their vision of perfection in an imperfect time, set out on an orgy of destruction. That horror is real enough, amply attested by the aftermaths of our century's revolutions. Still, the argument which invokes it remains essentially a historicist argument, based on the relative disvalue of historicism in the order of time.

A far more basic reason for questioning the utilitarian justification of the historicist vision is its effect on the only lives that humans actually live, those of the perennial present. The power of the historicist vision is that it seems to endow that present with a time-relative meaning. It does so, however, only at the frightful cost of draining the present of all absolute, perennially present meaning. As the present becomes purposeful and valuable as the means to a future, it loses all intrinsic value as a present, as real in its own right, not phenomenal only. That disvaluation of the present is what makes the sacrifice of entire generations to the perennially future "better tomorrow" appear acceptable. It is, however, no less a matter of personal life drained of all intrinsic worth as it is lived in a posture of anticipation, of a discontent nothing can satisfy since it is precisely the anticipation, not its consummation, which bestows the relative, historical meaning on human lives. Consummation then cannot but be an anticlimax which can be countered only by escalating expectation—in ideology as well as in the acquisition of possessions. If the *now* is not good intrinsically, in terms of the eternity which intersects it, it can be redeemed only by a constant future reference.

That is the power of the vision of life as "progress," currently crudely acted out in consumerism: it endows the present with meaning by relating it to a future. Such a regression may well be infinite; our lives, however, are not. Our lives are finite, leading to the moment which has no future reference, the moment of death. The historicist posture, as Martin Heidegger recognized, inevitably leads to the nihilism of being toward death, giving Sartre grounds for his assertion that human life is always a failure because humans die. A prolongation of that finite time into a putative infinite temporality of immortality, as Saint Thomas recognized for his part, compensates the intrinsic nihilism of being within time only illusorily. Once we lose sight of the eternity perennially intersecting time, even an infinite prolongation of time cannot redeem its futility. "Natural immortality," he tells us, is little to be desired.[32] Amid the loss of all sense of absolute meaning, the intense grasping at the relative meaning of history may be understandable, but it is no less futile. It sacrifices the sole real value, the eternal value of the present, as a means to an ever-receding future about which we have only one assurance: that it will lead to death. Hope—not as a transcendental virtue, to be sure, but as a transcendent, temporal one—is Pandora's most ambiguous gift.

It is tempting to conclude with a graffito of some years ago, that "History is a communist plot," and to praise the ahistoricity of phenomenology's eidetic vision as a virtue rather than a failing. Such a conclusion, though quite understandable in the bleak morning after the orgy of "better tomorrows," obscures the complex relationship between eternity and time, between human morality and historicity. History, though it must be placed within phenomenological brackets, is not excluded by them but represented as experience instead of being posited as a putative cause. As the depth of being human, history shares in the transcendence-in-immanence that Husserl recognizes as a trait of the transcendental dimension of our subjectivity, the "pure I."[33] Humans do bear their historicity within them, both as retention and protention and as recollection and anticipation, and their moral humanity is unthinkable without it. That historicity, however, unlike the alienated, absolutized historicity of the historicist vision, does not stand in a contradiction to human morality, the eternity of being human. It is intimately linked to it. Only because we are capable of a vision of eternity—and to the extent to which we are capable of it—are we also capable of experiencing succession as history and our presence as historicity.[34]

There is an entirely mundane recognition at the base of that aphorism. Temporal continuity alone simply is not enough to generate a sense of history. Though the lives of those who came before us may be contiguous with ours, the continuity soon grows tenuous in the order of time. The facticity of human lives changes far too rapidly, the familiar factual landmarks are swept away and "the place thereof knows it no more." Were we, with historicism, to consider persons as a product of their time, we could not recognize the humans of long ago and far away as kin and ancestors, their story a part of our history. Were historicism true, there could be no history. Only because humans are not locked within their time, because they are capable of transcendence, recognizing the eternal intersecting all times, are they able to recognize the far away and long ago as kin. Only because we recognize the story of King David, Uriah the mighty warrior, and Bathsheba his wife as not simply a product of its time but as an instantiation of a perennial pattern of love, coveting, and remorse, that the story remains relevant and intelligible. Any awareness of temporal continuity of our times with, say, the events of the Trojan War or even of far more recent happenings has faded long ago. We are aware of it only because we recognize those events as instantiation of the same eternal patterns as those which render our lives meaningful—just as we recognize an intelligibility in events involving social wholes only because, with Plato, we perceive them as persons writ large.

The Renaissance conception of history as not a sequence but a canvas on which the story of noble deeds, of the realization of value in time, is writ may not be sufficient, since it offers little clue to the processes which have shaped the conditions for this or that instance of the ingression of eternity in time. Still, it is necessarily the first, most basic recognition, essential to any adequate philosophy of history, since it does provide a clue to the constitution of historicity. Factual historical processes are no more autonomously, intratemporally meaningful than are individual human lives. The story of, say, the industrialization of the West and the rise of a stratum of humans alienated from love and labor, the "proletariat" of Engels's and Marx's writings, is of itself no more than a fact. Only when seen in the perspective of the realization and destruction of perennial human values—the perspective, we could say in a self-conscious paradox, of eternity—does it become meaningful as history. For all their invocation of historical relativity, it was only because Marx and Engels saw the "condition of the working class in England" in the absolute moral terms of indignation at injustice that they could present it as a reason for action. There is, finally, history only because there is eternity intersecting time and rendering all times contemporaneous.

In that sense, it would not be inaccurate to say that the being of morality is absolute, the being of historicity merely phenomenal. It would, admittedly, be misleading, since in our ordinary usage "morality" does not suggest the dimension of the eternal, the axis of good and evil, but only its very transient articulations in particular, historically specific moral codes. That is a basic difference. The reason why a particular age articulated the perennial vision of justice as it in fact did is a specific empirical one, the question concerning it one which can be answered only in the context of empirical historical research. But while only so can it be answered, it can be posed at all only thanks to the prior, eidetic vision of a moral ideal which enables us to speak of the variables of history in terms of a common moral denominator. Thus while it may be crucial to study, say, the Bolshevik revolution in terms of historical continuities, that study is significant only in the context of the eidetic vision of human greed and injustice, which provoke despair, violence, and self-perpetuating terror—and for the purpose of recognizing the same eidetic pattern in our own present time and place.

For that is the obverse of the intimate relation of history and eternity. As the vision of the eternal enables us to see the order of time as history, so in turn history enables us to distinguish the perennial pattern of being human from the specific facticity of our time. In the myopic vision of the present, it is all too easy to perceive the real as the rational, the actual as the necessary. It is precisely the recognition of historical relativity of fact which enables us to recognize the eternal validity of the *eidos*. The Marxists could present their vision of the relativity of good and evil as convincing, in spite of the horrors it implied and justified, because during a century of frozen history between the Congress of Vienna and the Russian Revolution Europe lost its ability to distinguish the eternal from the merely familiar and was unable to recognize that, in a changing time, it is precisely the eternal moral law which demands changes in transient mores.[35]

As the failure to recognize that it is eternity which gives sense to time and the moral law which gives force to custom is the downfall of all historicism, so the failure to recognize that convention is but a historically specific, transient embodiment of that law is the perennial failure of moral realism. The paradoxical contribution of historical relativism to our moral humanity is not the absolute truth claimed for it by its adherents but rather the clarity it can give to our vision of the eternal. The "Austro-Marxists" who claimed that it is just the absolute, eternal moral law which demands revolutionary changes in changing times were surely far wiser than the orthodox Marxists who saw that demand as rooted in and determined by "history" alone—or than their conservative opponents who invoked the eternity of the moral law to interdict all change in time. Historicity is not the opposite of morality, any more than time is the opposite of eternity. It is, rather, morality acted out in time. It is as eternal that humans constitute history—and as historical that they become aware of eternity. Only a philosophy which does justice to the morality of being human can do justice to its historicity as well.

The vertigo of temporality, like the spell of the demon, does not, finally, unveil before us some deep and hiden truth of being human. It, too, is a product of the loss of confidence in our personhood, directly linked to the loss of a living sense of its reality. Europe's nineteenth century, opposing nature to history, managed to convince itself, as Collingwood was to testify much later,[36] that as humans substitute a world of artifacts and constructs for the living cosmos, they can also substitute history for nature and even freedom for necessity. It was a brave and a failing vision. Without the vision of eternity, there can be no tenable vision of history and no freedom, only a historicism which entraps humans in the order of time. But there can be little vision of eternity in a world of artifacts and constructs, since these, precisely, are the product of the order of time and wholly enclosed within it. Karl Marx's vision was truly what he claimed for it, the ideology of the Industrial Revolution, the gospel of the age of production and consumption. As such, it remains instructive, a precise diagnosis of the total dehumanization entailed by that age, masked for the moment by affluence but acted out starkly in the lands ruled by Marx's heirs. The "kingdom of freedom" lies not in its future.

Here Kant, not Marx, was right: freedom is the noumenal reality of time's phenomenal actuality, not its extension in a future time.

The attempt to conquer rather than accept the dark horizon of history ends inevitably in the nihilism of a surrender to history. The motivation of that attempt, unlike that of the German "national" version of socialism, is not demonic. It is, as Reinhold Niebuhr recognized long ago, a paradoxic extension of the ageless human strategy, the affirmation that "all things work together for good. . . ." It is, nonetheless, as false as that affirmation itself becomes in the order of time. For it is not of that order: in time, even a time prolonged into a Kantian immortality, it is false necessarily, because the idea of a transient good is a contradiction in terms in theory and a bitter mockery in practice. If there is an answer humans can give to the vertigo of history it is in the recognition of the eternity which intersects time and gives it meaning. Historicity then, as depth and horizon, is a gift of eternity, not its contradiction, and passing is not a failure.

All that and more can be said: unlike Karl Jaspers, I do not believe that philosophy must retreat into silence in face of skepsis.[37] Still, all that can be said will not constitute an argument, nor will arguments convince. Borden Parker Bowne may well have been right when he wrote that all knowledge rests on faith. That faith, though, is neither arbitrary nor irrational.[38] It is an expression of a vision, a clear expression of a truth clearly seen. Arguments are crucial to it: they make the difference between critical faith and naïve dogmatism. It is in analysis that philosophy assures itself that its initial vision is not fallacious and that its articulations can come to terms with the claims of its alternatives. Arguments are reasons for *not disbelieving* what we believe because we have seen.

Arguments, though, are not of themselves sufficient reasons for believing. Only seeing, the confrontation with a truth evidently given, can provide a reason for belief. It must be tested and sustained in arguments, certainly—but the primary impetus and ultimate confirmation is clear awareness, the recognition of ourselves as Persons in a personal world, bearers but not the products of our passions and our historicity. In a real sense, the affirmation in face of skepsis remains an act of faith—*credo.*

5. Credo

Nature's God and Mine

It would be neither meet nor right to speak of conclusions in a book which seeks not to argue but to see and to evoke a vision, pleading with the reader to pause and ponder rather than to argue and agree. An argument can lead to a conclusion; an evening does not. Slowly, imperceptibly, the forest grows still, the sounds of the day, the hum of the insects and the song of the birds, the sound of the wind and the sounds of the creatures of the forest, all mellow into silence. Only the sound of the river tumbling over the boulders, the backdrop of the day, stands out in the evening silence, while the bats under the eaves embroider their twitter upon it. The sky darkens gently and the tree line merges with it, while the occulting flies of Saint John mirror the stars piercing the sky above.

The evening becomes night. Yet the night is not a conclusion drawn from the evening, as death is not a conclusion drawn from a life. Neither is the night the fruition of the evening, as death is not the fruition of life. There is evening, and there is night, each of them eternal in its own right and mode. Neither the evening nor the night lasts forever: there is evening, but then there is night. Nor is the point that though *this* evening might pass, evenings recur in principle. The eternity of the evening has nothing to do with the forever of endless time, just as the eternity of which we speak when we confess to believing in life eternal is not a condemnation to endless temporality. Eternity is a present quality, a dimension and a glory of being that now is, of this evening. The sense of this evening is not a function of a temporal reference. When, fascinated with time, we teach ourselves to think of the evening as a transition, as the conclusion of the day and the anticipation of the night, something to pass through in order to get from the former to the latter, we lose the evening itself. So, too, we lose a journey when we think of it as something to be endured in the transition between here and elsewhere, and the days of our lives when we think of them as time not to be cherished but to be endured from *x* until *y*. Instrumental value—though indubitably real enough—then overshadows intrinsic value, robbing our lives of the profound worth present in them in exchange for the ephemeral promise of value to come, giving rise to the illusion of a "value-free" reality. To recover the truth of value it is crucial to bracket the reductive framework of temporal sequence and to see being in its reference to the eternity which ever intersects with time, defining the *now* within it. Within time, that *now* would be indistinguishable from the endless series of such *nows*. It stands out as the moment in which eternity intersects time.

The articulation of such a vision in radical brackets is an essential task of philosophy. It is here that philosophy finds its access to reality. R. G. Collingwood's conventional division of labor, according to which "science" is assigned the task of seeing while philosophy, itself unseeing, is charged with reflecting on the principles of the seen,[1] has proved seductive but also destructive. The problem is not simply that the endeavor of science is not one of seeing, though in truth it is not. It is a highly selective inquiry, intrinsically interpretative, taking as its starting point not the lived experience of nature but rather a particular perspective which both assumes and implies a particular nature construct.[2] Even Collingwood, though he entitled his book *Idea of Nature*, dismisses that primordial idea, the sense of nature in meaningful experience, in a few pages, and turns for the rest of the volume to Greek *theories* of nature, conceived in surprisingly modern terms. The same is true even of theoreticians of nature like Schrödinger, Eddington, or Whitehead, who are least prone to positivistic reductionism. Their reflections are genuinely aimed at discovering the sense of nature, not simply constructing an explanation of observed phenomena. Their datum, however, is again not nature as primordially present, the meaningful, living cosmos of which we are a part, but nature as observed by the sciences, conforming to Collingwood's division of labor. Their philosophy, a reflection on principles, sets out with an immense burden of covert assumptions built into its data. Even in the case of Whitehead, who was perhaps most persistent of them all in his stubborn attempt to make room for subject experience within the framework of a theory of reality, that theory remains a theory of nature as reconstructed by the sciences, not of nature as lived experience. So too, Ernst Cassirer, who took nature as experience seriously, in the end wrote it off as the "mythical" view of nature. The conceptualization of nature within the symbolic system of the natural sciences here retains the claim to being a privileged mode of representing reality.

The sterility of such a conceptualization, however, is at the root of our predicament. It has amply shown its utilitarian value for the purposes of manipulating our psychophysical environment and so has established its validity as a special case theory for the special task of manipulation. Its broader claim to validity for the purposes of understanding the ultimate sense of reality and of our place within it, however, has left us bereft of a moral perspective which would enable us to inquire into the purpose of manipulating reality. Metaphorically, the more we know about the techniques of constructing nuclear devices, the more are we at a loss as to how to use them. Our conceptualization of reality as value-free and material, so useful for the purposes of *technē*, provides no context for judgments of value on which all our purposeful activity depends.

Unlike the romantics, I do not believe that the activity of conceptualization is itself at fault: my perception of the sense of nature is indebted to Robert Frost, not to Henry David Thoreau.[3] *Technē*, too, is an authentically human activity, conceptualization, the will to *theoria,* is an authentically human way of knowing. Nor do I believe, with Husserl's more romantically inclined followers, that faithfully articulated seeing of itself constitutes an adequate conceptualization: in the jargon of the trade, that descriptive phenomenology is all that philosophy can, need, and ought to be. Husserl's own claim seems to me far more perceptive. As he understands it, phenomenology is the necessary propaedeutic of all *scientia*, all rigorous knowing, both general and special. Or, reverting to our earlier terminology, radical seeing, the seeing in radical brackets, is the necessary foundation of all conceptualization. Without it, conceptualization remains no more than a cunningly devised fable. The search for a more adequate conceptualization of nature and of our own humanity must, I am convinced, begin with a radical seeing, encountering the cosmos and ourselves within it in the full richness of meaningful experience. Only on such a basis can we hope to generate a conceptual framework which would enable us to make not only effective judgments of *technē* but, more broadly, to raise and answer the question of the moral sense of *technē*.

Still, seeing, even radical seeing faithfully articulated, is not yet of itself a *theoria*, an adequate conceptualization. Though I am convinced that it is *prima philosophia*, the perennial ground of philosophy, it is not yet an *ultima philosophia*. The critical task of philosophy, analysis, critique, reformulation, are all yet to come. That is why I cannot entitle the final chapter of this volume "Conclusions." I have opted instead for the title *Credo*, not as a noun, a creed offered for assent, but as the first person singular of a verb—I believe. For these are not conclusions, only convictions that have emerged out of years close to the land, years lived in radical brackets. They are, to me, the incoercible givens, the outlines of a reality which any adequate conceptualization of nature and our humanity would have to acknowledge if it were not to be but a cunningly devised fable.

To speak of the incoercible presence of God may at first appear marginal in the context of the conceptualization of nature. Nature appears dead to us in great part because we have grown accustomed to thinking of God as "super-natural," absent from nature and not to be found therein. That, though, is itself a measure of how far our quest for theory has deviated from the reality of lived experience, not ours alone, but that of humankind throughout history. For, in lived experience, in the radical brackets of the embers and the stars, the presence of God is so utterly basic, the one theme never absent from all the many configurations of life's rhythm. The most basic trait of the world that confronts a dweller in the radical brackets of the forest clearing is that it is God's world, not "man's," and that here God is never far. The heavens declare His glory, the creatures of the forest obey His law, the human dweller gives thanks for His grace. "Though I take the wings of the morning and dwell in the uttermost parts of the earth, even there Thou art with me"—even the language that harmonizes most easily with life close to the land is that of the Králíky Brethern, translating God's word into Czech so that it may be understanded of the people in the sixteenth century, or of their English counterparts who, a century later, gave us the King James Bible. The moral sense of nature, and not that alone, but all whereof we have spoken, is not its own, generated by its processes. It is the presence of God—the Christians would speak of the Holy Spirit—and a gift of Nature's Creator. Nature's gift to humans, in turn, is not its own but God's gift which nature mediates. The segment of our phenomenal field revealed by the radical brackets is privileged not intrinsically but because here humans have not obscured the epiphany of God's presence. The miracle of nature is the power and grace of God which confront the dweller therein. That is the most basic given, the gift of the dusk.

The recognition of that given is at the same time our most basic conceptual task. Both in principle and as a matter of historic fact, alienation sets in when humans lose their awareness of the presence of God and persuade themselves to view the cosmos no longer as a creation, endowed with value in the order of being, a purpose in the order of time and a moral sense in the order of eternity, but as a cosmic accident, meaningless and mechanical. Then nature comes to appear as absurd and we ourselves as futile within it. In fact, we first desanctified nature by exiling God into the "supernatural," only to discover that its very intelligibility became problematic thereby. Immanuel Kant provided us with an interim solution, attributing to human reason the godlike power of endowing nature with intelligibility. When we discover, all too quickly, how ill-equipped we are for that task, we grasp at straws, hoping that History or passion will come to our rescue. When that hope failed—as "real" and "national" socialism respectively acted out a metaphor of that failure—we resigned ourselves to absurdity. Absurdity, however, necessarily self-destructs. If we are to escape its self-destruction, no conceptual task is more urgent than that of recovering our awareness of the presence of God and of nature as His creation. A book concerned with the conceptualization of nature ought surely to speak prominently of the presence of God, whether or not such is the current philosophic fashion.

Yet of God, more than of aught else, humans can speak truly only by indirection. God is never present as an object, a being among beings. Paul Tillich, in the tradition of German idealism, opted for the phrase, "the Ground of Being," and the usage has much to recommend it, though no usage can be definitive. The experience words here seek to evoke is not so much one of a thematic focus as one of a pervading presence, awareness of nature as the poetry of God.

Poiēma theou, the poetry of God: when Diogenes Laertius ascribed that phrase to Thales, it was not a play on words.[4] The verb *poiein* referred generically to the activity of making, molding, shaping, rather like the archaic English "wrighting," which could be used to describe equally the activity of a wheelwright and a playwright, so that a wheel and a poem could equally be said to be wrought. In the double brackets of a forest clearing at dusk, no metaphor points to the sense of nature's presence as faithfully as that of God's *poiēma,* indicating, by happy coincidence of words, both God's works and His poetizing. The sense of nature's presence, ultimately, is the sense of the presence of God.

For there still is night, and there is dawning, a new day. There is a rightness between the rhythm of nature's time and the eternity of the sky, between the embers and the stars. The turbulence of passion and the turmoil of history find their place, subsumed within the peace of nature's God.

To speak of "nature's God," to be sure, may well seem suspect. Western thought had to struggle strenuously to free its vision of God from the reductive tendencies of nature-worship which echo still in the Renaissance equation, *Deus sive natura*—God, that is, nature. Speaking of "God's nature" may well seem safer. In what sense, after all, can God be said to be "nature's"? Does the skunk know there is God? Of all the night creatures who pass through the clearing, he is the most graceful, his wide white stripe undulating in the moonlight. Or the porcupine, the *porc-aux-pins* of the early voyageurs—does he know? He comes lumbering from across the river: once one of them spent over an hour with me, watching the moon. Or the huge turtle who came to lay her eggs in the sandbank before the house: she covered them so carefully before disappearing in the river. She will never know her children. Does she know God?

In our customary frame of mind, even posing the question may seem cute, a disingenuous affectation. Of course, we assume with Descartes, animals do not "know": the turtle is a programmed organism, a natural process unfolding before us. To speak of animals—never mind trees and boulders—as knowing, especially if we equate knowing with human reflection and articulation, seems a contradiction in terms.[5]

Or so it seems, in the city. When the intimate presence of nature dissolves the wolf-fog of human arrogance, that prejudice dissolves with it. Just the opposite comes to seem obvious. Of course animals know. Their knowing may be of a different order than human reflection, conceptualization, and articulation, but their purposeful behavior in the context they treat as meaningful testifies both to a highly differentiated cognition and to an ability to store and transmit information. Not animals only: insects, trees, plants, though much more humbly, recognize the presence of a world of others and respond to the cycle of day and night and to the rhythm of the seasons. We have as little warrant for conceiving of them as mechanisms, as nature's artifacts, as we do of higher animals. In fact, once the usual order of asking is inverted and we acknowledge, on good Jamesian grounds, reasons for suspecting presence of mind, it becomes extremely difficult to find evidence which would warrant denying it. With higher organisms, the behaviorist dogma is credible only as dogma, as an initial assumption. In fact, it is difficult to deny a sense of inwardness, the "subjective aim" which Whitehead made into a technical term, even to the ageless boulders. Seen through Whitehead's eyes, even the boulder prehends, focusing a world around it, constituting an *Umwelt:* much more so the growing and the moving creatures around us. Not humans alone, but all creatures *know*—and if they know, in whatever sense, why assume that they do not know the Holy, the presence of God which pervades the life of all nature? After all, even humans, though notoriously the species endowed with the dullest senses and the greatest capacity for self-deception, do know God.

For, as a species, humans do know God. Of all the illusions of the world of artifacts and constructs, the most facile and the most palpably false is the claim that the awareness of God's presence—in our inept phrase, "believing in God"—is the peculiarity of certain individuals, an opinion contingently held by some members of the species. The obverse is true. It is the blindness to God's presence that is exceptional. Humans, as a species, throughout the millennia and all over the globe, have been worshipers of the Holy. The awareness of God's presence is and ever has been the most persistent specific trait of our species being.[6] Even secular anthropologists use the evidence of worship as the distinguishing mark of a human rather than simply higher primate presence. Both empirically and eidetically, humans are beings who know God. The real question is not the very recent one, why some humans believe, but rather why some humans profess to be blind to God's presence. In fact, the theories that purport to explain the putative "causes of religion"—whether the Marxian claim that religion is a mystified ideology justifying exploitation or the Freudian conception of projection—explain not so much the universal fact of human worship as those distortions of faith which make it inaccessible to some humans. As for accounting for the fact of worship itself, the explanation most readily available and most parsimonious is far simpler: humans worship because the evident presence of God in nature and history is the most primordial given of lived experience.[7]

The question that humans have posed through the ages is not whether there is a god but rather, "What does the Lord require of me?" Locked in the monad of our constructs, we tend to lose sight of it, but the question, "Is there a god?" only arises when humans interpose a mental artifact, a "god-construct," between themselves and the living presence of God, effectively blocking it from view. Then the question no longer has to do with the awareness of God's presence. It has nothing to do with God. All it asks about is the extensional reality of an object described by the god-construct—and is truthfully answered in the negative. Animals, I am convinced, know God because they do not formulate constructs which would blind them to the reality of God's presence.

Beyond the world of artifacts and constructs, the speculative question fades, hopelessly artificial, displaced by an overwhelming sense of God's presence, by a realization of the utter impossibility of God not being. It is not that the mind considers and rejects the possibility: rather, between the embers and the stars, the possibility is unthinkable. One global awareness remains: God is.[8]

That is the awareness, though the attempt to express it by saying that God's existence is "self-evident," as theologians in the tradition of Saint Augustine have at times done, though true, has little evocative power for most hearers. Self-evidence, in our present usage, has come to function as a logical, not an experiential category. As such, it applies to our concepts rather than to our categories. It can be said of a proposition whose contrary is self-contradictory. On the formal level of propositions arbitrarily severed from the realities to which they point, however, there is nothing self-contradictory about the proposition "God is not," any more than about the proposition "The sky is not blue"—even though the day is clear and cool and the sky so evidently is so. Here an experiential category like Husserl's *Evidenz*[9] is more appropriate. As Husserl uses it, the term recaptures some of the original experiential sense of the term "self-evidence," as indicating something that carries its own warrant in its evident givenness, like Descartes's clear and distinct idea. Such is the experiential force of the proposition "The sky is blue," uttered not as a low-order hypothesis but as the amazed, wondrous acknowledgment of the intensely blue presence of the sky on an August day, a presence that will not be denied. That, too, is the experiential force of the proposition "God is," uttered again not as a hypothesis but as the recognition of the overwhelming presence of God. It is not that the proposition as such is self-evident: rather, the reality is undeniable. The truth to which it points is so overwhelmingly evident that the question of God's "existence" pales into utter artificiality. In that sense, though in that sense only, we can say with Saint Anselm that the existence of God is self-evident.

Saint Thomas, sagacious as ever, sought to make the distinction by distinguishing between self-evidence in itself and self-evidence for us. The existence of God, he acknowledged, is evident in itself, the living presence of Being which is wholly incompatible with the very notion of being-not, thus giving Saint Anselm's ontological argument its due. Intrinsically, God evidently could not not be. It is only for us, who know God not in his essence but only in his attributes, that the utter evidence, evident givenness of God's being, can appear as not evident—since, as finite intellects, we interpose a phenomenal veil of constructs between ourselves and God's living presence. There is, therefore, room not only for Saint Anselm but also for the fool.[10]

It is a distinction usefully drawn. In the busyness of our days, amid our artifacts and constructs, we can indeed lose the sense of God's presence behind the veil of our god-constructs. There is a self-imposed blindness which can become invincible. Still, the very possibility of making the distinction which Saint Thomas makes should make us hesitant about attributing that blindness intrinsically to the finitude of the human intellect, thus making it insurmountable in this life at least. Humans can and do, in this life, confront the awesome majesty of God's evident presence—or, more accurately, they are able to recognize God's presence when it confronts them in moments of openness. The limits of that ability, reflected in the possibility of doubt, seem rooted elsewhere: in the human capacity for alienation, for inserting a layer of constructs between themselves and all living presence, including that of others and of nature. That, though, is a capacity, not a necessity, and though in history it may have become inevitable, yet it is not essential. Certainly the loss of the direct sense of presence, as noted already, need not simply be a matter of an arbitrary personal decision, as Pelagius vainly taught. It can be that—and is, when a human chooses to harden his heart to blind himself to God's presence so that he can follow the desires and devices of his own heart, undisturbed by a twinge of conscience. Perhaps all of us have done it—and have lived to regret it. When conscience is blocked, sickness becomes a sickness until death, or, in the terminology of the tradition, "a sin against the Holy Spirit," incurably deadly since it rejects healing. Sin, metaphorically speaking, may be always original—but sometimes Pelagian as well. Still, it is not always the latter. The vicissitudes of life projected into temporality, the burden of guilt and grief as well as the estrangement of reflection and its constructs, can scar human life even without any personal ill will—and in fact do, leaving their marks on all of us, even those whom we venerate as saints. Still, though that may be a universal condition, it is not an essential, structural one, an inability to see, to acknowledge the evident presence of God that shines through both nature and history. Humans are capable of blindness, yet, in privileged moments, they are also capable of receiving the gift of sight. Then they know, with utter evident givenness: God is.

How, though, can we *speak* of the presence of God? Earnest young men, carefully groomed and endearing in their earnestness, stop by my house at times. For a long time they were my only visitors when neither the righteous nor the religious would follow the abandoned wagon road to my dwelling place. God enters a house with a guest—may they be richly repaid! Like Jacob at the brook Jabbock, they were convinced that they had learned the secret name of God to whom they witnessed and eagerly read me their pamphlets, proving their point with an odd mixture of innocence and sophistry.[11] They are such good people, and much of what they would teach to a disoriented generation is the perennial truth of the ages. Yet doctrines grow sterile: the presence of God is much more direct, independent of textual proofs in its evidence, and far harder to speak of than coining a name out of the consonants of one word and the vowels of another.

There is, most basically, the presence of God in the very fact of the world. In a living world, the cycle of generation and perishing is a constant reminder of the utter contingency of the beings of this world. None of us are our own, self-made and self-sustaining. The illusion of our own necessity may seem tenable in a context in which our dependence on our human and natural world is so thoroughly mediated as to become invisible. It becomes far more evident with self-sufficiency: solitude teaches thanking. We are, though only by a hair. We could easily not be. The stark white glow of the January moon, pressing down on the frozen forest, sears away the illusion of necessity. Then again, perhaps when humans grow immersed in the order of time, they can avoid the recognition of the utter contingency of being by conceiving of the present as necessitated by a preceding past, and so on, ad infinitum. When, however, eternity intersects with time, presenting all time in the perspective of a copresence, the vacuity of regress becomes evident. All of us, humans together with all creation, *need not be.* There is, in nature and in human mind, no ultimate reason why the massive boulder, the oak sapling rising beside it, the chipmunk searching for seed, and I, the human who watches them in wonder, should be rather than not be. And yet, *we are*—and our being testifies to its Creator. It is not an argument, and would fail if so presented. Rather, it is a testimony, the presence of God made manifest.

The order of the created world is that, too. The natural world, abandoned by a human dweller, does not disintegrate into a meaningless aggregate. It may seem that way as the ridge of the abandoned barn sags and caves in, the laboriously erected stone fences yield to the winter frost, and the forest reclaims the hard-won fields of yesteryear. That, though, is only the human order passing. The forest that replaces it has an order of its own, in the rhythm of the seasons, the cycles of its flora and fauna. Nothing is random here. When humans give up the arrogance of trying to be the measure of all things, they begin to perceive in a world of a different order. The nature abandoned by humans is yet not abandoned. It is not simply that it is lawlike in performance, manifesting observed regularities. Its order is far more intimate than that. It is the order of a sphere of *mineness.*

That metaphor points to something more than the intricate design which the Reverend Mr. Paley noted in the watch he found on the wind-swept heath of his example. It is also a sense of caring, of mattering, the sense that each twig of the forest is precious. It is a sense of a presence such as humans experience on entering a home in the dweller's absence. Unlike the abandoned, looted dwellings left in the wake of revolutions or the gutted shells of the inner city, the refuse of law and order, a dwelling, though empty, feels cared for, as if there were a cherishing and a rightness. The house *belongs:* on entering it, we sense its order not simply as an order, but specifically as the order of a *Lebenswelt,* of an inhabited context ordered by a caring presence. Trying to cook in a strange kitchen brings it home: things have their places, unknown to us, but not arbitrary. The house is a sphere of someone's mineness.

So, too, the forest meets the dweller, not simply as an order, but as a sphere of mineness. Not my own: though parts of it can become that, the forest is too vast, too autonomous for that. Nor does it belong to the animals who dwell therein, not even to the trees that make it up. Walking down from the orchard, past the cellar hole to the boulder at the narrows where the first wheel may have stood, the recognition comes slowly—the mineness is God's, the world is God's household, *die Lebeswelt Gottes.* That again is not an argument, and becomes vain when we seek to reconstitute it as such, as the "argument from design." Far more, it is another mode of God's presence.

So, too, is the tangible reality of the moral order in its continuity with the vital order of the creation. Kant saw it, but so did my neighbor, a good man who has never heard of Immanuel Kant. He set down his beer on the stoop on a night of the new moon with the words, "The stars are going out of their mind. It goes to show you, you can't have things just any way you want." I did not press him for an elaboration. It seemed no less evident to me than to him. The periodicity of the seasons, the rightness of the order of time, all the ethic of utility and appropriateness, are anchored in an intrinsic rightness, in the evident goodness, truth, and beauty of Being. That value is not the value of nature. It, too, is one of the modes of God's presence—not an argument, but a mode of presence and a mode of speaking thereof.

Through the years I filled many pages with notes on the presence of the Holy. Yet all I wrote seemed trite. It had all been written before. The nineteenth century tried to formalize it; impressed with the natural sciences of their time, religious thinkers sought to formulate the sense of God's presence as "arguments for the existence of God." It was a bootless effort—the strength of philosophic propositions is evocative, their ability to evoke an experience. When they are presented as hypotheses, seeking to win consent through argument, they become empty. I doubt that anyone was ever convinced into believing by the traditional arguments. But then, that is not really their point. The concern with intellectual conviction and verbal assent reflects the insecurity of humans amid the man-made world of constructs. In a world which is not yet "man's," the point is different: to see, to recognize God's presence in His creation. Saint Thomas, finally, may well have known that. Though he couched his testimony to the modes of God's presence in the world in the form of arguments, he concluded each with an appeal to evident insight—and this all men know to be God.[12]

They do, and they have always known. The sense of God's presence is an intrinsic, inseparable trait of their species being, their doubt a measure of their alienation. As humans recover the moral sense of life, they recover the sense of God's presence no less. I have watched the process among survivors of life's shipwrecks, rebuilding shattered lives on New England homesteads. There is a ready-made ideology of Mother Nature and of "folk" ways, made up of shards of "the 'sixties," small-print calico, organic gardening, and the perennial romanticism in the heart of all humans. As a life raft in shipwreck, there could be worse.

Still, those who persist develop a deeper awareness which, not inappropriately, could be articulated in symbols not unlike those of Karl Jaspers's "philosophic faith." God is. There is a moral law. The human dwells in a nature which is God's poem, at the intersection of time and eternity.[13] Shipwrecked humans find ways to God.

Still, those survivors seeking the *vis medicatrix Dei in natura,* God's healing power in nature, seldom recover the traditional symbols of religious faith. It is simply a very, very long journey from that perennial philosophic faith to what seems to be the all too mundane reality of religion at work and worship. Philosophers, for the most part, have been loath to undertake it. Work and worship in act are always particular, marred by the imperfection of all particularity. "We have this treasure in earthen vessels," the Scriptures tell us, and anyone who was ever associated with a parish can testify how utterly earthen, how utterly imperfect they are. To disparage "organized religion" in the name of the unsullied purity of religious experience is not only easy. It is also always justified: the vessels are all too earthern.

So, though, is this earth, the good earth. Only in the dreamland of romantic imagination is nature a forest of Ardennes where swains and nymphs gambol—for some reason, that is what they invariably do—to the tune of a shepherd's pan-pipe, as you like it. The forest and the earth of human dwelling is a place of love and labor—and a great deal of labor. It is not "nobler" or "more natural" to draw water from a well, to split wood to heat it, to feed the goat and milk her—for milked she will be, whether you would or not—and to do the hundred chores that must be done before the dweller can take down a book and light a lamp—which must also be filled, trimmed, and cleaned. It is, however, definitely far more work, and the results are much less uniformly perfect than what even fairly primitive technology can deliver. If there is virtue in home-made cheese or home-brewed beer, it is not the flavor, only the loving care that goes into them, the all too earthy mingling of love and labor. As the Apostle James knew, it is labor that makes love real and love that makes labor meaningful. Alienation, more than aught else, is the dissociation of love and labor, leaving love an empty sentimentality and labor a drudgery. Each time we sacrifice the tangible goodness of self-labor for the perfection of mass production, we lose something of ourselves.

The appeal of romantic nostalgia suggests that we are not unaware of it. Perhaps the greatest irony of human effort is that it is not greed but good will, the striving for perfection, which introduces the gap of alienation into our lives. For the perfect, the effortless and the flawless, is also all too often the emptiest. People do not always buy commercial greeting cards because they do not care enough to draw or write their own. As often as not, they would feel ashamed of a home-made card: they have, after all, long been enjoined to *buy* "when you care enough to give the best"—as if their love and care were second best. A professionally produced greeting card is flawless—and meaningless. The person who sends it is not in it. We seek to compensate by purchasing ever more expensive greeting cards, investing more of our wages in them, yet in vain. The mediation is too great to let the presence shine through. In the process, we enact, in microcosm, the self-defeating frustration of consumerism. In a quest for perfection, we drain the fruit of our effort of all human presence, of all meaning.

Be ye perfect, we are bade in the Scriptures. We have interpreted that injunction in our own manner, as the perfection of a product of our *technē*, flawless and effortless, free of all traces of human fallibility. In a world of artifacts, the products of *technē*, that may well be the appropriate and only meaning the idea of perfection still retains. The perfection which living creatures seek, however, is of a wholly different order. The porcupine, lumbering along the edge of the clearing beside her mate, does not seek the perfection of the flawless and the effortless product. Neither do trees aspire to that perfection, nor the table I fashioned out of spruce tailings. Visitors proud of their new "dining room set" cannot understand my preference for things cherished by reason of age and labor invested—nor I their preference for the products of technology. We both seek perfection, the one I seek, though, is that of full incarnation, of the optimal presence of spirit *in carne*—and there is little spirit in what machines make. Romanticism, revolting against the soullessness of mechanical perfection, simply inverted the scale, treating rudeness as a virtue. I can understand the impulse, but not share it: rudeness and crudeness, be it of manner, of workmanship, or of care, can be as much of an obstacle to the manifestation of presence in love and labor as the sophistication of the product. The point is different—to let stand out the reality of presence, the ideal in the real, eternity in time, meaning in being. The perfect is not simply the ideal, as a perfect marriage is not simply a storybook meeting of souls. It is rather the optimal incarnation of spirit, the point at which the presence achieves maximal concreteness and the actual lets the presence shine through most clearly. Perhaps that, too, is the meaning of the Cross.

It is not the quest for perfection which has led us astray, but the kind of perfection we have sought, the flawless manuscript, the perfect argument with nothing to give, or the perfect "sincerity" devoid of all grace and generosity. So, too, we have insisted that the Church be perfect. Yet we believe that God became man, and we ourselves are beings who dwell at the intersection of eternity and time. Incarnation is our perfection as well; our glory is the ability to render being meaningful and meaning actual. Perhaps the problem is precisely that the intersection is not only the Nativity but also the Cross. The love which dares become actual becomes at the same time all too vulnerable; the act which attempts to embody the ideal places itself under the judgment of failure. It is infinitely easier to give up the attempt to be perfect, seeking no more than simply *to do:* there is, then, no risk of falling short. Alternately, it is so much easier to give up the attempt to do, conceiving of perfection as an alternative to actuality rather than as its sense. Yet if we are to believe the tradition, our Lord chose to become a man, born of a woman and hanged on a cross.

The perfection of which the tradition of faith speaks, whether it uses the symbolism of God become man or of divine Wisdom becoming the law which does not think even the order of the kitchen beneath God's notice, is of a different order. So is the perfection of the owl and the oak, of all incarnate nature. Its glory is neither the fact of the embodiment nor the ideal it embodies, but the ever-failing, all too earthern attempt to embody the ideal. The wonder of living nature, in which humans may share, is literally the *in-carne*-ation of the ideal, that here the sense, the ideal, becomes actual in the intense particularity of the beaver working on his dam at dusk while the actual becomes an epiphany of the ideal.

All this we know, in a thousand ways throughout our lives—that perfection is the optimal point of incarnation, the ideal becoming actual, the actual becoming meaningful. Why, then, should we expect the Church to be perfect in a wholly different—and rather strained—way? Why should we condemn the actuality of the worshiping community because it is, admittedly, all too flawed and all too earthern a vessel, rather than glorying in it because in it the Word becomes actual in speaking? The act of love itself is never pure *agapē:* like the acts of Jesus' ministry, it is always incarnate as particular, bearing witness in particular terms, in response to particular needs, healing humanity in particular humans while seeing the universal significance of particularity. Actuality is always particular: without the courage of particularity, the ideal remains sterile.

We could, to be sure, undertake a phenomenology of religious experience in principle, as van der Leeuw, James, or Otto have done, seeking to isolate its eidetic structure. The task is always legitimate.

Such reflection, however, is rather different from the act of worship, of the acknowledgment of God's presence in act and word. That is why, in the radical brackets, the reflection on the presence of God must always remain open-ended. In one sense, all it could say has already been said. Nature has no theology of its own to teach. Years of life close to the soil, of the dawn over Barrett Mountain and moonlit nights, have not, for me, added a single proposition to what stands written in the Scriptures and the Book of Common Prayer. They add depth to what has already been written or, perhaps more accurately, they help open up the depth of what has been written. They add nothing to it. *It has all been written.*

Yet it cannot all ever be written. As Jaspers knew so well, the presence, the truth *ab solo,* can never be reduced to a set of true propositions, valid for all possible readers, nor can faith be reduced to *a* religion. I do not mean that the truth is in some sense ineffable, that it defies articulation. It is not. Just the opposite: it can be so readily articulated—and in so many ways! Each articulation, however, is as particular as being and as language, its validity a function of an encounter beween the truth that speaks and a hearer who acknowledges in sentence and in metaphor. The image of the "mighty fortress" is as culture-specific as that of the mist-shrouded iceberg. Either can be a bearer of the living truth, though neither can be universal. I am an heir of the Czech reformation and its moral earnestness. But, in spite of the tragedy of the defeat of 1620, mine is also a Catholic nation, heir to Baroque Catholicism and its sense of the beauty of holiness.[14] The metaphors of the Church of England speak to me truly—and Being is true, beautiful, good.

To others, other metaphors may speak truly. In rare and precious moments of sharing in the worship of others, at Mass, in a synagogue, I have seen glimpses of the holy in entirely different traditions and metaphors. I think them no less true for not being mine. They speak, each in its own way, of a truth that is indeed catholic, all-embracing. Churches, liturgies, and creeds, though, speaking to particular humans, can be catholic only as they become transparent, testifying in their plurality to the one truth. The expression, any expression of that truth becomes opaque when it claims to be universal—and wholly vacuous when it seeks to be interdenominational. The act of worship, intensely personal, must needs be particular.

I am convinced that all beings need to worship. Of humans, I know it. It is so in spite of the inevitable particularity it entails, the much-bemoaned rending of the seamless robe of Christ. The great mystery of being, its sense, its incarnation, love becoming actual in labor, faith in life and worship. The radical awareness of God's presence, which stands out so powerfully in the radical brackets of the forest clearing, witnesses to it. It does not, however, provide an infallible guide to denominational preference.

What it does provide seems to me far more basic, the fundamental clue: *God is.* The nature which surrounds us is never empty of His presence, never material and value-free. It is good. Any attempt to conceptualize nature as value-free—except as a special case theory for admittedly special purposes—is flawed from the start. The moral perspective, encountering the universe as a cosmos, value-laden and value-ordered, is not a superstructure which we might or might not add to our conception of reality, as we please. It is the most fundamental given from which all our conceptualizations must start if they are not to be idle fables. Within the conception of the cosmos as value-ordered—earlier we spoke of it as the personalistic perspective—there is surely also the room and the need for vitalistic and physicalistic perspectives as well, since reality ingresses both in the order of time and the order of being. It is, however, the personalistic perspective, recognizing the cosmos as a creation, which is primary. Our relation to nature—be it to our fellow humans, to the furry inhabitants of the forest, or to its trees and boulders—is first of all a moral relation, governed by a moral law. Only secondarily, within that moral matrix, can we designate nature also in terms of utility or in terms of sheer being.

An evening, unlike an argument, does not lead to a conclusion. That is why a reflection on the living presence of God must remain open-ended, leading at most to a confession, not to a conclusion or a denominational preference. Clues, though, do arise within it. Perhaps the most basic among them is that *God is.*

Being, Time, and Eternity

God is—that is the all-pervasive clue, an awareness which precedes and underlies all subsequent inquiry and which emerges in the guise of a conclusion at its end once humans rediscover the moral sense of nature. Other clues, though, emerge with it, unobtrusively, irresistibly. In seeking to speak of them, it is tempting to resort to a Heideggerean aphorism—testifying, even in dissent, to the grandeur of his vision—and to speak of the radical recognition that *Being is not time.* Being is value born of the intersection of time and eternity.

Aphorisms, to be sure, pay a price in accuracy for their conciseness. Were we to strive for accuracy, we should have to speak of the irreducibility of the sense of Being to the sequence of its instantiations, or of something even more awkward. Regardless of the metaphor we employ, that recognition remains central. It is not simply the awareness that Being is not matter, a point which the functionalist theory of science has come to recognize no less than process philosophy, but that, contrary to Heidegger and the philosophers of life before him, *Being* really *is not time.* Its sense includes, irreducibly, a dimension of eternity that subsumes both the temporality of life and the atemporality of inanimate being. The meaning of temporality and of matter alike is the ingression of value, of eternity, in time, making being meaningful and meaning actual.

The reference of being to matter, as articulated in the austere ontologies of physicalism, is surely legitimate. It is, however, also no less surely secondary, a special case theory suited to the description of certain phenomena for a special purpose, not a clue to the ultimate nature of reality. Likewise the reference of being to temporality, stressed by vitalist theories, philosophies of life and process, seems no less legitimate but also no less secondary. The temporality of being, though crucial for certain special purposes, is again a false clue to the ultimate sense of being. It is the reference of being to value, to eternity, capable of subsuming all being and all special theories of being within it, that stands out as definitive. The ultimate sense of being is the ingression of the Idea of the Good, of beauty, truth, goodness, of holiness, justice, tenderness, love, into matter and time, becoming actual within them and bestowing meaning upon them.

Perhaps that is the insight at which Alfred North Whitehead arrived in reflecting on the tragic death of his son. He, too, must have known the clear vision which is the gift of solitude and pain.[15] Or perhaps not: there are grounds for arguing that Whitehead still tended to conceive of the dimension of the personal as a special case of the subjective aim of all being, rather than treating nonpersonal being as a progressively less distinct incarnation of the personal. Though with his recognition of the eternal objects Whitehead moves significantly beyond vitalism and process philosophy, he remains deeply indebted to them. Here an interesting argument could be made, and an argument is what is in order.

What we have sought to present, though, is of a far more modest order—a vision, an initial evident insight that presents itself far less insistently, closing in like the dusk, gathering up the dweller like the all-reconciling darkness of the night, at peace in silence, glowing with embers and bright with stars. Perhaps that really is a necessary propaedeutic, even for understanding Whitehead's insight. Whitehead's argument, so prominent on the philosophical scene two score years ago, has drifted into academic inattention. It was not "refuted"; genuine insight, as Heidegger notes, never is.[16] It seems far more likely that it simply could not be heard.

That is not surprising. The dual reference of being to matter and time—or, more prosaically, the habit of explaining being in terms of a reference to its material instantiation or its temporal duration—is one we imbibe with our earliest experiences long before it is formally taught and theoretically justified in our schools. A parent typically consoles her child's pain over a shredded doll with phrases such as "It was just a rag" or "Tomorrow we'll buy a new one." Here the material reference and the instrumental reference, respectively, are painfully obvious. The initial ineffectiveness of such consolation testifies that the child knows how utterly irrelevant both are to the irreducible fact of the broken doll, of love whose eternal clarity stands out with even greater intensity when its material presence in time is shattered.

Still, no practicing parent would think of what is perhaps the only response adequate to the situation, "We will pray together to thank God for all the years Dolly was with you." At most, a parent attempts to act out that response in giving the doll or the guinea pig a Christian burial, lining the shoe box that serves as a coffin with scraps of soft, bright cloth and placing a garland of ribbons beside its head. Understandably: any response which does not explain away eternity, the infinite preciousness of goodness and beauty, by a material or a temporal reduction, also demands a willingness to bear an immense pain, the very pain that the Stoics sought to avoid even at the cost of love itself. The people who are willing to bear that pain, not escaping by devaluing the loss, are to be treasured. They preserve for the cosmos a great goodness. They are also rare. By the time we reach the age of reason, we have, for the most part, been thoroughly conditioned to the costly comfort of our familiar double reference, the reduction to materiality and instrumentality.

The power of that double reference, to be sure, is not simply a function of social conditioning. It is also the power of the consolation it offers, based on a truth which it can genuinely claim. It is, after all, never the outright falsehood, the cunningly devised fable, which misleads. Since it does not coincide with the truth, it cannot cover it, hide it. It is always the superficial truth which hides the depth of truth. The material and the temporal references have been able to mislead Western thought only because, in their own superficial way, they are also true.

There is a truth to the material reference. Incarnation is not an accident. Being is present as incarnate, and so all being includes a dimension of the material, the atemporal, and the inorganic. The point, though, is that in lived reality the dimension of the inorganic is always present as subsumed within the organic and, taken in itself, becomes an abstraction. In the literature of the physical sciences, there is little clear consensus as to whether even a theoretical reduction of the organic and the animate to the inorganic is possible at all. But let us assume, for the moment, that it were so—that the entire functioning of the body of a human or a porcupine could be "explained" in terms of elementary chemical interactions. Such a reduction would still do nothing to help us understand the living reality of a porcupine. A porcupine is a *life,* the reality of lived subject experience. It includes the cautious grazing by the full moon, the warmth of mating and the care of the young, the fear and the pain, the comfort and the contentment, the familiarity of a home territory and the ancestral burrow, the sorrow of aging and dying. The reality of a living being is a life which, though subsuming within itself the atemporal, inorganic dimension, is not reducible to it. Its reality is of a higher order, a process which cannot be understood without a temporal reference.

It is really not possible to speak of a porcupine atemporally. The being of a porcupine is inseparable from a temporal density. It is a span of life, not an atemporal reality *en soi* like that of an inorganic compound. It can subsume the atemporality of the inorganic but cannot be reduced to it. It is, if anything, the inorganic which can be reduced, subsumed within the categories of the organic as its zero-limit, much as rest can be understood as zero motion, though motion cannot be understood in terms of rest.

That was in fact the central insight of vitalism, of the philosophies of life and the philosophies of process derived from it. Bergson with his conception of an *évolution créatrice,* Teilhard de Chardin, seeing all reality *sub speciae evolutionis,* have elevated that basic insight into the definitive reference for understanding being. Being, they argue, is not a state but a process and must be understood in terms of a duration and a progression from a before to an after. Or, as Heidegger, in this respect the last of the philosophers of life rather than the first of the philosophers of existence, concluded, *Sein ist Zeit*—being is time, and time is being.[17]

Admittedly, even the porcupine is not wholly reducible to a life. He is a life, as surely as he is also an aggregate of organized matter. He is, though, something more—an epiphany of value. Still at the edge of a moonlit clearing, he is a miracle of being standing out against the ever-pressing sense of nothing, a witness to God's glory. The grief humans experience over the bloody remnants of animals along our highways is not simply utilitarian. Nor is it empty sentimentality, except in those humans who feel no similar compassion for the sorrows of their fellow humans. It is, rather, a recognition of the transcendental dimension of all being—that in its perishing, something absolutely valuable is laid waste. Nature, in addition to vitality, bears within it also a dimension of eternity.

Less poetically, we could express that same recognition by saying that while the temporal reference is legitimate, it is not sufficient. Instrumental value is not self-sustaining: without an absolute reference, process could not be progress, only busywork. John Dewey, at once one of the most persistent and most thoughtful of the philosophers of process, sought to resolve the problem somewhat in Aristotle's fashion, interpreting the terms "ends" and "means" functionally, so that the "ends" of one stage become the "means" of another, ever justified by new receding means and ends. In his thought, the transparent weakness of that schema was redeemed not simply by a faith in the intrinsic value of process—characteristically, Dewey preferred the vitalistic term, "growth"—but by a conception reminiscent of Whitehead, that of enjoyment or, simply, joy. That motif, introduced in Dewey's most phenomenological work, *Experience and Nature,*[18] received relatively little attention among Dewey's contemporaries, perhaps because it represents a perception which deviates radically from the spirit of instrumentalism. Joy or enjoyment is noninstrumental. The experience it describes serves no purpose beyond itself, it is not a function of the experiences which led up to it. It breaks out of the entire instrumental chain as a moment of encounter between a human and an Other, be it an entity, an act, a person, in cherishing, appreciation, enjoyment. It is precisely the experience of eternal reference. Whitehead attempted to integrate that dimension within a naturalistic metaphysics, subsuming it to a cosmic scheme. Dewey is, perhaps, wiser: he introduces it as the moment of fulfillment. Extrapolating within the bounds of legitimacy, we might claim that Dewey's instrumental scheme escapes the absurdity of the treadmill of process because, in each of its moments, enjoyment justifies process in an encounter with the eternal.

To the age of "progress," Dewey's reference to joy might have appeared as a trivial aberration. It was Dewey's conception of growth that seemed central. In the wake of a second apocalyptic war followed not by peace but by the subjugation of half of Europe and the cold war, the confidence of Dewey's contemporaries in the irresistible workings of "progress" becomes hard to sustain. But then, what remains to justify process? B. F. Skinner ends up speaking of "survival."[19] Though he introduces the concept almost surreptitiously, it is crucial—the one absolute value which provides instrumental justification for all human doings, including, presumably, the surrender of freedom and dignity or the "etherization" proposed by Skinner's predecessor, J. B. Watson.[20] Yet survival of a life devoid of intrinsic worth—in our terms, of the eternal reference—is of dubious value. The incidence of suicide suggests that humans in fact do not regard individual survival as an absolute, all-overriding and all-justifying value. It is itself valuable only instrumentally. Yet to what purpose? If the putative purpose of sacrifice is survival which serves as an instrument to further survival, we are reduced to a classic *circulus viciosus.*

Should we then claim that individual survival is instrumental to the survival of the species? The claim has been made, yet the concept of "species survival" is entirely an artificial construct, designed to account for certain types of animal behavior, but reflecting no lived experience. It is highly problematic to what extent we are ever justified in attributing to animals, on the basis of wholly external observation, motivations of which we find no trace in ourselves, especially since the behavior cited as evidence is by no means uniform. Many animal mothers will kill their offspring when placed in an environment in which, as we would say in human terms, life is no longer worth living, in conditions of scarcity, danger, captivity. Still, instances of self-sacrifice for the sake of offspring and kin do occur in animals, including humans, giving the concept of species survival some tenuous legitimacy.

Even though legitimate, the concept of species survival is of little help in answering the question of the ground of value. Why should a species, our species, survive? Of the bee, we can say that its survival has a purpose in the economy of the universe, perhaps in the humble yet crucial task of pollination. What, though, is the task of humans? What makes our species worthy of survival and justifies the immense cost which other species pay for our survival? What good is the "good of humanity"? Is it anything but species egotism?

That question, which we raised earlier, marks the limits of vitalism and its temporal reference. It cannot be answered, as we found, without recourse to a different, eternal reference. The ancients spoke of *thaumazein,* the philosophic wondering, which confronts being not in the instrumental sequence of time but in its reference to eternity, as the presence of the eternal in time.[21] Wonder, though, is still ambiguous. Not without reason. As early as in Democritus Western thought succumbed to the temptation to confuse the eternal with the atemporal, the inorganic. Certainly wonder can describe the awestruck gaze of

Kant beholding the moral law in the wonder of the heavens, but it can describe no less the speculations of Descartes about the superficial analogy between humans and the mechanical statues in a garden. To the *thaumazein* of Athens, we might do well to add the *agapē* of Jerusalem. The uniquely human stance is the loving wonder which can knowingly cherish the beauty, truth, and goodness of the creation. Using a metaphor which in truth may be the most literal statement of which we are capable, we could say that God placed humans in this world to cherish its goodness, to love its beauty, and to know its truth. The ultimate justification of being human is the ability to perceive the eternal in the temporal, inscribing time into eternity.

For *being is not time.* It is value, the ingression of eternity into time. Certainly time is not a mere illusion, a veil of *maya.* It is as time that eternity is present. Love becomes actual only as the process of a life shared; life becomes actual only as the series of acts which, individually, seem mundane; a melody becomes actual only as a sequence of notes—and the good *ab solo* only as a history of relative value. Still, love is more than the seasons shared, a life more than the sequence of acts and passions in which it is acted out, the good more than the values which instantiate it. Without that transcendental reference, temporality becomes absurd—and in turn, without ingression in time, the eternal remains merely potential. Still, *being is not time.* It is the intersection of eternity with time whose locus humans can be. It is the privilege and the task of humans to recognize and to act out the presence of eternity in time.

The cosmos is not an accident, being is not time—and reality is not matter. That is another clue whose aphoristic formulation sacrifices clarity to conciseness. The point is not whether "matter is real" in a natural scientific sense, that is, whether the concept "matter," whatever that may mean, is or is not useful or necessary for the purposes of a scientific description of physical phenomena. Perhaps it is, perhaps it is not—in any case, it is strictly a formal question. Nor is the question whether "matter is real" in a commonsense, experiential sense: evidently it is, as Dr. Johnson stoutly maintained, kicking the kerb stone. We have our being and encounter that of others as material, effectively present as extended, resisting force and integrated in a causal order. Meaning is acted out in space as well as in time. The recognition, though, is much more basic. Reality is not matter: being is not reducible to its factual material presence.

The small sturdy dog, tan and white, who curls up against me as I sit, watching the full moon, is so tangibly material. Still, were nothing left of him but the matter in and as which he is incarnate, it would be he no longer. The reality of that dog, the abused, abandoned mutt, craving affection, who took up residence with me, is not matter but a meaningful presence of which materiality is but one component. It is a person-al reality, not an impersonal one, a focused complex of meanings whose name is Míša, Mikey. Any conceptual or physical reduction of that subject presence to the ideal or the material component would present not a reality but an abstraction.

Perhaps, paraphrasing Nagel, we should not say that reality is not matter, but speak instead of the *primacy of meaningful being* in the order of reality.[22] For the purposes of guiding our lives, of understanding and deciding, the realities that matter are never merely material but always an intersection of matter and meaning. They are as they mean, and the meaning is not secondary to their effective presence. A home is not a synonym for a house so that we could sell one and buy another. Humans can sell a home, but they can buy only a house. A wife or husband is not a synonym for the person I live with so that humans could, at will, divorce one and substitute another, attaching the same meaning. The meaning is not attached to autonomous matter: it is a primordial trait of reality.

That we have long striven to forget, in our doing and our knowing alike. If the purpose of knowledge is control—and it surely so appeared in the wake of the collapse of the great medieval synthesis—then it is easier that way. Matter is so much easier to manipulate, possession of physical entities so much easier to attain than the bond of belonging. Continuing our metaphor, we could say that we have substituted houses for homes, the material embodiment for the meaningful reality, because objects make no demands while meaningful beings do. I can, without a pang of guilt or regret, neglect a house, though not a home. Objects, however, also give nothing. We end up, hollow men in a wasteland, urgently needing to rediscover that matter is not reality.

The reality of God and a moral order, the reality of value ingressing in time, the reality and primacy of meaningful being—such are the clues of the radical brackets and the starting points for a reconceptualization of nature, and not for that alone. Not only the philosophy of nature, but most of Western thought in all its dimensions has for some three centuries operated on the assumption that the cosmos is an accident, that matter is the ultimate reality, and that meaning is an afterthought produced by history. In an archaic idiom, we might say that it has attempted to reduce being to becoming—and becoming to efficient rather than final causality. The clues that emerge in the radical brackets, however, suggest that both of those assumptions are mistaken: that reality is the intersection of being and becoming, that it is value that makes final causality—and efficient causality, its backward reading—intelligible. Or, to introduce yet another metaphor into the cluster, perhaps neither epistemology nor metaphysics but rather ethics, the vision and theory of value, is the starting point of understanding. Perhaps Kant's second *Critique* should have been the first.

Ultimately, though, those metaphors converge on a basic recognition: being is value ingressing in time as persons dwell in the *Lebenswelt Gottes.*

The Days of Our Years

"Seek not to venture forth: turn within—truth dwelleth in the inner man."[23] So counseled Saint Augustine amid the collapse of the power that for centuries had been Rome. When Edmund Husserl selected that line as the conclusion of his *Cartesian Meditations,* his critics and his sympathetic readers alike seized upon it as evidence that his "transcendental turn" had led phenomenology into an invincible solipsism. To this day, that remains a part of the conventional wisdom of a flourishing Husserl industry.

Yet the intent of Saint Augustine's line clearly was not solopsistic, nor was that its effect. Saint Augustine's work bears no trace of the self-centered, self-indulgent preoccupation with private moods and dispositions which we have come to associate with the inward turn. Quite the contrary: his "inward" vision spans the full range of reality—the presence of God, the sweep of history, the works of humans. If anything, it was the Roman world around him, scorning all inward turn in a feverish preoccupation with the gratification of all its greed, that today seems locked in an invincible solipsism of both pure and practical reason, a lonely crown of insatiable monadic egos, each heedless of all but itself.

Nor has the injunction to turn within always led to solipsism in our time. Husserl's vision, too, spans the whole scope of Western history. His emphasis throughout lies on *Einfühlung* and *Eindeutung*, the emotive and the cognitive reaching out to the other in a self-transcending empathic understanding. In the world of our days, it is not those who follow Saint Augustine's injunction, whether in prayer or in the radical brackets of a forest clearing, who are typically locked in the self-centered consumer mania of *solus ipse*, acknowledging no reality beyond their feeling and the flickering image on an electronic screen. Quite the contrary, they are the ones who tend to be sensitive to the plight of their fellow humans and the devastation of the natural world, willing to encounter the other with a respect for his integrity and to subordinate their whim to a good clearly perceived. Far more typically, it is those who boast of the no-nonsense objectivity of their world view who are likely to go bulldozing through their world, both social and natural, transforming it into a wasteland in a heedless quest for gratification. There is, surely, a difference between solipsism in theory and practice and an openness to the other, but the time-honored metaphor of the "outer" and the "inner" no longer evokes it adequately.

There is a reason why the metaphor will no longer serve, even though it served not only Saint Augustine but countless others as well, Jan Amos Komenský no less than Alfred North Whitehead.[24] In Saint Augustine's or Whitehead's usage, the distinction of "inward" and "outward" did not suggest a compartmentalization of entities into two categories, the world of objects, conceived as the region of meaningless matter in motion, and the world of meanings, locked within the privacy of each individual's mind or even brain. In their usage, both terms apply equally to all being, referring not to classes of entities but to modes of being and modes of understanding anything that is. It is not the case here that a boulder is an "outward" reality and a thought an "inward" one. Nor can anything else be so qualified. The woodchuck at his grazing in the cool of the morning after a night's rain can be considered simply an entity, a component in an aggregate of organized matter propelled by a blind though lawlike force. He is that, too. He is, however, also a *subject*, and we can also understand him as such, in terms of his "inwardness" in Whitehead's sense, or, in our terms, as a Person-al being, a focus of meaningful relations with a rightness and an integrity of his own. We can approach him as an object, blind to all but his outward presence. We can, though, also approach him in respect, recognizing the integrity of his being much as we recognize the "inward" integrity of our fellow humans. The crucial distinction is not between an "outer" and an "inner" reality but, as Bergson recognized, between understanding any and all reality *from within* and explaining it superficially from without. The significance of Saint Augustine's injunction is not to lead us to some funky, touchy-feely solipsism but to an understanding of reality "from within" in this sense, in terms of its meaningful being rather than in terms of categories arbitrarily imposed upon it from without.

So understood, the Augustinian inward turn—the turn of radical brackets—is the very opposite of solipsism. It calls for a radical opening of our life and thought to the world of others, human, animate, inanimate, in the integrity of its otherness and the meaningfulness of its being. It is what we have come to think of as the objective "outward" turn which leaves the subject an isolated alien, considering the world solely from without, an object of our doings, asking not for the inner rightness of its being but subsuming it high-handedly under the arbitrary categories of our cognitive and practical utility. When we so approach the world, each subject finds himself locked in the solitude of his own purposes, taking in nothing, imposing his will on others until he in his turn comes to see himself solely in terms of the surface of his own being. The inward reality of his own self then appears as an illusion, at best a "merely subjective" reflection of the putatively objective "public" reality. If we were so to understand the categories of "outward" and "inward," we might well say, consistently with both Augustine and Husserl, that the sickness of our age is the externalization (or, with Hannah Arendt, the banalization) of being—we have lost sight of all but the most superficial outward semblance of reality, becoming ourselves Eliot's "hollow men" amid a wasteland of hollow objects. Then we might speak of our urgent need as one of turning inward.

For better or for worse, though, that is no longer how we understand the terms "inner" and "outer." In our ordinary usage, those terms have acquired a distinctively spatial significance, as if they designated regions of entities rather than modes of being and understanding. We speak of the "outer" world as the "objective" world, the world of physical entities, of stones, animals, and human organisms, conceived as essentially "outer" in all their being. We then wonder whether, in addition, enclosed within certain of such "outer" entities there might not exist another set of different "inner" or "subjective" entities such as thoughts, values, or emotions. We might even claim, with the "humanistic" trends in our social sciences, that the second "subjective" realm is of relatively greater importance. Still, it avails little. If this is how we conceive of "inner" and "outer" reality, we face only a choice of two solipsisms. The objectivistic perspective is solipsistic intrinsically. Since it conceives of reality as consisting solely of surfaces, it permits neither *Einfühlung* nor *Eindeutung*, neither cognitive nor emotive empathic understanding of the other in his integrity. The other necessarily appears as an object, and the ego as *solus ipse.* Then "turning within" appears as a turn away from the world which necessarily leads to a subjectivistic solipsism, a sticky, self-indulgent preoccupation with the subject's putative "feelings." Such an option then constitutes a mirror image of the objectivistic solipsism, not an alternative to it. It would be hard to decide which side of the coin is less attractive. If philosophy is to avoid degeneration to an objectivistic or a subjectivistic triviality, it must, willy-nilly, seek new metaphors.

In an age whose language is no less polarized than its conception of reality, such metaphors are hard to come by. The terms "subjective" and "objective," once useful, have long since become no more than synonyms for the terms "inner" and "outer" in their worst sense. When Husserl speaks of transcendental subjectivity, his readers for the most part no longer hear him speaking of an intrinsic meaning structure of our being but simply of a merely private, "inward" reflection of outer reality to which, incomprehensibly, he seems to be attributing an absolute validity. It is little wonder that they then dismiss the very idea.[25] Were subjectivity no more than that, it could claim little philosophical significance. I am convinced that it is a grievous misreading of Husserl's intent, yet attempts to overcome it by reviving the Augustinian sense of subjectivity by verbal devices such as the Saxon genitive, "subject's," to replace the the adjective "subjective," invariably come to grief on the shoals of current usage. The categories of the subjective and the objective, too, have become philosophically unavailable.

Romanticism offered us a pair of less well-defined categories to which I have often resorted, those of the *natural* and the *artificial.* As metaphors, they are not without their virtues, especially since they have a clear counterpart in lived experience. In a real sense, nature is itself a metaphor. There is an intuitively evident difference between a physical object like a tree and an artifact like a hat-rack, between an animal and a mechanical toy, between a person and a robot embodying the latest marvels of computer technology. The porcupine is a living being, a subject whose life has an integrity of its own. The robot remains meaningless matter propelled by a blind force, creating an illusion of meaning by re-presenting the intentionality of its human maker. The difference is striking, and useful in reminding us of the integral reality of meaningful being amid the meaninglessness of our artifact and construct world. The choice of a forest clearing as the root metaphor of radical bracketing is not arbitrary. It is here that the "inwardness" or "subjectivity" of reality, in Augustine's and Husserl's sense, stands out most clearly and is hardest to deny.

Still, even that metaphor is flawed. The brackets of the forest clearing provide a clue to recovering the moral sense of the days of our lives, but they do not constitute an alternative to their everydayness. On an overpopulated globe, Thoreau's hut at Walden, Kant's retreat at Moditten, or my own cherished corner of New Hampshire is incredibly privileged, not only cognitively, but in a wholly practical sense as well. When the romantics express their call for moral renewal in the metaphor of a "return to nature," they restrict their appeal not only because artifice, too, is an intrinsic part of human nature, but also because such a return is simply not an option for most of their hearers. Philosophically, the metaphor of the forest clearing can be a valuable tool in recapturing the philosophic vision. As philosophy seeks to articulate that vision, though, it must move beyond it.

That is why, though with trepidation, I have resorted to the metaphor of the *personal* and the *impersonal*. That, too, is flawed. Though we may insist that by "personal" we mean "person-like" in certain crucial aspects, the term can still evoke images of the simply private, of my own, and all the connotations of subjectivism. Still, I would run that risk, calling up the dictum of older personalists that "Person" is the most basic philosophical category, modifying it to read that "Person" is the root philosophic metaphor.[26] The person, as a moral subject, is the clearest instantiation of meaningful being, at the intersection of being and meaning, of time and eternity. To speak of the world as "personal" means to conceive of it as structured in terms of relations best understood on the model of meaningful relations among persons. It is to conceive of it as peopled by beings who are similarly best understood on the model of persons, modified as needed, rather than on the model of matter in motion, raised to infinite complexity. It is the conception of being as structured by a moral law.

In recent philosophy, it was Martin Buber who expressed this most clearly in positing two models of relating and being. One of these, the relation of mutual empathy and respect between two subjects, he described as "I and thou." He speaks of its opposite, the asymmetric relationship of a subject to an object within his world, as one of "I and it." What typifies the former is that it is essentially a personal relationship, while in the latter the object and even the relationship itself appear as impersonal, devoid of all autonomous integrity, defined entirely by the subject's whim and convenience. That is a privative mode of relating. The authentic relation between beings is the personal encounter of mutual respect, with its cognitive counterpart of a quest for empathic understanding and its ethical presumption of a fundamental order of a moral law rather than of individual or collective utility. What Augustine once described as the inward turn might well be described as a quest for a vision of the world structured after the mode of persons.

Such is the traditional perception of the world as a creation—at least as long as we take "creation" as designating a mode of being rather than as a hypothesis concerning the origin of organized matter. To speak of the creation as personal would, to be sure, be either trivial or false if we were to interpret it as endowing all created beings with a "soul" or some other duplicate of human consciousness. For all the striking similarities between humans and porcupines, both subject beings, there are still some fundamental differences. Those differences are greater still between the being of humans and the being of boulders. Still, when we conceive of the world as God's creation, we cannot dismiss even the boulder as "dead matter" in our modern sense. Even the boulder is an expression of God's loving will, testifying to the glory of its maker—and, as such, to be approached with respect. Its relation to us is personal in the sense that it, too, is a part of a value-endowed, meaningfully oriented cosmos. In such a cosmos, the human, whether in his knowing, his feeling, or his willing, cannot proceed as a sovereign master of a meaningless reserve of raw materials. His being in the world is ordered by a moral law. He owes his world respect as a dweller therein. In turn, in such a world he is never an alien, never a stranger. His being, too, as well as his conception of it, are basically personal and personalistic.

By contrast, we could describe the development of Western thought as one of an ongoing, systematic depersonalization of both our conception of the world and of the world of our ordinary life itself. We have progressively built up around us an impersonal world, social as well as physical, in which no respect for the integrity of its objects need constrain our arbitrary will. Step by step, we have extended our conception of reality as impersonal, derived from a world of artifacts, to the world of living nature until we have come to think of trees on the model of telephone poles, of woodchucks on the model of mechanical toys—and of ourselves on the model of our robots.

To rant against the works of technology as the source of all evil is not only futile but also false. Technology is not the source of anything, though it does multiply human capabilities for good and evil alike. It is, however, crucial not to let ourselves be deceived by the impersonal meaninglessness of the fruits of *technē* into losing sight of the integral, personal sense of our being. The great gift of the radical brackets is not a putative alternative life-style but rather the liberating recognition that the impersonality of our world is no more than a mask of a real world, a personal world that can be the home of persons. The forest with its creatures, the boulders, the entire world of nature between the earth and the sky, are not a senseless, impersonal aggregate of matter in motion. That world is intensely personal; it has a life, a rightness and an integrity of its own. There is room for humans within it, not as natural robots but as persons in a personal world. Here the all-corroding depersonalization of nature is unmasked as an illusion. We are still persons, there still is a living personal world in which we, as persons, can dwell in peace.

That recognition may initially prompt simply an escape to nature from the shipwreck of our depersonalized world. At the end of their tether, humans do tend to seek at least the solace of a park or a zoo. Though so many of our zoos are little more than animal prisons, their inmates, more generous than we, their jailers, can still comfort us, as ambassadors of another, personal world.[27] Pets, too, though often little more than slaves, have that power. In the time of heartbreak after the Soviet occupation of Czechoslovakia, the number of pet dogs in Prague rose so precipitously that the regime recruited an army of pensioners in a vain attempt to impose on dogs the same tight discipline it imposes on its human subjects. Until a kindly editor reminded me, I had utterly forgot the author of the lines, quoted by William James in his *Varieties of Religious Experience* from Walt Whitman's *Song of Myself*, part 32, "I think I could turn and live with animals, they are so placid and self-contain'd, I stand and look at them long and long," yet the thought was often with me.

The strategy of escape, though not generalizable, remains valuable because it suggests a different, viable strategy—that of a purposive repersonalization of our lives and our life-world. As we have extended our conception of reality as impersonal from the world of human making to the world of nature, so, too, we can extend the recognition of reality as personal to the world of our making. There is no intrinsic reason why the object of utility cannot be at the same time an object of cherishing respect—or why we should not think of its latter status as normative, the former as derivative, rather than vice versa.

There is, to be sure, a reason why we do not, though it is an extrinsic one. It takes time, patience, and effort to build up a personal relationship with the other, be he human, animate, or inanimate, and it requires a willingness to honor his demands as well as ours. Most of the time we possess and covet far more than we can care for and cherish. Yet if the point is to recover a sense of the world as personal, one in which we can be at home, then such a posture is counterproductive. Beyond the point of satisfying need, redundant capacity becomes a burden, not a gain. Greed, the attempt to fill an empty spirit with possessions, is a great producer of depersonalization.

Our preoccupation with labor saving, beyond the elimination of soul-destroying drudgery, is no less counterproductive. To have without doing corrodes the soul: it is precisely in investing life, love, and labor that we constitute the world as personal, as the place of intimate dwelling. In our earlier metaphor, the idea of buying a home is an illusion: it is a house we buy; we make it a home by giving ourselves to it. Generosity of spirit personalizes as greed depersonalizes.

The repersonalization of the inanimate world grows slowly, imperceptibly. Seeds of it, to be sure, are present in all our days. It may be the day when a person, clearing a trail, decides to lead it around a boulder which would yield to a bulldozer, simply out of respect, because that is where it has been these many seasons. Or it may be the day when a person decides to refurbish a tool he was going to discard, perhaps because he noted the intricate carving with which an unknown craftsman decorated it long ago, perhaps because discarding, wasting, is an act of disrespect, depersonalizing the world.[28] It is out of such moments that the recognition grows that the world is not an impersonal store of raw materials from which to take but rather a personal world to which to give. If we honor it, we may become less affluent for it, yet also far richer.

Certainly, as there are choices, there will be compromises. The world of nature is not only a metaphor of God's glory, it is also a source of raw materials. There will be times to discard a tool, to fell a tree, or dislodge a boulder, as there are times when it is legitimate to think of the world as an aggregate of matter in motion or as a process of utility, for the sake of works of necessity or charity. The point, though, is that we recognize them as compromises, between equivalent claims, not as unilateral decisions. Recognized as compromises, they can lead the user to cherish what he uses, knowing that it is bought with a price, and to use it with respect and thanks, not wastefully. Waste is an act of disrespect to the creation. The New England adage, "Use it up, wear it out, make it do, do without," is not only a counsel of poverty. It is also an excellent guide to ecological ethics—and a basic principle of the ethics of dealing with the world around us in general.

What is true of inanimate nature is no less true of animate reality. In one sense, it is even more true, since animals share so much of our own being as persons. While in the case of inanimate being there is a striking contrast between the way we conceive of it for the purposes of manipulation and the way we conceive of it as personal, for the purpose of charting our course with respect to it, in the case of animate being the personalistic perspective is continuous with the vitalistic and can provide a useful guide to animal psychology. Though affected by the absence of verbal communication, the behavior of the animals who ingress into our lives can be understood far more adequately in terms of the personalistic psychology of William James or Wilhelm Stern than by extending to it the principles of material interaction.[29]

That, though, is not the central point. The repersonalization of our relationship to our animal world means, far more basically, approaching it with respect, as ordered by a moral law, not only by our convenience. Yes, there will again be compromises, but let them be perceived clearly as compromises. We need to recognize that the suffering we impose on animals is not automatically justified by our convenience. The two claims must be measured and adjudicated, much as the conflicting claims of two humans. If anything, since our animal kin cannot speak for themselves, we need to recognize our obligation to speak for them, to protest the heedless slaughter of whales and seals as much as the moral scandal of the needless suffering of laboratory animals and the brutality of the "biomechanism" approach to raising food animals. Again, we may be less affluent for it, much as the feudal lord would have been much less affluent if he recognized the moral claim of his subjects, but we shall be much richer, much more human for it.

It may, finally, seem ironic to speak of the repersonalization of the world of persons, yet it is no less needed. We have grown so used to the impersonality of our world of persons that we are often not even aware of it, yet it is no less destructive than the depersonalization of the world of nature. That depersonalization is not simply a matter of superficial interpersonal relations or of using social security numbers in place of names on our records. Nor is the repersonalization of our personal world a matter of the forced familiarity of addressing strangers by first names or of the impertinence of probing their feelings as a conversational gambit. Slavery in all its forms is viciously depersonalizing, even though masters typically do address slaves by their first names. To treat humans as persons means most fundamentally to approach them with a deep respect for the integrity of their being, conceiving of our interrelation with them as governed by a moral law, not simply by utility and consent. The great achievement of Martin Luther King was not that he won some advantages for black Americans, but rather that he enabled all of us, whites perhaps even more than blacks, to place our mutual relationships on the basis of mutual respect rather than on the impersonal accident of skin color. Here, too, Kant's profound insight retains its validity, regardless of that of the rest of his conceptual system—the command of the moral law is to treat reality as an end, not as a means merely, recognizing its integrity and the respect due it.

Kant, incidentally, inserted an important clause: "whether in your own person or that of another." We need to repersonalize our conception of ourselves, respecting the integrity of our own being as well. That, again, is not a counsel of self-indulgence, any more than the "as thyself" in Jesus' summary of the law. Rather, it is a matter of perceiving ourselves as persons, set free by a moral law. We destroy our own personhood when we sacrifice the integrity of our conscience to a lie, when we subject it to the bondage of utility rather than the freedom of the good. We, too, need to rediscover ourselves as persons, not as need-gratifying organisms.

All that is implied in the fundamental shift from an impersonal conception of reality, whether mechanistic or vitalistic, to a personalistic one. Though we retain impersonal conceptions as special case theories of high utility, we are not simply modifying a theory but profoundly altering the moral sense of our being. The rediscovery of the moral sense of nature and of our place in it is nothing less than the most radical revolution possible, a revolution, in Karel Havlíček's words, of minds and hearts.[30] Were that to come about, not merely our conceptualization of nature but our very mode of being would be radically transformed.

Yet can any "revolution of hearts and minds" ever succeed? It is a firm part of our conventional wisdom that, of course, it cannot. We are firmly convinced that only a "real" movement in the "real" world can bring about a "real" change. Throughout, we identify the word "real" with the impersonal, the institutional, the "objective." It is consistent with our underlying conviction that the dimension of meaning, the personal world of our lived experience, is but an *Abbild,* a reflection of our constructs. That is what leads philosophers to organize political parties, that is the theoretical justification of ideological coups, as in the classic case of Lenin's coup within the Russian Social Democratic Party in 1903. As Lenin saw it, that coup transformed the party from an impractical debating society of unrealistic dreamers into a hard-hitting vanguard of class struggle. More than anything else, it was that coup which enabled the Bolshevik faction of Russian Social Democracy to seize power in a coup within the Provisional Government and to establish what Lenin's heirs have come to call "real" socialism. Did not Lenin succeed where the dreamers were doomed to fail? But for him, communism would have remained a vision and Russian Social Democracy would wield no more power today than Social Democratic parties in, say, Austria or Germany. Thanks to Lenin's realism, the revolution succeeded . . . or did it?

Since we are used to measuring as the world measures, we tend to take it for granted that the revolution succeeded: Lenin seized power, and his heirs wield it more firmly than the czars ever did. We forget that, in terms of what it set out to do, the revolution proved a dismal and bloody failure. Yes, Lenin seized power—and used it to establish an empire that dominates half Europe and intimidates the rest. Its police hold Soviet society in a grip far tighter than any ever achieved by the old czarist *Ochrana.* There are labor camps to deal with labor unrest, and orthodoxy and autocracy rule supreme. Russia's social and economic development, though slow and in all likelihood far slower than it would have been had the revolution not happened, is still sufficient to support the empire and to provide its rulers with privileges and affluence undreamt of by the czar's boyars.

That, though, is surely not at all what the revolution was all about. There are people still alive who remember the long-ago hopes, who know that the hope was not one of more of the same under new management, more relentless power more deeply entrenched. It was a hope of a more humane society, of more personal lives amid the depersonalization of an industrial society. The driving force of the revolutionary hope in the hearts and minds of millions was not one of changes in personnel but of a transformation in the hearts and minds of people and their relation to each other and their world. It is ever that—the one powerful hope, the hope of a personalization of our life world, not of tinkering with the abstract impersonal world of social artifacts. If that hope is ever to succeed, it must not become distracted by the chimera of "success" on the level of social artifacts. It can succeed only as a revolution of hearts and minds, transforming the moral sense of the world of persons and nature alike. If the term "success" is appropriate at all, it must be a success on its own terms.

In that sense, the question is not academic: Can such a quiet revolution ever succeed? In truth, it has been precisely such quiet revolutions of hearts and minds that have succeeded in bringing about genuine change in the quality of human lives. At that task, institutional revolutions fail inevitably. Institutional changes can be significant only when they are a reflection of a change of mind and heart. Thus did the spread of Christianity transform Europe, fundamentally and deeply. Not, notice, the growth of ecclesiastical institutions: those have often served precisely to perpetuate old institutions and old orders. Established churches served to sustain established states; princes religious blessed the tyranny of secular princes. It was the Gospel seeping into the hearts and minds of humans that changed the sense of human lives in the lands of the European heritage. It was the piety of the Czech Brethren that provided the foundation of modern Czech national and moral consciousness. It was the vision of Martin Luther King which transformed America, freeing those of its people whom it touched, white and black, from the bondage of racial stereotypes. The vision of Rachel Carson, penetrating consciousness, is challenging the destructive, depersonalizing logic of consumerism. If anything can preserve the Czech nation from the "Biafra of the spirit" today, it is the clear moral vision of its human rights movement which does not even aspire to an institutional revolution but seeks, in Václav Havel's words, to live in truth.[31]

To live in truth—can that be called a success? Probably not, as we have learned to measure success, in terms of spectacular transformations of the institutional superstructures of our lives. Václav Havel served a four-year prison term. It is the people willing to repeat the lie who are writing their success stories. That mode of thought, though, is predicated on the assumption that being is time, that value is utility, and that the line of time is and should be the same as the line of value. Personally, I think that a deeply problematic conception on the part of finite beings whose personal time line leads only too soon to death. If "real" value were only the value that endures through time, it would have to be impersonal value, the value of artifacts, of institutions and constructs which last while humans die. Humans, marked by mortality, would be doomed to failure.

Perhaps we need to learn to judge success in wholly different ways, not in the succession of time but in its intersection with eternity.

Perhaps real success is not that time is transformed in its flux but that, in each moment, value ingresses in it, that in each moment humans glimpse the glory of the true, the good, the beautiful, the holy. The miracle of children—it is not that it lasts for ever. It would be tragic if it did. Children are beings who pass through our lives to disappear into adulthood. The miracle is the moment of joy in which they open to us a vision of eternity. Or the wonder of truth: its precious worth is not that ever thereafter philosophers to come will repeat that formula. They won't, and should not. The grandeur of truth is not that it persists in time but that it opens to its hearers a glimpse of the eternal. Or again, the immensely brave men and women of the civil initiative, killed, jailed, exiled, are unlikely to bring down the impersonal edifice of Societ rule. Their great achievement is that, before all eternity, they have spoken the word of truth in time. Revolutions of hearts and minds do not succeed by changing the externals of the world but by opening it up to eternity, bringing moral value into it. Their success, whatever the "results," is in having been at all, in having spoken the word of eternal truth amid the complexity of time.

For the truth, for all its complexity, is in a sense utterly simple, as simple as the embers and the stars. We fear unknowing, yet the greater danger may well be that of forgetting, of losing sight of the starry heaven and the moral law, dismissing the truth because it seems so naïvely simple. That is why it seems to me so urgent that philosophy should ever return down the long-abandoned wagon road amid the new growth, not to speculate but to see, hear, and know that there still is night, star-bright and all-reconciling, and that there is dawn, pale over Barrett Mountain, a world which still is God's, not man's, a world where the human can be a dweller at peace with himself, his world, and his God. Though it cannot remain there, philosophy must ever return down the wagon road, in the golden glow of the autumn. Not to find a new truth. The reason is far more modest: lest we forget.

Once more it is autumn, when the sunlight grows golden with the turning leaves and the air heavy with fruition and decay. Somewhere the grapes grow rich on the vine. The leaves of the red maple, whose color all summer anticipated the fall, grow tan; the fresh pine straw softly blankets the corner of memories beneath the white pines. Around the clearing the forest floor lights up with the gold of freshly fallen leaves; the river bed is bright with them beneath the clear water.

How many autumns since the agonized cry with which humans protest the unacceptability of the inevitable? It is vain to count. Humans must ever make peace with the ending of a life, the parting of the loved, with the raccoon wasted on the pavement, struck down by an unheeding motorist. The anguished cry of a child's futile love focuses the helplessness of love in face of the flow of time no less than the agony of the woman who in vain would enfold with the angel's wings of her love the man plummeting to his death, sixteen stories below, on the refuse-stained concrete of the alley. That aching love is so human—and so vain in the order of time. The fulfillment of life cannot be in its future. That future is always an end. We know that: we ought not to wonder that something perishes. We hurt when we forget that the point of life is not that it should last forever. Its overlooked wonder is that once it was; there once was a man, there once was a raccoon. That is the miracle, that is the point.

The altar hangings on the Eve of All Saints' are not purple, the color of mourning. They are richly, lovingly embroidered, in a pattern of deep joy. All Saints' is not a day to grieve for all who have died. It is a day to rejoice in all who have lived. The fulfillment of time is not where we seek it in vain, in its endless future. It is where we find it, in its perennially present eternity.

The golden leaves line the river bottom, setting the water aglow in the autumn sun. The forest dies and is renewed in the order of time; the sparkling river bears away grief. In the pained cherishing of that transient world, the human, a dweller between the embers and the stars, can raise it up to eternity. That is the task of humans. The moral sense of nature is that it can teach us to cherish time and to look to eternity within it.

Sharon, New Hampshire
All Hallows' Eve, A.D. 1982

Postscriptum

I hesitated for a long time whether to include my marginal notes in the final verson of this book. They were an integral part of the work of thought, white half-sheets inserted in the yellow lined pads on which, each morning, I would transform the retention of the evening into recollection ("Insert fn.: Brentano, *Psych. empir. Stand.;* Husserl, *Zeitbewusst.*"). Contrary to Wundt's and Titchener's assumptions and experiments ("Insert fn.: James, *Princ. Psych. I,* "Time" and "Memory" chs"), I do not believe that the difference between retention and recollection is quantitative, so that memory would retain the form of retention for 8.6 seconds and be transmuted into recollection at 8.7 seconds. The experience of retention, the nonreflective, direct persistence of an experience which continues to "vibrate"—James's metaphor is apt—in consciousness is real enough. It is not, however, restricted in clock time. Melodies and olfactory stimuli, I find, are capable of evoking a memory of an event years removed with precisely the nonreflective immediacy which defines retention. The cry of a wild goose literally reawakens, re-presents the lived experience, the stillness of the reflection on the pond above the beaver dam on a late autumn afternoon, the three Canada geese which appeared without warning, winging low over the clearing and disappearing beyond the tree tops, and all I was living at that time, long ago. That memory has about it none of the traits of a recollection—of an active, reflective reconstitution of time passed. In spite of the intervening years, it represents itself with a nonreflective lived immediacy.

What transforms retention into recollection, I have found, is not the passage of time but the thought-work ("Insert fn.: Freud, *Traumdeut.* ch. VII") of explicating its sense in a network of associated significances. It may begin by linking the flight of the Canada geese with the image of the bird's flight through the banquet hall in *Beowulf,* go on with Proust's *A la recherche du temps perdu,* then on to Bergson's concept of the density of the present and on to Husserl and Gadamer. Consciousness in the mode of retention is linked solely and directly to lived experience. It is transformed into recollection by being situated in a second, intersecting context of reflective meanings.

That transformation of retention into recollection appears to me as the crucial work of philosophic thought. Kant's reflection on the relation of intuitions and concepts is to the point here. Thought which does no more than re-evoke experience in the mode of retention may not be wholly blind, but it remains essentially poetic. Its great merit is rescuing reality for thought out of the ever-rolling stream of time, but no more. Concepts without intuitions, conversely, are surely quite empty. Thought which does no more than manipulate concepts, perhaps with consummate skill but wholly devoid of all lived experiential reference ("Insert fn.: Derrida re. verbalizations as the referent of discourse") may dazzle but is never more than a cunningly devised fable. Philosophy must fuse: it would be most metaphoric but not entirely false to say that the chief task of philosophy is to write footnotes to the text of experience.

That is why I believe that footnotes are not wholly inappropriate even in a volume which self-consciously sets out to *see* rather than speculate. Still, any set of footnotes is inevitably deficient. Some of the deepest bonds of the spirit inevitably remain unacknowledged. In all this volume, there are virtually no footnotes to the poetry of Robert Frost. Yet it was Frost—not Thoreau, not Tolstoy, emphatically not Rousseau—who shaped my experience most powerfully. I memorized his poetry while I was still struggling with the rudiments of the English language, and it has been with me ever since. It was Frost who helped me find a second home in the forests and stony fields "north of Boston." Frost, too, was rather less than a success as a farmer: his crop was insights and reflections into the very core of love and pain. It was from him that I learned sensitivity to the *sense* of nature and of human life. Husserl, Rádl, and others gave me the tools of my trade, and I cite them often. It is Frost who provides my basic impetus. Yet there are few footnotes to Frost, and there cannot be more. It is too basic.

Then, too, footnotes are inevitably personal. They are a testimony to the way a thinker integrates his retentions in a web of recollections. They can be helpful, but they cannot be normative. The work of thought cannot be done second-hand. It is a highly personal task: each reader must, in effect, write his own footnotes, integrating the text within his own network of meanings. One writer's footnotes can at best serve as clues, opening up avenues of reflection.

It is in that spirit that I present my own notes—not as an exhaustive catalogue of associations, but as a series of openings from the experience of the text on the horizon of thought. Yet wide margins are as crucial to a book as dense notes, for it is the reader, who, in the last instance, must write his own marginalia. A book succeeds when its margins are full.

Notes

Unless otherwise stated, all notes refer to editions listed in the bibliography.

Prolegomenon

1. "We walk on asphalt . . ." is a quote from a contemporary Czech philosopher, Milan Machovec, formerly a professor at Charles University in Prague. Since the Soviet occupation in 1968, he has been banned from all academic employment as well as from all forms of publication. The quotation comes from an unpublished text. Several of Machovec's earlier works, however, have appeared in translation in the West (see bibliography).
2. My perception of the spiritual crisis of the West is deeply influenced by Edmund Husserl, though not so much by the familiar "egology" of his *Cartesian Meditations* as by the personalistic humanism of his letter to Arnold Metzger, of his *Ideen II* and of his Prague and Vienna lectures, which appeared posthumously as *Die Krisis der europäischen Wissenschaften.* I have been no less influenced by two less familiar sources, Emanuel Rádl's *Útěcha z filozofie* and Jan Patočka's *Kacířské eseje o filozofii dějin.* Emanuel Rádl (1873–1942), a Czech biologist and philosopher, made me aware of the continuity of the vital and moral orders. Jan Patočka (1907–77), another Czech philosopher, forced me to recognize that the crisis is deeper than it appeared to Husserl or even Heidegger, and that the "natural world" which radical reflection must seek need be not only prescientific but, in a sense yet to be explained, prehistorical—or, better, *prehistoricist.* Cf. Patočka, *Essais hérétiques sur la philosophie de l'histoire,* and the superb preface to that volume by Paul Ricoeur.
3. Sir Charles Sherrington captured the horror of nature with poetic power in his *Man on His Nature* (pp. 266–75), essential reading for anyone contemplating the wonders of creation, even though Sherrington's protoexistentialist conclusion seems problematic. For the conception of *technē* as also an authentic human possibility, cf. Martin Heidegger, "Die Frage nach der Technik," *Vorträge und Aufsätze,* pp. 16ff.
4. The classic presentation of "nature" as a construct, *Korelat der Naturwissenschaften,* is Husserl's in *Ideen II,* § 1, and again in *Krisis,* § 9. Others,

however, note as much as well, as Rádl, *Útěcha,* pp. 76–85, or Philip Rieff, who writes that "a theoretician is the artificer of reality" (*The Triumph of the Therapeutic,* p. 84).

5. Here, especially Patočka, who is conscious of the appeal of historicism as offering at least a vision of a relative sense to a generation whom the loss of absolute sense confronted with the abyss of the nihilism whose coming Nietzsche proclaims—but who is no less aware that a relative sense is absolute nonsense (*Essais hérétiques,* pp. 65–88).
6. I have qualified the assertion with respect to Kant because of the clearly speculative, deductive approach which marks his *Theorie des Himmels.* To Rádl (*Útěcha,* pp. 74–75), Kant appears as a personification of the post-Galilean hypothetico-deductive approach. Still, the intuitive power of the opening sentence of the conclusion to *Critique of Practical Reason,* with its vision of "the starry heavens above and the moral law within," stands out in poetic grandeur regardless of the verdict of Kantian scholarship.
7. Calvin Schrag, *Radical Reflection and the Origin of the Human Sciences,* p. x. Schrag gives a new vitality to Husserl's search for the primordial experiential reality in which all reflection and speculation is grounded—and of whose problems a number of commentators write (as David Carr, "Husserl's Problematic Concept of the Life World," *American Philosophical Quarterly,* 7 [October 1970]: 331–39). I am not unaware of the criticisms which have been leveled at this conception (as Richard Rorty, *Philosophy and the Mirror of Nature,* p. 26, where Rorty denies any "original text of lived experience"). I am, however, no less aware that philosophies which sought to deny that original text and to build on their own speculation, no matter how cunning, have regularly ended up in a wistful denial of their own competence.
8. Let me hasten to stress that I do not regard a metaphor as "mere." I am convinced that philosophical metaphors do refer, and that in a way peculiarly suited to philosophy. Cf. Jaspers, *Philosophy,* vol. 3, pp. 147–91, but esp. Ricoeur, *The Rule of Metaphor,* study 8.5.
9. Husserl, *Crisis,* § 7, with which I fully identify.

Chapter 1

1. Heidegger's term is *Dasein,* usually translated as "dasein," the lowercase "d" indicating that the word is now English. The virtue of such translation is that, in English, the word means nothing and so does not introduce any prejudicial connotations. Its flaw is that it appears as a mysterious but technical term, indicating "what 'man' really is"—clearly not Heidegger's intent. The relevant passage is *Sein und Zeit,* § 4 (*Being and Time,* pp. 32–35). Let the reader judge.
2. The classic statement is that of Sir Charles Sherrington in *Man on His Nature,* the more striking since, unlike many of his fellow scientists, Sherrington fully acknowledges both the reality of mind and the teleology of nature. Though the existentialists tended to perceive and present their thought as wholly discontinuous with earlier philosophy, reading Sher-

rington makes existentialism appear as a philosophical reflection of the philosophy of science of a generation ago, with the sense of a moral man cast as a stranger into a material, amoral universe. Cf. esp. chap. 12, "Altruism," pp. 262–98.

3. Max Scheler's personalism was explicit and noted as such in the subtitle of his *Formalism in Ethics and Non-Formal Ethics of Values, A New Attempt toward the Foundation of an Ethical Personalism* (see esp. chap. 6, pp. 370–583). Husserl's personalism has been obscured by other aspects of his work, but it is no less pronounced in the second volume of his *Ideen* cycle, *Phänomenologische Studien zur Konstitution.* If anything, it is more explicit, since what Husserl proposes is not simply a theory of persons but a personalistic perspective on reality. See esp. part 3, §§ 64–66, and Beilage 12.2.

4. *Sein und Zeit,* §§ 1–4 (*Being and Time,* pp. 21–35). One of Heidegger's leading commentators, William J. Richardson, questions this, distinguishing a more "existentialist" Heidegger I (in *Sein und Zeit*) from an ontologically oriented Heidegger II of the later works. Heidegger, in his *Vorwort* to Richardson, *Heidegger: Through Phenomenology to Thought,* tactfully avoids endorsing that view (pp. xxii–xxiii).

5. The *Geviert,* which Richardson translates as the "quadrate," the earth, the sky, the gods, and mortals, might be read as an attempt to provide categories—though Heidegger rejects that term—to replace those of metaphysics which Heidegger thinks have been surpassed. Cf. "Das Ding" and "Überwindung der Metaphysik," *Vorträge und Aufsätze,* pp. 157–80 and 67–96; English translation in *Poetry, Language, Thought,* pp. 163–87.

6. In *Being and Nothingness,* Sartre clearly introduces the category of being-in-itself, *l'être en soi,* as describing a mode of being, not a set of entities (pp. 617–24)—though it is a mode of being coextensive with a set of entities, nonhuman nature. In the evocative description of the protagonist's hand or of the tree roots as sheer senseless being-in-itself in *Nausea,* however, being-in-itself is presented simply as nature as it putatively "really is," of itself, not rendered meaningful by humans—in a striking parallel to Sherrington's view of nature and the place of humans therein.

7. The phrase, "*existence* comes before *essence,*" occurs in Sartre's lecture, *Existentialism and Humanism,* pp. 26–27. It makes little sense in the traditional sense of those terms. If, however, we give the term "essence" the rather naïve interpretation suggested by Sartre's example of the paper-cutter (ibid.) the assertion becomes little more than a reaffirmation of Bergson's claim of the creative powers of evolution: the process of becoming gives rise to novelty which can be described in terms of a pattern.

8. I should have preferred to speak of the *regional ontology* of physics, but for the unfamiliarity of that term, introduced by Husserl in *Ideen I* §§ 9–16 and explicated further in *Ideen II,* part 1. Ontology here refers to an inventory and an ordering of what is taken to be. A general ontology would have to include all that presents itself and functions as real in lived experience, including intentional objects. For the purposes of a special inquiry, however, whether it is chemistry, physics, or psychology, the researcher necessarily restricts the totality of the phenomenal field to the region of whatever is relevant to the inquiry. Such a restriction is essential,

but it means that the ontology of that inquiry is regional, a correlate of particular science (cf. Husserl, *Ideen II,* §§ 1, 11). The legitimate exclusion of, say, aesthetic experience from physics is a special, not a general science, and so cannot serve as a basis for metaphysical generalizations.

9. Many authors have commented on the exclusion of the subject. The presentation of the mathematical physicist, Erwin Schrödinger, is particularly useful because the author links it to the idea of self-forgetting. Cf. *Nature and the Greeks,* chap. 7, p. 91.

10. I am indebted to Quine's classic, *Word and Object,* for the terms "rich" and "austere" ontology. Quine is one of the most articulate spokesmen of what I would describe as reductionism. He acknowledges the actuality of the full phenomenal field and the utility of intentional language, but considers it derivative—the useful German term is "*fundiert*"—rather than primordial and prefers to restrict the term "real" to an irreducible conceptual minimum (cf. § 43, § 45). Quine is a brilliant thinker and an elegant writer, his work the noblest foil for anyone seeking to rediscover a "rich" ontology.

11. Husserl's university studies focused on mathematics and philosophical psychology rather than on the history of philosophy. His acquaintance with Plato would be likely to have been heavily influenced by the two standard texts of the time, Wilhelm Windelband's *A History of Philosophy* and Friedrich Ueberweg's earlier work of the same title. Windelband, especially, gives an explicitly dualistic reading of Plato, interpreting the "realm of ideas" not only as analogous to Kant's noumenal realm but actually far more on the model of the medieval parallel of the "natural" and the "supernatural." Husserl's rejection of Platonism (as in *Ideen I* § 22) in fact applies far more to Windelband's interpretation of Plato than to Plato's writings.

12. In fairness to Heidegger, we should note that the analysis in *Sein und Zeit* §§ 14–21, to which we are referring, is presented explicitly as a description of "average everydayness," the ordinary experience of an urban dweller in the twentieth century. When Heidegger comes to write his "way of truth" rather than "way of seeming," as in his analysis of nearness in "Das Ding," *Vorträge und Aufsätze,* pp. 157–80, his description is far closer to what Ernst Cassirer describes as the "mythico-religious" perspective (*An Essay on Man,* pp. 72–108) and what we shall term the "personalistic" perspective, typified by the stance which, modifying Kant, we could describe as "treating reality, whether in your own person or that of an Other, as an end and never a means merely."

13. This was not only the implicit, but the explicit assertion of behaviorism. Thus J. B. Watson bids us "to think of man as an assembled organic machine ready to run" (*Behaviorism,* p. 269). Similarly, B. F. Skinner explicitly rejects the conception of the human as a person, a moral subject, providing, in the course of naming his opponents, a very reasonable bibliography of writers who represent the personalistic (in our sense, below, pp. 122–30) conception of humans and nature, such as Joseph Wood Krutch or C. S. Lewis (*Beyond Freedom and Dignity,* p. 200).

14. Banned by the new Communist regime two years after its publication, Rádl's *Útěcha z filosofie* remained a cherished possession of Czech readers

but never became widely available in translation. A very limited private printing of a bilingual Czech-English edition was produced by Czech exiles in the West in 1983. It will, I hope, become the basis for a German-Czech edition and, in time, for a regular English one as well. As of this writing, however, the book remains unavailable.

15. *Útěcha z filosofie,* chap. 2. Rádl's philosophical views, though today they appear idiosyncratic, were in fact consistent with those of his teacher, the vitalist biologist Hans Driesch, though augmented by a dimension of moral rather than merely vital being, much along the lines of his contemporary, Max Scheler, with whose work Rádl was quite familiar. Cf. Max Scheler, *Die Stellung des Menschen im Kosmos*, esp. chap. 3 (*Man's Place in Nature*, pp. 56–87).
16. Skinner, *Beyond Freedom and Dignity,* pp. 185–202. The unwitting service of behaviorism may be that, having stripped being human of all intrinsic value, it forces the reader to confront, starkly, the ultimate question: Why should this species survive? We shall return to this below, pp. 91–103.
17. So Bergson, *Creative Evolution,* and Teilhard de Chardin, *The Phenomenon of Man.* The latter writer tells us that humans are "nothing else than evolution become conscious of itself" (p. 221). Interestingly, in spite of his "point Omega," in his concluding part 4 Teilhard in effect acknowledges survival as the ultimate value reference *pro statu isto.*
18. That is not Heidegger's conclusion—he is lead, rather, to acknowledge the transtemporal dimension of reality. I have seen the statement attributed to Sartre but have not been able to locate it.
19. Husserl, *Ideen II,* part 3; Scheler, *Formalism in Ethics. . . ,* chap. 6; most explicitly, *Man's Place in Nature,* chap. 2.
20. *Process and Reality,* part 1, chap. 3. Charles Hartshorne worked out that conception in *The Divine Relativity,* pp. 60–115.
21. *The Phenomen of Man,* part 4, esp. pp. 255–71.
22. Jan Patočka, *Kacířské eseje o filosofii dějin,* study 2 (*Essais hérétiques sur la philosophie de l'histoire,* pp. 70–71).
23. Cassirer, *An Essay on Man,* chap. 7. Cassirer insists on treating the "mythico-religious" mode as an earlier phase rather than an alternative (cf. p. 207), though the evidence he presents does not bear out that contention. Here Kurt Hübner seems more adequate (*Kritik der wissenschaftlichen Vernunft,* pp. 395–426; English translation, *Critique of Scientific Reason,* tr. Paul and Hollis Dixon [Chicago: University of Chicago Press, 1983]).
24. The theme of murder/suicide, the killing of the other or the killing of oneself as the desperate response to the solipsism of the modern age, recurs on several occasions in Masaryk's writings, though, as with most of Masaryk's philosophic reflections, typically in the margins of social commentary. Cf. *The Spirit of Russia,* vol. 2, § 191, pp. 473–74.
25. The distinction made by writers like E. F. Schumacher (*Small Is Beautiful,* pp. 53–78) between high and low technology is, surely, absolutely crucial in practice. The possibility of "low" technology may be the condition of the survival of our species. In the present context, though, the crucial distinction is not between high and low technology or even between technology and some putative pretechnological state: even a sharpened stick is technology. Rather, it is the distinction between the fact and the sense

of both nature and technology. Thus not Thoreau, seeking a low-technology life-style, but Robert Frost, seeking the sense of life and nature, serves as my guide, though my conclusions differ from his.

26. *Vorträge und Aufsätze,* pp. 13–14. English in "The Question Concerning Technology," *Basic Writings,* p. 228.
27. This is one of Emanuel Rádl's favorite themes—that the task of philosophic critique is not to abolish but to preserve by grasping the good in what at first may appear absurd. Thus again, Frost, not Thoreau (*Útěcha,* chap. 5b).

Chapter 2

1. Martin Heidegger made those two terms, poetizing and thinking, into virtually technical terms in "The Thinker as Poet" *(Poetry, Language, Thought)* and again in *On the Way to Language.* I am using them somewhat idiosyncratically to distinguish philosophic reflection, *denken,* from the instrumental rationality of daylight "thinking." In such reflection, however, it is still a person, a moral subject, who thinks. Thinking is still an act. Poetizing, as I am using the term, comes closer to being a passion in the classical sense derived from *passio:* a stream of consciousness borne along by the wonder of Being. Cf. also Heidegger, *What Is Philosophy?,* p. 95.
2. It is in this sense that Jaspers describes philosophy movingly in his radio lectures published as *The Way to Wisdom* (pp. 9–11). Husserl states it more prosaically in his insistence that such philosophic reflection is the essential propaedeutic for philosophy, generating, in another terminology, philosophy's data base. It is thanks to such seeing that philosophy is a first-order activity. I would vehemently deny Collingwood's division of labor according to which the sciences see while philosophy reflects on their results (*The Idea of Nature,* pp. 1–3). That is not to deny the validity of the subsequent philosophic task of critical articulation and speculative construction. Without them, *denken,* would slip into *dichten,* philosophy into poetry. Without the grounding in radical seeing, however, it would become a delightful, civilized, but entirely sterile game, a conclusion reached independently by Jacques Derrida in *Speech and Phenomena* and by Richard Rorty in *Mind and the Mirror of Nature.* To be sure, were nature what Rorty takes it to be, the mind could not mirror it.
3. *Ideen II* § 47. I have sought, as much as possible, to avoid the term "objectivity" because in ordinary usage it fuses two meanings that should be kept distinct, the legitimate meaning of the incoercibility of the given which Nicolai Hartman aptly terms "die Härte des Realen," the hardness of the real ("Zum Problem der Realitätsgegebenheit," *Philosophische Vorträge* no. 32), and that of the consensus of subjectivity which Husserl criticizes in *Formal and Transcendental Logic.* The earlier reference, "truth is in communication," is to Karl Jaspers, *The Perennial Scope of Philosophy,* pp. 180–83. What Jaspers seeks to present, however, is not the elevation of subjectivity to dogma by consensus but the negation of the absolutist pretensions of individual terms in the process of communicating.

4. The key here is the recognition of the *presence* of the other, not exhausted in the sum of observable traits which we readily grant in the case of persons but which John Findlay calls us to recognize in the case of all beings, including inanimate objects. This is a central theme of his *Kant and the Transcendental Object*, as pp. 9–16, 166–70, 350–54 et passim.
5. Kant's restriction of the moral law, to treat as an end and not as a means merely, to persons to the exclusion of all other beings is consistent with his conception of the realm of nature as a realm of utility (*Lectures on Ethics*, p. 239; *The Fundamental Principles of the Metaphysics of Morals*, second section, § 56). If, however, Findlay is right (preceding note), then the command would have to be extended to all beings *an sich*, including things.
6. Ecclesiastes 4:9–12.
7. Heidegger, "Das Ding," in *Vorträge und Aufsätze*, pp. 157–81; English in *Poetry, Language, Thought*, pp. 163–87.
8. I use the term *Umwelt* in the special sense it has acquired in phenomenological writings, as the effectively present context structured by a subject's presence. Perhaps the term "functional environment," recalling Uexkül's "*Funktionskreis*" (Cassirer, *An Essay on Man*, p. 23), might serve as an English equivalent.
9. Ricoeur, *Interpretation Theory*, p. 15. In fairness to Ricoeur, let me stress that the quotation is an offhand remark made in the context of a wholly different argument, not a matter of a thematic focus.
10. I do not mean to claim that affect is a necessary component of knowledge in what Husserl calls the "doxic-theoretic" mode (*Ideen II* § 3). Here, however, I am using the term "understanding" in a much broader sense, as what Husserl, on analogy with *Einfühlung*, empathy, calls *Eindeutung*. Theodore Klein, translator of Husserl's *Ideen III*, uses *interpretation*, set in italics, as a translation. That, however, seems misleading. *Empathic understanding*, though clumsy, seems closer to the literal sense of *meaning into* (on analogy with *Einfühlung*, feeling into, empathy) of the term *Eindeutung*.
11. As used in most psychological writings, "mastery" indicates competence and confidence in a situation rather than domination (cf. Andras Angyal's methodologically superb volume, *Neurosis and Treatment*, pp. 75). Still, that psychology should have seized upon a term whose ordinary connotations are those of domination is suggestive.
12. Ricoeur criticizes Derrida for holding that "language does not refer to anything outside itself, it constitutes a world for itself" (*Rule of Metaphor*, p. 313). Derrida, however, does not consider that a criticism, affirming explicitly that "*there is nothing outside of the text*" (*Of Grammatology*, p. 158) and that "the thing itself is a sign" (p. 49).
13. Ricoeur: "Something must be for something to be said," *Rule of Metaphor*, p. 304.
14. Husserl, *Ideen I* § 66. It is the confidence in the possibility of univocal articulation which Jaspers seems to have in mind when, in spite of his evident close spiritual kinship with Husserl, he denies the possibility of philosophy as a rigorous science.

15. Schrödinger advances his hypothesis of identity of being in this 1960 essay, "What Is Real?" sections 2 and 5 (*My View of the World*, pp. 67–81 and 104–10).
16. Cf. Husserl's identification of being and meaning as abstractions from the primordial given, meaningful being, in the latter portions of his *Formal and Transcendental Logic*, as in §§ 50, 72, 86.
17. That is the notorious "we are the true positivists" passage of *Ideen I* § 22. Heidegger offers a striking characterization of the special sciences as special in the "nothing but" passage in "What Is Metaphysics?" (*Basic Writings*, p. 97).
18. *Ideen I* § 66, where Husserl identifies univocal conceptualization independent of the original insight as a hallmark of science.
19. Ricoeur provides an authoritative inventory of the problematization of language in *Rule of Metaphor*, esp. studies 7 and 8. Cassirer complements it with a survey of theories and philosophies of language in *Philosophy of Symbolic Forms*, vol. 1, pp. 117–76 and in *An Essay on Man*, pp. 109–36.
20. If Heidegger means that it is the tongue, the mother tongue that enshrines a nation's spiritual heritage and identity, that speaks, rather than the individual speakers who happen to instantiate the nation at a given time, then his assertion "Die Sprache spricht" is not in the least trivial. Cf. also Hans Georg Gadamer, *Philosophical Hermeneutics*, pp. 59–81, 236.
21. This stands out when we contrast the Saussurean conception of the autonomy of language as a sign system (Ricoeur, *Rule of Metaphor*, pp. 120–25) with J. B. Watson's conception of its autonomy as a set of laryngeal habits (*Behaviorism*, pp. 224–51). Watson can deny the reality of meaning and still construe language as unified by bodily behavior, but would be hard put to account for the intelligibility of a *text*. Saussure's problem would be the precise opposite.
22. "Co měsíc dal," *Studie* (Rome) 15, no. 69 (fall 1980): 260–64, and "Sigmund Freud by Moonlight," *Journal of Religion and Health* 19, no. 4 (winter 1980): 260–67.
23. The crucial point here is that the text is defective discourse, not vice versa. The autonomization of a text is here analogous to the autonomization of the artifact, and creates the same illusion. As Husserl insisted that the justification of a theory is that it leads back to seeing (*Ideen I* § 69), so, with Ricoeur, I would say that the justification of discourse is that it enables us to "rediscover reality by the roundabout way of heuristic fiction" (*Rule of Metaphor*, p. 247).
24. Cassirer, *An Essay on Man*, pp. 107–36. Cassirer appears to waver between considering the various symbolic systems as alternatives and treating them as stages. The implied progression, however, is one from words as symbols, sharing in and evoking a lived reality, to words as autonomous designators of entities, leading to the logical positivist conclusion that any use of language other than the doxic-theoretic is "meaningless"—which Cassirer would surely have to reject.
25. Jaspers, *Philosophy*, vol. 3, pp. 147ff. Ricoeur's own statement of metaphoric reference (*Rule of Metaphor*, p. 247, *Interpretation Theory*, p. 58), though far more sophisticated, remains profoundly Jaspersian in this sense.

26. Cassirer, *An Essay on Man,* pp. 110ff. I read Cassirer's assertion as descriptive not only of mythical usage but also of the sense in which the actual presence at a moment can be the metaphor of the sense of a life, the raccoon in the clearing a metaphor of the life that is the raccoon, I at this moment a metaphor of the man and life I am.
27. Cf. Maurice Grajewski, *The Formal Distinction of John Duns Scotus,* pp. 71–96. John Duns Scotus used the notions of "formality" and "formal distinction" to explicate the mystery—and the experience—of the Trinity: of a God who is so profoundly One and yet encounters us so differently as Father, Son, Holy Spirit. I am borrowing it for dealing with the primacy of meaningful being. In that context for instance, Peter as a father, Peter as a teacher, and Peter as an amateur carpenter are not three separate persons, yet, assuming he is passionately devoted to all three frequently incompatible roles, neither is it adequate to speak of one person who contingently happens to exercise three activities: each of the roles is definitive of Peter's entire identity. Hence it is useful to speak of them as "formalities," not merely virtually distinct, *de mente,* not quite really distinct, *in re,* but formally distinct, as distinct meaningful being.
28. Paul Ricoeur's massive study, *The Rule of Metaphor,* may mark the end of an era to the extent to which the "problem of language" is a product of the assumption that reference must be of the doxic-theoretic variety. Were that the case, language would either distort or fail to add anything—the statement "P is true" would be reducible to "P." Ricoeur's conception of *metaphoric reference* (ibid., pp. 239, 247) combines the recognition of the autonomy of meaningful discourse with its essential referential grounding, which Husserl affirms in insisting on the reducibility of predicative to prepredicative evidence in *Formal and Transcendental Logic* § 86. Having so come to terms with its linguistic tool, philosophy can, perhaps, return to dealing with substantive issues.
29. The relevant passage comes in *Ideen I* § 69. Unlike his existentialist heirs, Husserl does not condemn theory—and, by implication, all of our conceptual and practical artifacts—as "inauthentic," the mark, as Rousseau would have it, of a depraved animal. His point is that theory is an instrument of seeing, not a higher stage of knowledge than insight or a substitute for it.
30. Ricoeur, *Interpretation Theory,* pp. 31ff. The point of the metaphor—as contrasted with the traditional metaphor of seeing—is that our knowledge is the product of an interaction, not simply the imprint of a signet ring on the wax tablet of our mind.
31. Perhaps through carelessness rather than design, Husserl at times uses the terms "*Sinn,*" and "*Wesen*"—meaning and essence—as interchangeable. So *Ideen II* § 15 and throughout Husserl's writings.
32. Sherrington traces that development in *Man on His Nature.* To him, the reduction of the order of nature to the vital and mechanical appears as progress—though, in virtue of it, the moral order of human life comes to appear as an anomaly (ibid., p. 282).
33. Rádl's presentation in *Útěcha z filosofie,* pp. 9–26, is especially helpful for its joint emphasis on the continuity and distinctness of the vital and the

moral law. Max Scheler's *Man's Place in Nature,* pp. 56–87, provides a parallel in English.

34. So stated, the theme sounds Kantian, and so it is, though with the reservations which Scheler elaborates: since Kant assumes a conception of nature devoid of value, the ingression of eternity can appear as an intrusion. It is the recognition of nature as value-laden that gives content to the moral law and makes it continuous with experience. Scheler, *Formalism in Ethics,* pp. 81ff.
35. There is a profound ambiguity in Freud between the mechanistic model of *The Project of Scientific Psychology* and the teleology of meaning in *The Interpretation of Dreams* (Ricoeur, *Freud and Philosophy,* esp. pp. 459–93). Thus our assertion does not hold of Freud as such, though I believe it to be accurate with respect to all mechanism in psychological theory.
36. Heidegger, *Sein und Zeit,* §§ 54–66. In distinguishing the "everyday" from the "authentic," Heidegger is going significantly beyond Husserl, recognizing, in effect, that the contrast is not simply one between experience and theory but between primordial experience and experience restructured by theory. Cf. Ricoeur, preface, in Jan Patočka, *Essais hérétiques,* pp. 7–15, and Patočka, ibid., p. 27, where Patočka goes in turn beyond Heidegger in speaking of natural world as the world prior to the discovery of its problematic nature.
37. The term is Heidegger's, though the concept was elaborated already by the vitalist biologist Uexkül. Cf. Cassirer, *An Essay on Man,* pp. 23—24.
38. The argument, to be sure, is circular. It is in the act of empathic understanding, Husserl's "meaning into," *Eindeutung,* that the moral sense of nature stands out. The very notion of "meaning into" in turn presupposes a moral sense, a meaning there to be grasped. When we conceive of the world as a *kosmos,* as creation endowed with meaning *ab initio,* then it follows that adequate knowledge must be an *Eindeutung,* grasping the meaning already there. If we conceive of knowledge as empathic understanding, then we are assuming a moral sense there to be grasped. The circularity, however, is not vicious. Metatheoretical arguments must be circular, self-confirming, since they seek to provide a global matrix of intelligibility—unlike theoretical arguments, which presuppose such a matrix. The condition is that the circle be wide enough to embrace all there is. Circles, much like dogs and other small animals, become vicious only when they sense that they are too small to cope with the task with which they are confronted.
39. In re "Idealizing Procedures," see *Ideen I* § 69. Like Husserl, I am using the term "reflection" in a weak sense. Cf. Kohák, *Idea and Experience,* pp. 113–20.
40. Writers in the latter half of the nineteenth century in fact often used the designation "historical" as an equivalent of what the eighteenth century designated as "moral," the free, personal dimension of being human, speaking, for instance, of the "historical sciences" to designate the "humanities" and contrasting natural and "historical" religion. Cf. Hübner, *Kritik,* pp. 304ff. This usage receives its theoretical justification in Collingwood, who argues that the idea of nature is, for humans, subsumed by that of History (*The Idea of Nature,* pp. 174–78).

41. Sartre's distinction here depends on the subsumption of what Scheler and the vitalists would call the "vital" realm within the "material" realm, a subsumption which Sartre assumes but never makes explicit (cf. *Being and Nothingness*, pp. 79–101). That is a subsumption which I find experientially untenable—and, since my conception of humanity as distinctive is not based on historicity, I find it theoretically unnecessary as well. However, compare below, pp. 171–74.

42. Teilhard de Chardin accepts Scheler's tripartite conception of being as material, vital, and moral. His point is that, on the material level, a physicalist explanation is equally adequate as a vital one, though not necessary. Only subsequent inquiry, he claims, proves the latter more adequate. Cf. *The Phenomenon of Man*, part 1, pp. 39–52.

43. Here a radical inversion of the way we conceive of moral commandments is crucial. To an age which conceives of nature as anarchic, lawless—symbolized by Freud's conception of the libido—the commandments appear as heteronomous restrictions on the subject's acts. If, however, we conceive of nature, including our nature and the nature of our being, as meaningfully structured, then a recognition of that structure—of its "rules"—is not a constraint but, in the words of Jan Milič Lochman, a "signpost to freedom," a guide how to live freely, avoiding conflict with the structure of being. Lochman argues this point of view persuasively in his *Signposts to Freedom.* I have focused on the latter seven rather than the first three commandments not because I think the first three less essential, but because I am deeply convinced that to those three crucial commandments humans must come as to conclusions, not as premises. Cf. below, pp. 182–88.

44. Bowne, *The Principles of Ethics*, pp. 221–25.

45. "To live in truth," to refuse to participate in the charade, is how Václav Havel, a Czech playwright recently released after serving four years of a four-and-a-half-year prison term, summed up the goal of the civil initiative in Czechoslovakia: to break free of the habit of pretense. Quoted from his samizdat essay, *Moc bezmocných*, widely reprinted in Czech periodicals abroad. English translation, "The Power of the Powerless," in *Crosscurrents 1983*, tr. P. Wilson (Ann Arbor: University of Michigan, 1983), pp. 3–22.

46. As should have become apparent by now, I am using the term *physis* in the etymological sense, designating nature as living, growing, as it was used in early Greek philosophy (cf. H. Leisegang, "Physis," in Pauly-Wissowa, *Realencyklopädie*, vol. 20, pp. 1130–64). Unlike Lovejoy and Boas, however, I do not regard it as in any sense a mark of primitivism (A. O. Lovejoy and G. Boas, *Primitivism and Related Ideas in Antiquity*). Cf. also F. Heinemann's classic *Nomos und Physis.*

47. *Process and Reality*, pp. 32 and passim. While it could be argued that Whitehead intended no more than to recognize the dimension of the eidetic, the fact remains that here, as with "feeling" and "subjectivity," he chose a philosophically loaded term, justifying at least an attempt at reading the term in its broadest rather than most austere sense. Cf. William Christian, *An Interpretation of Whitehead's Metaphysics*, pp. 193–220, 258–82.

48. Scheler, *Vom Ewigen im Menschen*, pp. 95–110, 673–706.

49. Sherrington makes a crucial point—that teleological ordering does not necessarily indicate or represent a value ordering. His description of the life cycle of the malaria mosquito is essential reading for anyone who wishes to take the teleologial argument seriously (*Man on His Nature,* pp. 267–75).
50. That is the unstated assumption of Bergson's *Creative Evolution* no less than of Teilhard's *The Phenomenon of Man.* Unamuno, in his *Tragic Sense of Life,* offers the opposite reading while Sherrington, in the work just cited, offers some evidence for it.

Chapter 3

1. Contrary to the claim of some writers on ecological ethics, the Renaissance inherited from antiquity the Stoic fear of nature as chaotic and the sense of a mission of imposing the order of reason upon it. Here I still prefer the two classic sources, Jacob Burckhardt, *Civilization of the Renaissance in Italy* and Johan Huizinga, *The Waning of the Middle Ages,* to more recent interpretations (as Peter Singer, *Animal Liberation*) which link the callousness toward nature with the much later rise of the natural sciences.
2. Though legitimate questions can be raised as to the historical accuracy of Peter Singer's claims concerning the medieval and the Renaissance view of animals, his *Animal Liberation* and subsequent volume, *Animal Rights and Human Obligations,* deserve high praise—and reading—both for raising the issue and for articulating the attitude of diffidence rather than domination toward other beings. Concerning his recent volume, *The Expanding Circle: Ethics and Sociobiology,* see p. 112n20, below.
3. Emanuel Rádl recounts the story of the Spanish anatomist Vesalius, condemned to make a pilgrimage to the Holy Land after a supposed corpse he was dissecting opened its eyes and stared at the audience in agony. Rádl writes, "What if the cosmos were to raise its head, stare at us and cry out, 'People, what are you doing to me?'—To what Holy Land would we then travel in a hair shirt to beg forgiveness?" *Útěcha,* p. 90.
4. E. F. Schumacher's writings, from *A Guide for the Perplexed* to *Small Is Beautiful,* argue this persuasively and sensitively. The contrast between his philosophical style and Peter Singer's far more intellectualistic presentation is instructive as well. In this context, see esp. Schumacher's insistence on the feasibility of "low" technology, *Small Is Beautiful,* pp. 53–78.
5. The theme recurs throughout Sartre's work. Perhaps the classic statement is in *Nausea,* pp. 128–29.
6. Admittedly, this recognition has been articulated repeatedly by religious writers, from Paul of Tarsus (Romans 5:8) to Paul Tillich (*The Courage to Be,* pp. 155ff). The theological statement of it, though, may well be too familiar to be convincing until we encounter the experience from which it stems—the peace which pervades the writings of Joseph Wood Krutch, the sense of acceptance as a lived experience rather than a doctrine. Hence the following pages.
7. William Carlos Williams, "Red Wheelbarrow," in L. Untermeyer, *Modern American Poetry,* p. 282.

8. Karl Jaspers outlines the triple perspective of being as sheer presence, being as the psycho-physical in time, and being as moral *(geistig)* in the perspective of eternity. Though I have learned much from him, a crucial component appears to me missing—the tangibility of the incarnation, the fusion of being and having. To Jaspers, the incarnation is a stumbling block. Here it is Gabriel Marcel who provides the missing link, in his *Being and Having*. See Jaspers, *The Perennial Scope of Philosophy*, but esp. *Way to Wisdom*, pp. 28–38.
9. I am using the term "temporalism" in a broad sense, to designate any philosophy which attributes value significance to temporality, whether by attributing a moral sense to history (below, pp. 97–101) or by attributing it to development. In the last category, it is the work of Lawrence Kohlberg, for example, *The Philosophy of Moral Development, Moral Stages and Ideas of Justice*, that has received most attention, though to me it appears flawed by its intellectualism, which reduces moral being to moral reasoning at its most abstract. In my own work, I have grown acutely aware that the variety of ethical positions does correspond to stages on life's way. The infants I have known have been ethical noncognitivists, their behavior accurately described by noncognitivist positions, emotivism and imperativism. As they learned to speak, they tended first to adopt an individual relativist position, equating "good" with "pleasing to me." Their next step was to social relativism, equating the good with peer-group preference, typically first their family, then their friends. It was only much later that they, or at least some of them, began to realize that good and evil, right and wrong are at times not a matter of anyone's preference but are objectively grounded in the nature of our being—brushing their teeth without being told, simply because they remembered their last visit to the dentist. In effect, they had grown up to moral naturalism, grounded in an ethics of utility. The last step to moral maturity, moral realism, the recognition of an absolute norm, grounded in self-respect and the respect of the integrity of the other, independent of utility and convention alike, I am convinced, is no longer an achievement but a gift.
10. Tomáš Baťa, (1875–1932), the founder of the worldwide Baťa shoe concern, well illustrates the missionary verve which, perhaps more than gain, motivated the great entrepreneurs of the industrial age: the conviction, every bit as powerful as that of Marx and Lenin, that the human lot can be improved, not by violence but by effort. Baťa set out to change the world for the better by shoeing the barefoot. In the process, he went from rags to riches—but Lenin, though not starting from rags, did not exactly die a pauper, either. Whether the world is better for their respective efforts may be the crucial question for all historicism. See Antonín Cekota, *Geniálni podnikatel Tomáš Baťa* (Toronto: '68 Publishers, 1981).
11. The German pastors Niemöller and Bonhoffer, martyred by the Hitler regime during the Second World War, are too familiar to require mention. Jaroslav Šimsa was a Czech pastor who died in a concentration camp. His testimony, *Úzkost a naděje*, bears witness to the courage of those years. His son, also a pastor, has been jailed by the Soviet regime in Czechoslovakia for human rights activities. Václav Benda, a Catholic layman, was just released after serving a four-year prison term for refusing to condemn

a civil rights manifesto without seeing it first. The quote comes from his *samizdat* essay, "Půlnoční kádrový dotazník."

12. Gabriel Marcel raises the distinction as a philosophical problem in *Being and Having;* Eric Fromm makes the two terms into psychologial as well as philosophical categories in *To Have or to Be?* (cf. esp. pp. 3–16).
13. Praxis of the regime in my native land convinces me that the slogan, "From each according to his ability, to each according to his needs," means in fact that every worker is to labor to exhaustion but is to be paid only as much as needed to keep him alive—and so is in truth a restatement of a basic principle of classical economics, that labor is a commodity priced according to its exchange value, as Marx points out in *Das Kapital,* vol. 1, chap. 8. Also Leszek Kołakowski, *Main Currents of Marxism,* vol. 1, pp. 280–81, and Erazim Kohák, "Possessing, Owning, Belonging," *Dissent* 19, no. 3 (summer 1972): 453–63.
14. Husserl, *Ideen II* § 21; Saint Paul, 1 Cor. 15:44.
15. The body, in effect, extends into a sphere of mine-ness. So Husserl, *Ideen II* § 51, elaborated in detail in Merleau-Ponty, *Phenomenology of Perception,* pp. 98–202.
16. In elevating industrial expansion to an ideology, communist regimes tend to evoke a ruralist reaction. Thus the work cited, Konstantin Rasputin, "Proshchanie s Materoi," in *Povesti,* pp. 15–195; or Mojmír Klánský, *Vyhnanství,* which consciously takes up a theme of the nineteenth-century classic, Karel Rais, *Zapadlí vlastenci.* Neither is available in English, but Willa Cather's works such as *My Ántonia* offer an English parallel.
17. The crux of the problem, I believe, is not the debate between John Stuart Mill and Immanuel Kant, mediated by Max Scheler, but rather the recognition of what I would describe as the *intrinsic value of utility.* There are times when being treated *as a means* is precisely the respect due to a being as *an end, an sich,* a denizen of the kingdom of ends. Though our age has little understanding of it, there is a joy and a pride in serving faithfully and well, a joy in service I know well. There have been times when I clearly saw the joy and pride of animals in performing tasks for which they were trained, a joy that cannot be reduced to a desire for a reward. Though I know the metaphor is far-fetched, I would speak also of a strong sense that things *deserve,* "have a right" to be used—that, in fairness, one ought to let one's pots take turns doing the cooking that none be ignored. The kernel of such fanciful metaphors is the recognition that the *value of utility is not itself utilitarian:* it is the *intrinsic* value of service. This is a common theme of devotional literature. See also J. N. Findlay, "They Think Not, Neither Do They Care" (publication pending). In that sense I interpret also the puzzling section on service in Rádl's *Útěcha*, pp. 19–22. I have elaborated this topic in "Creation's Orphans: Toward a Metaphysics of Artifacts," *The Personalist Forum* vol. 1, no. 1 (Spring 1985): 22–42.
18. Martin Heidegger's "Ein Brief über den Humanismus" ("Letter on Humanism" in *Basic Works*, pp. 189–243) appears to me as a devastating and definitive criticism of the facile "humanism" of the postwar years—though, as Heidegger is aware, it is really a critique of our conception of being human.

19. That there is genuinely something that we can distinguish as a Czech philosophical tradition rather than echoes of world philosophy in the Czech lands stands out most clearly in T. G. Masaryk's *Česká otázka,* now available in an English translation by Peter Kussi, *The Meaning of Czech History.* It is a tradition of moral humanism whose origins lie in the Czech Brethren reformation (Comenius) down to recent figures like Masaryk, Rádl, and Patočka. It is in Rádl that the kinship with American religious personalism is most apparent. The perspective of this volume, though drawn from many sources, stands spiritually in the mainstream of historic Czech thought. See also Masaryk, *The Ideals of Humanity.*
20. The critical weakness of Lawrence Kohlberg's potentially valuable attempt to link ethics with developmental psychology, notably Piaget's, appears to me to be the hopelessly abstract intellectualism of the ethics which he uses, evident in Rawl's *A Theory of Justice* (cf. esp. section 11). Peter Singer, whose attempt to link ethics and sociobiology *(The Expanding Circle: Ethics and Sociobiology)* places him in this tradition, defines ethics as the "form of reasoning which develops in a group context, building on more limited biologically based form of altruism" (p. 149). Yet were ethics a "form of reasoning," it would be the exclusive domain of a narrow intellectual elite—and since it is not, that equation restricts the validity of Singer's exposition. Most unfortunately, since the basic recognition—moral growth as the progressive extension of respect from near kin to all persons, then all animate beings, then to all being as such—is valuable. It would be interesting to take, say, Lawrence Kohlberg's "Stage and Sequence: The Cognitive Developmental Approach to Socialization" (in D. A. Goslin, ed., *Handbook of Socialization Theory and Research*) and do the work over, using a more adequate model of motivation and morality that would take into account Husserl, Merleau-Ponty, and Ricoeur.
21. This may be the reason why Windelband, otherwise such a scrupulous scholar, does so little justice to Stoicism in his *History of Ancient Philosophy,* pp. 303–18. It took an age purged by the tragedy of romanticism to appreciate the Stoics, as Tillich does in *The Courage to Be,* pp. 9–17.
22. I am following Rudolf Bultman's reading as he presents it in his *Theology of the New Testament,* vol. 2, pp. 201–3, interpreting the contrast not as one of "flesh" and "spirit" but of *life ordered according to* the flesh as against life ordered by the spirit, noting that the word is not *sōma,* body, but *sarx,* bodily lusts (perhaps libidinal drives?) which is being rejected.
23. That is Rádl's criticism of Kant (*Útěcha,* pp. 74–75, 79–80; *Dějiny filosofie,* vol. 2, pp. 291–310). Rádl was no Kant scholar, and his reading has been criticized as superficial. A similar criticism has been leveled against Husserl's reading of Kant (*Crisis,* §§ 28–32). Still, a valid point remains: given Kant's conception of nature as impersonal, his moral point of view cannot but appear as nonnatural and so grounded in speculation rather than insight. Scheler, however, did study Kant intensively and sees the dilemma in which his impersonal conception of nature places him. His attempt, in *Formalism,* chap. 1, to make Kantian formalism possible, is based on the reintroduction of value into nature.
24. To Kant scholars, for the most part, this aspect of the *Foundations of Metaphysics of Morals* seems marginal. To me it does not: in appealing to

the moral intuition of the man in the street, Kant acknowledges what Scheler will insist on more than a century later: the primordial givenness of values. Kant, "Foundations," in *Kants Werke,* vol. 4, pp. 388–91; Scheler, p. 71n34, above.

25. What may seem obscure in philosophic texts like Husserl's *Ideen I* §§ 1–3 stands out clearly in Köhler's *Gestalt Psychology,* pp. 174ff.—that the presentation of the sense of a configuration ("Gestalt") is a given of direct rational intuition, *Wesensanschauung,* not a construct.
26. Here one of the classic early critiques of positivism—Edna Heidbreder's critique of John Broadus Watson's *Behaviorism*—makes the point most clearly: positivism owes its impact not to its theories but to the moral fervor to which it is heir—and which its theories would disqualify (*Seven Psychologies,* pp. 359ff.).
27. Stanislav Mareš, *Báje z nového světa* (Toronto: '68 Publishers, 1978), p. 9. New English translation, Paul Alpers, *The Singer of the Eclogues,* (Berkeley, University of California Press, 1979), p. 11.
28. Ever since the work of Pavlov and Yerkes early in the century, the assumption in psychological circles has tended to be that behavioristic explanation unproblematically applies to animals—in spite of Köhler's findings (*Gestalt Psychology,* chap. 4)—but not to humans. My own observation leads me to suspect that just the opposite is the case. In the absence of a neocortex or its mental equivalent, animals cannot separate their acts from the dimension of the moral. It is only humans who can separate the moral and the vital dimension and so are capable of purely vital acts—and thus of purely behavioristic explanations. In animal acts, the dimension of the moral, though not separately defined, is always present. That, however, is no more than a hunch—and an experiment to test it would be rather difficult to design, since the hunch depends on the recognition of a moral dimension in the being of animals.
29. The definition of personality in terms of needs is prominent in MacDougal's correlation of needs and instincts and in subsequent writers who compiled lists of needs as a key to understanding personality. I am indebted to Gordon Allport's overview of the problem of individuality in *Pattern and Growth in Personality,* pp. 311–75. I am not sure, however, that Allport's attempt to account for individuality as a unique synthesis of traits (his "personal disposition") is any more adequate than, say, Cattell's positing of "unique traits" (*Description and Measurement of Personality,* chap. 3) unless we interpret the synthesis as the act of a Person, as Bertocci does. Cf. Allport, pp. 30–31. Subsequent reference to Ricoeur is to *The Voluntary and the Involuntary,* pp. 93–99.
30. In the United States, Personalism did generate something like an orthodoxy in the form of "personalistic idealism," thanks largely to the efforts of the remarkable "Boston B's"—Lotze's American pupil, Bordon Parker Bowne, his successor at Boston University, Edgar Sheffield Brightman, and the current Borden Parker Bowne Professor (Emeritus), Peter Anthony Bertocci. Its impact in the first half of this century was considerable: Martin Luther King was among its products. A lively Personalistic Discussion Group still meets within the American Philosophical Association, though both specifically Personalistic journals, the California *Personalist* and the Boston-based *Philosophical Forum* (O. S.) are now defunct, replaced by a new journal, *The Personalist Forum,* edited by Thomas Buford at Furman

University in Greenville, S.C. In France, Emanuel Mounier made personalism a live option, while in Germany Max Scheler subtitled his *Formalism in Ethics* "An Ethical Personalism," and Edmund Husserl made it his masthead in *Ideen II,* as the concluding part 3 testifies. In Czechoslovakia, both T. G. Masaryk and Emanuel Rádl were strongly influenced by personalist themes though neither used the label—largely because Czech lacks a word which would embody the happy ambiguity of personhood and personality of "Person"—*osobnost* means specifically "personality." In present-day Poland, Karol Wojtyła, who identifies himself as a personalist in the tradition of Max Scheler, is making his impact today. See Albert B. Knudson, *The Philosophy of Personalism;* John Lavely, "Personalism," in Paul Edwards, ed., *The Encyclopedia of Philosophy,* vol. 6, pp. 107–10.

31. The phrase, here taken from Brightman, *An Introduction to Philosophy,* occurs in several contexts. Here it is "The essence of (personalism) is that the whole universe is a society of intercommunicating selves or persons, of which God is the creative centre . . . ," p. 293.

32. The aspect of Bowne's Kantian heritage which here concerns me is the conception of nature expressed in *Foundations of Metaphysics of Morals,* § 56, in which Kant restricts intrinsic worth or "dignity" to persons while writing off the world of nature as having only a utilitarian value, to be used arbitrarily by this or that will.

33. Bowne speaks of the duty of humans to cultivate nature (*Personalism,* pp. 276–77), but denies it ultimate reality and thus dignity of its own—nature, to him, remains merely phenomenal (*Metaphysics,* p. 260).

34. Brightman asserts that "nothing is real save purposing beings, namely, persons," but attributes a low degree of personhood to a grasshopper and describes even the mosquito and amoeba as "conscious selves or unities of mental activity" (*An Introduction to Philosophy,* pp. 262, 200–201).

35. Frederick Ferré, "Personalism and the Dignity of Nature," presented at the Personalistic Discussion Group, American Philosophical Association, Baltimore, Maryland, 28 December 1982. Publication pending.

36. Cf. my "I, Thou and It," *The Philosophical Forum* (new series) vol. 1, no. 1 (fall 1968): 36–72; more recently two articles in *Environmental Ethics,* John Talmadge, "Saying You to the Land" (winter 1981), and John Kultgen, "Saving You for Real People" (spring 1982). Concerning the last two, see the reservation expressed above, pp. 112n20.

Chapter 4

1. The distinction between philosophy and theology reflects the distinction between the "natural" and the "supernatural," whose legitimacy we have been denying throughout. Even apart from that, the concept of the Fall has been amply legitimated as a philosophical category, as in Paul Ricoeur's *Phenomenology of the Will, Fallible Man* (chap. 1.2 and conclusion) and *Symbolism of Evil* (part 2, chaps. 3.2 and 5.4).

2. "In the present state," a phrase commonly used by John Duns Scotus to indicate that the world we know is not necessarily a true embodiment of its true being but at the same time is not wholly discontinuous from it.

Paul Ricoeur in effect takes over the concept, though not the term, when he speak of the vicissitudes of existence and the "empirics" of the will, as in the preface to *Fallible Man* and throughout the *Phenomenology of the Will.*

3. *Statesman,* 269–74. This image calls into question the image of the prisoner making his way out of the cave (*Republic* 509–17) by reasoning. Were the Fall as radical as the *Statesman* passage suggests, no reasoning could lead from the actuality to the true being of reality.
4. Quine's may be the most perceptive modern variant of the theme. If "physical things . . . become known to us only through the effects which they help induce at our sensory surfaces" (*Word and Object,* p. 1), then it would seem that conceptualization would be a constitution and our knowledge a knowledge of conceptualizations. Quine seems to respond in effect with an imposing coherence theory of truth which the book elaborates and § 56 sums up (pp. 270–76).
5. Tomáš G. Masaryk, *Počet pravděpodobnosti a Humeova skepse* (Prague: J. Otto, 1883).
6. In fairness to Matthew Arnold, we should note that the sense of the phrase "sweetness and light" in his text is not at all that which the words acquired later, but rather the decision to trust of which we spoke earlier. Cf. Matthew Arnold, "Sweetness and Light," *Culture and Anarchy, Works of Matthew Arnold* (New York: AMS Press, 1970), vol. 6, pp. 5–43.
7. Philosophically sophisticated practitioners of the art of measurement in the human sciences recognize that the step from the average to the normal to the normative is unwarranted, yet the implication remains. Measurement against the average of a population is conventionally called a "normative measurement" (Cattell, *Description and Measurement of Personality,* p. 148).
8. "Exterminate all the brutes!" Conclusion of Mr. Kurtz's report to the Society for the Suppression of Savage Customs in Joseph Conrad's *Heart of Darkness* (*Great Short Works of Joseph Conrad* [New York: Harper and Row, 1967]).
9. I take that to be the significance of the dramatic shift from an emphasis on *Entschlossenheit,* resoluteness, in *Being and Time* §§ 54–60, to an emphasis on listening, on letting be, only a few years later in "Vom Wesen der Wahrheit," *Wegmarken,* pp. 73–97 (*Basic Works,* pp. 117–42).
10. Rádl here reflects and generalizes Masaryk's critique of the revolutionary illusion—that humans need but destroy the bad and the good will emerge spontaneously. Cf. *Masaryk on Marx,* § 147, Rádl, *Útěcha,* chap. 3.
11. John Hospers, "What Means This Freedom?" in Sidney Hook, ed., *Determinism and Freedom in the Age of Modern Science.* Today that piece is, admittedly, a bit dated: subsequent interpreters of Freud, notably Paul Ricoeur in *Freud and Philosophy* and Alfred Lorenzer in *Die Wahrheit der psychoanalytischen Erkenntnis,* have cast serious doubt on such a mechanist reading of Freud. I cite it not as an adequate interpretation but as an extreme statement of psychoanalytic determinism. The reference to contents which cannot cross the threshold of clear consciousness "wegen

psychologischen Hemmungen" is Husserl's oblique acknowledgment of psychoanalysis in *Ideen I* § 69.

12. Freud's German actually sounds less impersonal than Strachey's English translation. Freud speaks throughout of the *ich,* with the connotations of the English "I," something *I am,* not those of the Latin *ego* which, in English, suggests something I have. In fairness to Freud, at his most prophetic he was also the author of the proclamation, "Wo Es war, soll Ich werden," legitimating Erik Erikson's "ego-psychological" rereading of Freudianism (*New Introductory Lectures,* in *Standard Edition,* vol. 22, p. 80; also Ricoeur, *Freud and Philosophy,* pp. 183–87, 443–45). I am presenting the hardest deterministic interpretation not because I think it most adequate but because it is psychoanalytic determinism, not simply psychoanalysis, that is the problem for personalism.
13. The case of Dora *(Dora: An Analysis of a Case of Hysteria)* is instructive. Freud cites patient recognition and cessation of symptoms as criteria of validity of a psychoanalytic interpretation. Dora's symptoms continued, intermittently, and Dora, a spirited young woman, stoutly rejected Freud's imputation, finally breaking off her therapy. Freud, however, does not treat either as a reason to reconsider his interpretation but as evidence of particularly stubborn resistance.
14. In his *Psychologie der Weltanschauungen.* Concise statement in English in *Reason and Anti-Reason in Our Time,* pp. 20–37.
15. Ricoeur, *Freud and Philosophy,* pp. 344–418. See also Ricoeur's earlier treatment of the topic in *The Voluntary and the Involuntary,* part 2, from which I have borrowed the term "the hidden."
16. Preface to Lorenzer's *Die Wahrheit der psychoanalytischen Erkenntnis,* elaborated in the last three chapters of the volume in the sense that the results of psychoanalytic cognition are to be treated as true if they conform to the finding of Marxist sociological critique. This conclusion, however, should not be allowed to obscure Lorenzer's superb sketch of the development of psychoanalytic interpretation in the first part of the book.
17. I have sought to elaborate this in "The Forest Lights: Notes on the Conceptualization of the Unconscious," *Journal of Religion and Health* 22, no. 1 (spring 1983): 49–57.
18. Cited and commented on in Heidegger, "Der Spruch des Anaximander," *Holzwege,* pp. 296ff.
19. Gordon Allport, in *Pattern and Growth in Personality,* establishes the concept of the autonomization of motives. Ricoeur, in the process of examining the role of needs as motives in part 1 of *The Voluntary and the Involuntary,* makes the point that in humans needs are indeed autonomously human, not disguised primitive needs.
20. Salvatore R. Maddi, "Freud's Most Famous Patient: The Victimization of Dora," *Psychology Today* 8, no. 4 (September 1974): 90–101, points out that in the nightmare context of an adulterous father whose mistress was her governess while her husband was seeking to seduce her, encouraged by her father, refusing to play along and dropping out via a reasonably mild neurosis, may well have been the most adaptive behavior. Freud kept probing for a "mental germ" in Dora's psyche, as if only an organism, a

body or a psyche, could be sick. In this case though, there is strong reason for concluding that the entire situation was sick and Dora, dropping out of it, the only sane member of the cast.

21. Angyal eliminates putative hidden causes or "unconscious" homunculi quite self-consciously; see *Neurosis and Treatment*, pp. 112–13. So does Viktor Frankl, *The Doctor and the Soul*, pp. 176–216. The classic text of personalistic psychology—other, I would say, than James's *Principles of Psychology*—is Wilhelm Stern, *General Psychology: Psychology from a Personalistic Viewpoint.* Angyal's work is most relevant in our context because Angyal specifically addresses our question: Can psychopathological phenomena be accounted for without positing hidden causes, in personal terms?

22. Freud's claim could be sustained only if we were to attribute to the past some objective reality. Yet even in that case its present effect is that of an *interpretation* of a past, as Ricoeur points out (*Freud and Philosophy*, pp. 88–101) and Freud admits, implicitly, in calling his work *Traumdeutung*, not "Traumwirkung."

23. Cf. David Carr, *Phenomenology and the Philosophy of History.* Carr argues that phenomenology includes its own "historical reduction" (pp. 111ff.).

24. Whitehead, *Process and Reality*, pp. 523–33, *Religion in the Making*, pp. 98ff. Whitehead's presentation lends itself to a reading which introduces a moment of process into the godhead in the form of a progressive accumulation of memories, as in Hartshorne, *The Divine Relativity*, pp. 86ff. I am assuming a more traditional reading, the copresence of all time in the eternity of God. Cf. Ivor Leclerc, *Whitehead's Metaphysics*, pp. 203–10.

25. I read this metaphor as overlapping the metaphor we used earlier, the intrinsic, nonutilitarian, nontemporal value of all that is, the "dignity" whereof Kant speaks. It may, however, be also the significance of the "peak experience" which appears so trivial when we read it as a peak of time rather than an intersection of eternity. Cf. Abraham Maslow, *Religions, Values and Peak Experiences*, pp. 19–29, 59–68.

26. Like its counterpart, psychologism, historicism covers a multitude of sins and even some virtues. I am using it in the broad sense established by Karl Mannheim ("Historicismus," *Archiv für Sozialwissenschaft und Sozialpolitik* 52; English in Paul Kecskemeti, trans. and ed., *Essays on the Sociology of Knowledge*), as the assumption that the meaning and value of all acts and events is a function of and to be understood in terms of their location within a process of history. Cf. also Ernst Troeltch, *Historicismus und seine Probleme*, and Karl Popper, *The Poverty of Historicism.*

27. *Essais hérétiques*, chap. 3.

28. *Being and Time*, §§ 12–13. The point is that the *in* is not a matter of location but of self-definition in interaction with remembrance and anticipation.

29. William James's may still be the most useful treatment of the relation of the sheer I-hood of my being with its empirical manifestations. This is usefully supplemented by Husserl's analysis of psychological and transcendental subjectivity in *Formal and Transcendental Logic*, § 99. The point

is that we are not dealing with two components but rather with two dimensions of personal being, as seen from the first-person standpoint. See James, *Principles of Psychology,* vol. 1, pp. 321ff.

30. I take Husserl to be speaking in epistemological rather than metaphysical terms, in light of the conclusion of *Ideen II* § 1, pointing out the ideality of our natural-scientific nature-construct rather than of experienced reality as such (*Ideen II*, pp. 496ff.).
31. Paul Tillich's moving classic, *The Courage to Be,* chapter 6, makes the point poetically. Viktor Frankl, in *The Doctor and the Soul* and in all his other works, elaborates it in psychological terms, yet the point is the same.
32. Saint Thomas, *Summa Theologica,* I, Q. 89 re. separated soul. Protestant pietism, with its moral emphasis and its conviction that immortality is necessary so that moral worth could be matched with reward as it is not in this life, lost sight of it, yet the New Testament hope is one of *resurrection,* the raising of being from time, including the present time, to eternity, not the perpetuation of some imperishable aspect of being human through endless time.
33. Aron Gurwitsch, *Studies in Phenomenology and Psychology,* p. xxiv.
34. Cf. Borden P. Bowne, *Metaphysics,* pp. 44–67, noting esp. pp. 63ff.
35. As in so much else, Rádl presents a classic instance here as well: in his anxious insistence on the eternity of the moral law, he finds himself defending highly transient manifestations of that law, as in *Útěcha,* pp. 21–22. It is painful instances like this that convince me that distinguishing the moral law from the law of custom is a crucial task of all moral philosophy.
36. Collingwood, *The Idea of Nature,* pp. 174–78.
37. Jaspers, *Way to Wisdom,* pp. 14–15; to see how such an approach appears to a morally earnest thinker committed to philosophy as the art of argument, cf. Rorty, *Consequences of Pragmatism,* pp. 37ff.
38. Bordon P. Bowne, *Theory of Thought and Knowledge.* Bowne's term, "creationism," most emphatically does not refer to the mechanics of creation—Bowne was prepared to leave that up to science—but to the present status of the created world: the world is purposefully ordered and value-laden. Cf. pp. 314ff.

Chapter 5

1. Collingwood, *The Idea of Nature,* pp. 1–3.
2. That is the classic Husserlian critique of the conception of philosophy as a second-order inquiry. Philosophy, Husserl claims, must be a "science"—that is, have an independent access to reality. Though Husserl's hope for philosophy as a *rigorous* science runs afoul of the metaphoric nature of philosophical language, his conception of philosophy remains valid. I take that to be the crucial aspect of Husserl's conception of philosophy as a "science" in his classic essay, "Philosophy as a Rigorous Science."
3. Thoreau was writing at a time when America, after nearly half a century of almost idyllic stability, was gearing up for a period of precipitous change. What he sought at Walden was an alternative life-style: his longest, opening chapter is devoted to the economic feasibility of a low-technology alter-

native, as he makes explicit in his argument with the Irish laborer, John Field. Such a quest can be legitimate, as in Schumacher's *Small Is Beautiful,* whatever our doubts about the way Thoreau set about it. My concern, however, is not with low-technology alternatives, though, from the moral point of view, they seem to me far superior and most desirable, but rather with the moral sense of our being, as acted out in the moral sense of nature. That I take to be Frost's concern—and it was from Frost that I learned to see sense in fact long before Husserl provided me with the technical apparatus for speaking about it. Frost, to be sure, arrives at a far darker vision of nature's sense, and were it not for the sense of God's presence, I might well share his conclusions. Hence the importance of the topic of this chapter.

4. *Poiēma theou,* the works of God or, prosaically, creation. The pun in English is fortuitous (and cannot be duplicated in Czech or German). Still, it is a fortunate one, and I am invoking poetic license to make use of it here.

5. In part, the question here is one of terminology. If, with William James, we define knowing as the ability to assess a situation and to respond appropriately to it, animals evidently do know, and, as Köhler's experiments suggest, even understand. The question which concerns me, however, is a substantive one, a question of root metaphor. Shall we think of knowing as a highly complex variation on the generic pattern of stimulus-response—or shall we think of such response as a greatly reduced variation of the generic pattern of understanding? The personalistic inversion leads to the second option. Hence, in asking whether animals know God, the question is not whether they know but whether their awareness includes that of the presence of the holy.

6. Scheler articulates this most explicitly, especially in his *On the Eternal in Man* (*Vom Ewigen in Menschen,* pp. 95–110) and in *Man's Place in Nature,* cited earlier, p. 71n34. Cassirer's treatment is quite striking: while recognizing the primacy of the mythico-religious symbolic forms as well as their universality, he yet stops short of the conclusion this suggests—that humans indeed know God (*An Essay on Man,* pp. 72ff.).

7. Emanuel Rádl, *Útěcha,* chap. 1 and passim. Rádl notes that a human who claims not to be aware of the reality of God is an anomaly in terms of the global history of humankind. Such a statistical argument, however, can elicit the response that so are people who believe the earth to be round—unless the sense of God's presence is an eidetic insight rather than a factual sense impression. Phenomenologically oriented writers like Rudolf Otto in *The Idea of the Holy* or Gerardhus van der Leeuw in *Religion in Essence and Manifestation* argue precisely that.

8. Cf. Karl Jaspers's conception of the "philosophic faith," *The Perennial Scope of Philosophy,* pp. 1–46.

9. *Formal and Transcendental Logic,* § 104–7. That, too, is the sense which the term had in its traditional use. "We hold these truths to be self-evident" refers not to their logical status but to their evident truth in the eyes of America's founding fathers.

10. Anselm of Canterbury, *Proslogium; Monologium; An Appendix in Behalf of the Fool,* trans. Sidney Norton Deane (Chicago: Open Court, 1903), pp. 7–10, 145–59.
11. The Jehovah's Witnesses I have known have been the most admirable of people. Like the Marxists, they place the Kingdom of God not in eternity but in a future time and, like the early Christians, believe that time to be imminent. In their case, the prophecy becomes self-fulfilling in a sense. In their devotion, their goodness, and the love they bear each other, they create, as it were, enclaves of the Kingdom. That, together with the fact that the Marxists so conspicuously fail to do so, bears on the concluding point, pp. 214–17 below. Transformed objective conditions do not create a transformed person, a "new socialist man." New, reborn persons, though, can create new objective conditions. Thus Havlíček and the primacy of the personal—the "revolution of hearts and minds." Cf. *infra,* 249n30.
12. *Summa Theologica,* I, Q. 2 A.3 and A.1–2.
13. In my paraphrase of Jaspers's philosophical faith I depart from his idealistic reading, "the reality of the world subsists ephemerally between God and existence" (*The Perennial Scope of Philosophy,* p. 34). That can be said of world as humans constitute and make it, not of the world God creates, and has serious negative consequences in the implicit denial of the intrinsic worth and dignity of the created world. See Frederick Ferré, "Personalism and the Dignity of Nature," pp. 6–8.
14. In 1620, the armies of the Czech estates were defeated by the imperial Austrian forces at the Battle of White Mountain. The victors resorted to a forcible conversion of the land, at the cost of over half its population, including virtually all of its intelligentsia, which was largely Protestant. Many Czech historians—Palacký, Masaryk, Pekař—see the meaning of Czech history in the Protestant-Catholic confrontation. While I would accept Masaryk's reading, I would interpret the polarity as fusion rather than confrontation. See Masaryk, *The Meaning of Czech History,* pp. 122ff.
15. Cf. the poetic conclusion of *Process and Reality,* p. 533, which recurs, with variations, in most of Whitehead's works.
16. "Any kind of polemics," writes Heidegger, "fails from the outset to assume the attitude of thinking." "What Calls for Thinking?" in *Basic Writings,* p. 354.
17. It may be that Heidegger's assertion sounds striking because he uses unfamiliar terminology, speaking of Being where philosophers were wont to speak of becoming. If that is so, his view could be read as a version of Heraclitus' identification of reality with becoming, and the title of the work restated as "Being and Becoming." Though philosophers may reject the doctrine of the Trinity, they must yet deal with the reality it seeks to express, the indissolubility and mutual irreducibility of being, of becoming and of the unity of the two, reflected in Act V of the Council of Chalcedon in A.D. 451, which is reprinted in the 1979 edition of *The Book of Common Prayer,* p. 864.
18. See Dewey in re enjoyment, *Experience and Nature,* pp. 78–90.
19. B. F. Skinner, *Beyond Freedom and Dignity,* pp. 184ff.

20. Watson, in a quaint passage, proposes the "etherization" of those judged unfit by boards of behavioral scientists; *Behaviorism* (p. 185).

21. I would read Husserl's characterization of European culture in terms of its drive to *theoria* as analogous to the traditional philosophic wonder, not as tendency to theorize, in light of Husserl's insistence that reflection is not identical with its doxic-theoretic mode (*Ideen II* § 6). See *Crisis of European Science,* §§ 2–6.

22. Ernst Nagel defines naturalism in terms of the "existential and causal primacy of organized matter in the executive order of nature," in his Presidential Address, "Naturalism Reconsidered," p. 7. That is the thesis I have set out to deny—though with reservations about the term naturalism. See above, pp. 7–8.

23. "Noli foras ire, in te redi, in interiore homine habitat veritas." Saint Augustine in *Of True Religion,* cited by Husserl, *Cartesian Meditations,* § 64. My subhead refers to Psalm 90:10, "The days of our years are three score years and ten and if by reason of strength they are four score, yet is their strength labor and sorrow for they are soon cut off and we fly away."

24. Jan Amos Komenský, *The Labyrinth of the World and the Paradise of the Heart,* trans. Matthew Spinka (Chicago: NUCPA, 1942). Whitehead makes the distinction in numerous works, for instance *Process and Reality,* pp. 238ff.

25. Even Aron Gurwitsch hesitates at this point. I have sought to deal with this elsewhere (Kohák, *Idea and Experience,* pp. 179–88).

26. I have sought to acknowledge my debt earlier, though with a critical difference. It may be well to stress that the point is the primacy of the personal to the material, not their discontinuity. Quite the contrary, I wish to stress their continuity. If, however, a robot of immense complexity were to begin to exhibit the full range of personal being, including psychic and moral spontaneity, it would not affect my argument. My conclusion would not be that moral being is "only" a complex configuration of material components, but rather that such material components are in fact and essentially components of meaningful being, accidentally taken out of context. Jerry Fodor's treatment of Turing machines and simulation is helpful here. Cf. *Psychological Explanation,* esp. pp. 132ff.

27. I am familiar with the argument advanced by Dale Jamieson, that the captivity of animals is slavery no less damaging to the moral fiber of the slave-owners than human slavery was. Still, I am not convinced that apartheid is the sole alternative. The point, to me, is the recognition of animals as respected members of a shared moral community. Robert O. Wagner speaks of captive animals as ambassadors of their kin in the wild—an appealing image but for the memory of captive savages exhibited in England less than three centuries ago. Cf. David Salisbury, "One Philosopher's Argument for Abolishing Zoos," *Christian Science Monitor,* 31 August 1982, p. 6.

28. I think this recognition crucial for an adequate answer to the charge that ecological ethics is an ethics of affluence excluding the impoverished. It could easily become that, were we to take use as such as sign of disrespect.

I do not believe that to be the case: things, I would argue, *deserve* to be used—in the terminology of Peter Singer's *Animal Liberation,* "have a right" to be used (see above, p. 108n17). Neither artifacts nor physical objects nor humans should be condemned to uselessness. Waste, however, is an act of disrespect. Hence a component of distributive justice, assuring use, avoiding waste, appears to me crucial in any environmental ethics. Cf. Ferré, *Personalism and the Dignity of Nature,* p. 5.

29. Experimentation on laboratory animals can tell us no more than experiments with inmates of high-security prisons could tell us about humans, since there is no reason whatever for assuming that captivity would distort animal behavior less than that of human beings. Hence the value of studying animal behavior by observation rather than experiment, in natural habitat, as in Cynthia Moss, *Portraits in the Wild* and others.

30. T. G. Masaryk, *Karel Havlíček.* Havlíček, a Czech journalist and political thinker in the first half of the nineteenth century, made moral, social, and cultural rebirth rather than violent upheaval the national program, earning the violent scorn of Karl Marx and the allegiance of T. G. Masaryk. Comparing Masaryk's Czechoslovak republic with the current Marxist regime suggests that Havlíček, not Marx,, was right. Cf. also Barbara K. Reinfeld, *Karel Havlíček* (New York: Columbia University Press, 1982).

31. The civil rights movement in Czechoslovakia, Charta 77, devastated by deaths, arrests, and exiles, self-consciously appealed to Rádl. Thus Rádl, *Útěcha,* pp. 22–24; Václav Havel, "The Power of the Powerless" (cf. p. 235n45).

Bibliography

Allport, Gordon. *Pattern and Growth in Personality.* New York: Holt, Rinehart & Winston, 1961.

Angyal, Andras. *Neurosis and Treatment.* New York: Viking Press, 1956.

Arnold, Matthew. *Culture and Anarchy.* In *Works of Matthew Arnold,* volume 6. New York: AMS Press, 1970.

Artz, Frederick B. *Renaissance Humanism.* Kent, Ohio: Kent State Univesity Press, 1966.

Bateson, Gregory. *Mind and Nature: A Necessary Unity.* New York: E. P. Dutton, 1979.

Bergson, Henri. *Les deux sources de la morale et de la religion.* Paris: F. Alcan, 1932. *Two Sources of Morality and Religion.* Translated by R. Ashley Audra and Cloudesley Brereton. New York: Holt, Rinehart & Winston, 1935.

———. *L'évolution créatrice.* 5th edition. Paris: F. Alcan, 1907. *Creative Evolution.* Translated by A. Ritchel. New York: Modern Library, 1944.

Bertocci, Peter Anthony. "The Person, His Personality and Environment." *Review of Metaphysics* 32 (1979).

———. *The Goodness of God.* Washington, D.C.: University Press of America, 1981.

———. *The Person God Is.* New York: Humanities Press, 1970.

Bertocci, Peter Anthony and Richard M. Millard. *Personality and the Good.* New York: David McKay, 1962.

Black, Max. *Models and Metaphors.* Ithaca, N.Y.: Cornell University Press, 1962.

———. *The Importance of Language.* Englewood Cliffs, N.J.: Prentice-Hall, 1962.

Bowne, Borden Parker. *Personalism.* Boston: Houghton Mifflin, 1908.

———. *Metaphysics.* New York: American Book, 1910.

———. *The Principles of Ethics.* New York: American Book, 1896.

———. *Theory of Thought and Knowledge.* New York: American Book, 1897.

———. *Philosophy of Theism.* New York: Harper, 1887.

———. *The Immanence of Good.* New York: Houghton Mifflin, 1905.

Brentano, Franz von. *The Origin of our Knowledge of Right and Wrong.* Translated by Roderick Chisholm and Elizabeth Schneewind. London: Routledge & Kegan Paul, 1969.

———. *Psychologie vom empirischen Standpunkt.* Hamburg: Felix Meiner Verlag, 1971.

Brightman, Edgar Sheffield. *An Introduction to Philosophy.* New York: Henry Holt, 1951.

———. *Religious Values.* New York: Abingdon Press, 1925.

———. *Moral Laws.* New York: Abingdon Press, 1933.

———. *Nature and Values.* New York: Abingdon Press, 1945.

———. *Person and Reality.* Edited by P. A. Bertocci. New York: Ronald Press, 1958.

Bultman, Rudolf. *Theology of the New Testament.* 2 vols. Translated by K. Grobel. New York: Scribner's, 1954.

Camus, Albert. *L'homme révolté.* Paris: Gaillard, 1951. *The Rebel: An Essay on Man in Revolt.* Revised translation by Anthony Bower. Foreword by Sir Herbert Read. New York: Knopf, 1956.

———. *Le mythe de Sisyphe.* Paris: Gaillard, 1942. *The Myth of Sisyphus, and Other Essays.* Translated by Justin O'Brien. New York: Vintage Books, 1955.

Čapek, Karel. *President Masaryk Tells His Story.* New York: Putnam, 1935.

Čapek, Milič. *The Philosophical Impact of Contemporary Physics.* New York: Van Nostrand Reinhold, 1961.

Carr, David. *Phenomenology and the Philosophy of History.* Evanston: Northwestern University Press, 1975.

———. "Husserl's Problematic Concept of the Life-World." *American Philosophical Quarterly* 7 (1970): 331–39.

Cassirer, Ernst. *An Essay on Man.* New Haven: Yale University Press, 1944.

———. *Philosophie der symbolischen Formen.* 2d edition. Darmstadt: Wissenschaftlichen Buchgesellschaft, 1953. *Philosophy of Symbolic Forms.* 3 vols. Translated by Ralph Manheim. New Haven: Yale University Press, 1953.

Cather, Willa. *My Ántonia.* Boston, New York: Houghton Mifflin, 1926.

Cattel, Raymond B. *Description and Measurement of Personality.* Yonkers, N.Y.: World Book, 1956.

Cekota, Antonin. *Geniální podnikatel Tomáš Baťa.* Toronto: Sixty-Eight Publishers, 1981.

Collingwood, Herbert W. *Adventures in Silence.* New York: Rural New Yorker, 1923.

Collingwood, R. G. *The Idea of Nature.* New York: Oxford University Press, 1960.

Comenius. See Komenský, Jan Amos.

Conrad, Joseph. *The Heart of Darkness and the Secret Sharer.* Introduction by Albert J. Guerard. New York: New American Library, 1950.

Christian, William. *An Interpretation of Whitehead's Metaphysics.* New Haven: Yale University Press, 1959.

Crane, Brinton. *Nietzsche.* Cambridge: Harvard University Press, 1941.

Derrida, Jacques. *De la grammatologie.* Paris: Editions de Minuit, 1967. *Of Grammatology.* Baltimore: Johns Hopkins University Press, 1976.

———. *La voix et le phénomène: introduction au problème du signe dans la phénomenologie de Husserl.* Paris: Presses universitaires de France, 1967. *Speech and Phenomenon.* Translated with an introduction by David B. Allison. Preface by Newton Garver. Evanston: Northwestern University Press, 1973.

Dewey, John. *Experience and Nature.* New York: Dover, 1958.

Dilthey, William. *Gesammelte Schriften..* Stuttgart: Teubner: Göttingen: Vandenhoeck & Ruprecht, 1914–72.

Driesch, Hans. *Der Vitalismus als Geschichte und als Lehre.* Leipzig, 1905. *The History and Theory of Vitalism.* London, 1914. *Geschichte des Vitalismus.* Revised German edition. Leipzig, 1922.

Ellenberger, Henri. *The Discovery of the Unconscious; The History and Evolution of Dynamic Psychiatry.* New York: Basic Books, 1970.

Ferré, Frederick. "Personalism and the Dignity of Nature." Presented to PDG, Baltimore, Md. 28 December 1982.

Findlay, J. N. *Kant and the Transcendental Object.* New York: Oxford University Press, 1981.

———. "Dialogue with Things or the Merits of Matter; 'They Think Not Neither Do They Care'." Boston University Institute of Philosophy and Religion Lecture. Boston University, 8 December 1982.

———. *Values and Intentions.* New York: Humanities Press, 1961.

Fodor, Jerry. *Psychological Explanation.* New York: Random House, 1968.

Frankl, Viktor. *The Doctor and the Soul.* Translated by Richard and Clara Wilson. New York: Random House-Vintage, 1965.

Freud, Sigmund. *Gesammelte Werke, chronologisch geordnet.* Edited by Anna Freud et al. London: Imago Publishing Company, 1942.

———. *The Standard Edition of the Complete Psychological Works of Sigmund Freud.* Edited and translated by James Strachey, Anna Freud, Alex Strachey, Alan Tyson. London: Hogarth Press, 1953–74.

Fromm, Erich. *To Have or to Be.* New York: Harper & Row, 1976.

Gadamer, Hans-Georg. *Kleine Schriften.* Tübingen: J.C.B. Mohr, 1974.

———. *Philosophical Hermeneutics.* Translated and edited by David E. Linge. Berkeley: University of California Press, 1976.

———. *Wahrheit und Methode: Grundzüge einer philosophischen Hermeneutik.* 2d edition. Tübingen: Mohr, 1965. *Truth and Method.* 2d edition. Translation edited by Garrett Barden and John Cumming. New York: Seabury Press, 1975.

Goslin, D. A., editor. *Handbook of Socialization Theory and Research.* Chicago: Rand McNally Press, 1969.

Grajewski, Maurice. *The Formal Distinction of John Duns Scotus.* Washington, D.C.: Catholic University of America Press, 1944.

Gurwitsch, Aron. *Studies in Phenomenology of Nature.* Evanston: Northwestern University Press, 1966.

Hartman, Nicolai. *Der Aufbau der realen Welt.* 3d edition. Berlin: Walter de Gruyter, 1964.

———. *Philosophie der Natur.* Berlin: Walter de Gruyter, 1951.

———. "Zum Problem der Realitätsgegebenheit." *Philosophische Vorträge* 32. Berlin: Kaufgesellschaft, 1931.

Hartshorne, Charles. *The Divine Relativity: A Social Conception of God.* New Haven: Yale University Press, 1948.

Heidbreder, Edna. *Seven Psychologies.* Englewood Cliffs, N.J.: Prentice-Hall, 1933.

Heidegger, Martin. *Basic Writings.* Edited by David F. Krell, et al. New York: Harper & Row, 1977.

———. *Die Einführung in die Metaphysik.* Tübingen: Niemeyer, 1953. *Introduction to Metaphysics.* Translated by Ralph Manheim. New Haven: Yale University Press, 1959.

———. *Die Grundprobleme der Phänomenologie.* [1927] Frankfurt: Klostermann, 1975.

———. *Kant und das Problem der Metaphysik.* Bonn: Cohen, 1922. *Kant and the Problem of Metaphysics.* Translated by James Spencer Churchill. Bloomington, Ind.: Indiana University Press, 1962.

———. *Nietzsche.* Translated by D. F. Krell. San Francisco: Harper & Row, 1979.

———. *Platons Lehre von der Wahrheit. Mit einem Brief über den "Humanismus."* Bern: Francke, 1947.

———. *Poetry, Language, and Thought.* Translated by Albert Hofstadter. New York: Harper, 1975.

———. *The Question Concerning Technology and Other Essays.* Translated by William Lovitt. New York: Garland Publishers, 1977.

———. *Der Satz vom Grund.* Pfullingen: Noeske, 1957.

———. *Sein und Zeit.* Tübingen: Neomanius Verlag, 1953. *Being and Time.* Translated by John Macquarrie and Edward Robinson. New York: Harper, 1962.

———. *Vom Wesen des Grundes.* Frankfurt: Klostermann, 1955. *The Essence of Reason.* Translated by Terrence Malick. Evanston, Ill.: Northwestern University Press, 1969.

———. *Vorträge und Aufssätze.* Pfullingen: Gunther Neske, 1954.

———. *Was ist das—Die Philosophie?* 3d edition. Pfullingen: Neske, 1963. *What Is Philosophy?* Translated by W. Klubacs, J. T. Wilde. New Haven: College and University Press, 1956.

———. "What Is Metaphysics?" Translated by R. F. C. Hall, A. Crick. In *Existence and Being.* Edited by W. Broch. Chicago: H. Regan, 1949.

———. *Zur Seinsfrage.* Frankfurt: Klostermann, 1958.

Heinemann, F. *Nomos und Physis.* Basel: F. Reinhardt, 1945.

Hospers, John. "What Means This Freedom?" In Sidney Hook, ed., *Determinism and Freedom in the Age of Modern Science.* New York: New York University Press, 1958.

Hübner, Kurt. *Kritik der Wissenschaftlichen Vernunft.* München: Karl Albert, 1978.

Huizinga, Johan. *The Waning of the Middle Ages.* Translated by F. Hopman. London: E. Arnold, 1924.

———. *Erasmus and the Age of Reformation.* Translated by F. Hopman. New York: Harper, 1957.

Husserl, Edmund. *Cartesianische Meditationen und Pariser Vorträge.* The Hague: Martinus Nijhoff, 1950; reprinted 1973. *Cartesian Meditations: An Introduction to Phenomenology.* Translated by Dorion Cairns. The Hague: Martinus Nijhoff, 1960. *The Paris Lectures.* Translated by Peter Koestenbaum. The Hague: Martinus Nijhoff, 1967.

———. *Erfahrung und Urteil.* Edited by Ludgwig Landgrebe. Prague: Academia, 1939; Hamburg: Meiner, 1974. *Experience and Judgment.* Translated by James S. Churchill and Karl Ameriks. Evanston, Ill.: Northwestern University Press, 1973.

———. *Formale und Transzendentale Logik.* Halle: Niemeyer, 1929; The Hague: Martinus Nijhoff, 1974. *Formal and Transcendental Logic.* Translated by Dorothy Cairns. The Hague: Martinus Nijhoff, 1969.

———. *Die Idee der Phänomenologie.* Edited by Walter Biemel. The Hague: Martinus Nijhoff, 1950. *The Idea of Phenomenology.* Translated by W. Alston, G. Nakhnikian. The Hague: Martinus Nijhoff, 1968.

———. *Ideen zu einer Phänomenologie und phänomenologischen Philosophie.* Volume 1: *Allgemeine Einführung in die reine Phänomenologie.* Halle: Niemeyer, 1913; The Hague: Martinus Nijhoff, 1950. *Ideas towards a Pure Phenomenology and Phenomenological Philosophy.* Translated by W. R. Boyce Gibson. New York: MacMillan, 1931; Collier, 1962. Volume 2: *Phänomenologische Untersuchungen zur Konstitution.* Edited by Marly Biemel. The Hague: Martinus Nijhoff, 1952. Volume 3: *Die Phänomenologie und die Fundamente der Wissenschaften.* Edited by Marly Biemel. The Hague: Martinus Nijhoff, 1971. *Phenomenology and the Foundations of the Sciences: Ideas Pertaining to a Pure Phenomenology and to a Phenomenological Philosophy.* Translated by Ted E. Klein, William E. Pohl. The Hague: Martinus Nijhoff, 1980.

———. *Die Krisis der europäischen Wissenschaften und die transzendentale Phänomenologie.* Edited by Walter Biemel. The Hague: Martinus Nijhoff, 1962; reprinted 1969. *The Crisis of the European Sciences and Transcendental Phenomenology: An Introduction to Phenomenological Philosophy.* Translated with an introduction by David Darr. Evanston, Ill.: Northwestern University Press, 1970.

———. *Logische Untersuchungen.* 2 vols. Tübingen: M. Niemeyer, 1968. *Logical Investigations.* 2 vols. Translated by J. N. Findlay. London: Routledge & Kegan Paul; New York: Humanities Press, 1970.

———. *Phänomenologische Psychologie.* Husserliana vol. 9. The Hague: Martinus Nijhoff, 1962. *Phenomenological Psychology.* Translated by John Scanlon. The Hague: Martinus Nijhoff, 1977.

———. *Philosophie als strenge Wissenschaft.* Frankfurt: Klostermann, 1965. "Philosophy as a Rigorous Science." Translated by Quentin Lauer. In *Phe-*

nomenology and the Crisis of Philosophy. Edited by Quentin Lauer. New York: Harper, 1965.

———. *Die Vorlesungen zur Phänomenologie des inneren Zeitbewusstseins.* Edited by R. Boehm. Halle: Niemeyer, 1929. *The Phenomenology of Internal Time-Consciousness.* Translated by James Spencer Churchill. Edited by Martin Heidegger. Introduction by Dalvin O. Schrag. Bloomington, Ind.: Indiana University Press, 1964.

———. *Zur Phänomenologie der Intersubjektivität.* Edited by Iso Kern. The Hague: Martinus Nijhoff, 1973.

James, William. *The Principles of Psychology.* New York: H. Holt, 1890.

———. *Varieties of Religious Experience.* New York: Modern Library, 1902.

———. *Will to Believe and Other Essays.* New York: Dover Publications, 1960.

Jamieson, Dale. "Reflections on Captive Animals." Cited in David Salisbury, "One Philosopher's Argument for Abolishing Zoos." *Christian Science Monitor,* 31 August 1982, p. 6.

Jaspers, Karl. *Philosophie.* 3d edition. Berlin: Springer, 1956. *Philosophy.* Translated by E. B. Ashton. Chicago: University of Chicago Press, 1969.

———. *Der Philosophische Glaube.* Frankfurt: Fischer, Bucherei, 1958. *The Perennial Scope of Philosophy.* Translated by Ralph Manheim. New York: Philosophical Library, 1949.

———. *Vernunft und Widervernunft in unserer Zeit.* Munich: R. Piper, 1950. *Reason and Anti-Reason in our Time.* Translated by Stanley Godman. New Haven: Yale University Press, 1952.

———. *Way to Wisdom.* Translated by Ralph Manheim. New Haven: Yale University Press, 1951.

Kant, Immanuel. *The Critique of Practical Reason.* Translated by Lewis White Beck. New York: Liberal Arts Press, 1956.

———. *Kant's Cosmogony.* Translated by J. Hastie. New York: Johnson Reprint, 1970.

———. *Kants Werke.* Akademie Textausgabe. Berlin: Walter de Gruyter, 1968.

———. *The Moral Law: Kant's Groundwork of the Metaphysic of Morals.* Translated by H. J. Paton. London: Hutchinson University Library, 1961.

Kaufman, Walter. *Nietzsche: Philosopher, Psychologist, Antichrist.* Princeton: Princeton Univeristy Press, 1968.

Kierkegaard, Søren. *Sickness unto Death.* Edited and translated by Howard V. Hong and Edna H. Hong. Princeton, N.J.: Princeton University Press, 1980.

Kirk, G. S. and J. E. Raven. *The Presocratic Philosophers.* Cambridge: At the University Press, 1957.

Klanský, Mojmír. *Vyhnanství.* Cologne: Index, 1976.

Koch, Sigmund. "The Nature and Limits to Psychological Knowledge." *American Psychologist* 36 (1981): 257–69.

Kohák, Erazim. *Idea and Experience.* Chicago: University of Chicago Press, 1979.

———. "Possessing, Owning, Belonging." *Dissent* 19 (1972): 453–563.

———. "Co měsíc dal." *Studie* (Rome) 15 (1980): 260–64.

———. "Sigmund Freud by Moonlight." *Journal of Religion and Health* 19 (1980): 260–67.

———. "I, Thou or It." *Philosophy from NS* 1 (1968): 36–72.

Kohlberg, Lawrence. *The Philosophy of Moral Development, Moral Stages and Ideas of Justice.* San Francisco: Harper & Row, 1981.

———. "Stage and Sequence: The Cognitive Developmental Approach to Socialization." In D. A. Goslin, ed., *Handbook of Socialization Theory and Research,* q.v.

Köhler, Wolfgang. *Gestalt Psychology.* New York: Liveright Publishers, 1947.

Kołakowski, Leszek. *Main Currents of Marxism.* Translated by P. S. Falla. Oxford: Clarendon Press, 1978.

Komárková, Božena. *Sekularizovaný svět a evangelium.* Zurich, 1981.

Komenský, Jan Amos. *The Labyrinth of the World and the Paradise of the Heart.* Translated by Matthew Spinka. Chicago: Northwestern University Press, 1942.

Krutch, Joseph Wood. *The Measure of Man.* Indianapolis: Bobbs-Merrill, 1954.

Lavely, John. "Personalism." In Paul Edwards, ed., *The Encyclopedia of Philosophy,* Volume 6, pp. 107–110.

Leclerc, Ivor. *Whitehead's Metaphysics.* New York: Macmillan, 1958.

Leisegang, H. "Physics." In Panly-Wissowa, ed., *Realencyclopedia,* volume 20. Stuttgart, 1941.

Lewis, C. S. *The Abolition of Man.* New York: Macmillan, 1957.

Lochman, Milic. *Signposts to Freedom.* Translated by David Lewis. Minneapolis: Augsburg Publishing House, 1982.

Lorenzer, Alfred. *Die Wahrheit des psychologischen Erkenntnis.* Frankfurt am Main: Suhrkamp, 1974.

Lovejoy, A. O. and G. Boas. *Primitivism and Related Ideas in Antiquity.* New York: Octagon, 1965.

Ludwig, Emil. *Defender of Democracy.* New York: R. M. McBride, 1936.

McDougal, William. *Introduction to Social Psycholoy.* London: Methuen, 1908.

Machovec, Milan. *Marxismus und dialektische Theologie.* Translated by Dorothea Neumarker. Zurich: EVZ-Verlag, 1965.

———. *A Marxist Looks at Jesus.* Translated by Peter Hebblethwaite. Philadelphia: Fortress Press, 1976.

———. *Masaryk.* Prague: Melantrich, 1969.

MacIntyre, Alasdair. *After Virtue.* Notre Dame, Ind.: University of Notre Dame Press, 1981.

Mannheim, Karl. "Historicismus." In *Archiv für Sozialwissenschaften und Sozialpolitik* 52 (1924). Translated by Paul Kecskemeti in *Essays in Sociological Knowledge.* London, 1952.

Marcel, Gabriel. *Being and Having.* Translated by Katherine Farrer. Boston: Beacon Press, 1951.

———. *The Philosophy of Existentialism.* Translated by Manya Harari. New York: Citadel, 1956.

Masaryk, Tomáš G. *Humanistic Ideals.* Translated by W. Penn Warren. Lewisberg: Buchnell University Press, 1971.

———. *Spirit of Russia.* Translated by Jan Slavik. London: Allen & Unwin, 1955.

———. *The Making of a State.* Translated by H. W. Stead. New York: F. A. Stokes, 1927.

———. *Masaryk on Marx.* Translated by Erazim Kohák. Lewisberg: Buchnell University Press, 1972.

Maslow, Abraham. *Religion, Values and Peak Experiences.* Columbia, Ohio: Ohio State University Press, 1964.

Merleau-Ponty, Maurice. *Phenomenology of Perception.* Translated by Colin Smith. New York: Humanities Press, 1962.

Nagel, Ernst. "Naturalism Reconsidered." In *Proceedings and Addresses of the American Philosophical Association* 28 (1955).

Nietzsche, Friedrich. *Beyond Good and Evil.* Translated by Walter Kaufman. New York: Vintage Books, 1966.

———. *On the Genealogy of Morals and Ecce Homo.* Edited by Walter Kaufman. Translated by Walter Kaufman and R. J. Hollingdale. New York: Vintage Books, 1967.

———. *Thus Spake Zarathustra.* Translated with an introduction by J. R. Hollingdale. Penguin Books, 1969.

———. *Werke.* 7 vols. Kritische Gesamtausgabe. Edited by Giorgio Colli, Mazzino Montinari. Berlin: de Gruyter, 1967–82.

Otto, Rudolf. *The Idea of the Holy.* Translated by John W. Harvey. London: Oxford University Press, 1950.

Patočka, Jan. *Kacířské eseje o filozofii dějin.* Munich: Edice Arkýř, 1980. *Essais hérétiques sur la philosophie de l'histoire.* Translated by Erika Abrams. Preface by Paul Ricoeur. Postface by Roman Jakobson. La Grasse, France: Editions Verdier, 1981.

———. *Dva eseje o Masarykovi.* Toronto: Sixty-Eight Publishers, 1979.

———. *Přirozený svět jako fiosofický problém.* Prague: Ústř. nakl. a Knihkup. učitelstva čs., 1936. *Le monde naturel comme un problème philosophique.* Translated by Jaromír Daněk. The Hague: Martinus Nijhoff, 1976.

Popper, Sir Karl. *Conjectures and Refutations: The Growth of Scientific Knowledge.* New York: Basic Books, 1962.

———. *The Poverty of Historicism.* Boston: Beacon Press, 1957.

Quine, Willard Van Orman. *Word and Object.* Cambridge, Mass.: MIT Press, 1960.

Rádl, Emanuel. *Útěcha z filosofie.* Prague: Čin, 1946.

———. *Dějiny vývojových theorií v biologii XIX. století.* Prague: J. Laichter, 1909. *History of Biological Theories.* Translated and adapted from the German by E. J. Hadfield. London: Oxford University Press, 1930.

Rais, Karel. *Zapadlí vlastenci.* Prague: Orbis, 1951.

Rasputin, Konstantin. "Proschchanie s Materoi." In *Povesti*, pp. 15–195. Moscow: Molodaja Gvardia, 1975.

Rawls, John. *A Theory of Justice*. Cambridge: Harvard University Press, 1972.

Reinfeld, Barbara K. *Karel Havlíček*. East European Monographs. New York: Columbia University Press, 1982.

Richardson, William J., S.J. *Heidegger: Through Phenomenology to Thought. Phenomenologica* 13. The Hague: Martinus Nijhoff, 1963.

Ricoeur, Paul. *De l'interpretation: essai sur Freud*. Paris: Edition du Seuil, 1965. *Freud and Philosophy*. Translated by Denis Savage. New Haven: Yale University Press, 1970.

———. *Histoire et vérité*. Paris: Seuil, 1955. *History and Truth*. Translated by Charles Kelbley. Evanston, Ill.: Northwestern University Press, 1965.

———. *Husserl: An Analysis of His Phenomenology*. Translated by Edward Bellamy, Lester E. Embree. Evanston, Ill.: Northwestern University Press, 1967.

———. *Interpretation Theory: Discourse on the Surplus of Meaning*. Fort Worth: Texas Christian University Press, 1976.

———. *Philosophie de la volonté* [The philosophy of the will]. Volume 1: *Le volontaire et l'involuntaire*. Paris: Aubier, 1950. *Freedom and Nature: The Voluntary and the Involuntary*. Translated by E. Kohák. Evanston, Ill.: Northwestern University Press, 1966. Volume 2: *Finitude et culpabilité* [Finitude and guilt]. Part 1: *L'homme faillible*. Paris: Aubier, 1960. *Fallible Man*. Translated by Charles Kelbley. Chicago: Regnery, 1965. Part 2: *La symbolique du mal*. Paris: Aubier, 1960. *Symbolism of Evil*. Translated by E. Buchanan. New York: Harper, 1967.

———. *La métaphore vive*. Paris: Seuil, 1975. *The Rule of Metaphor*. Translated by Robert Czerny et al. Toronto: University of Toronto Press, 1977.

Rieff, Philip. *The Triumph of the Therapeutic*. New York: Harper & Row, 1966.

Rorty, Richard. *Consequences of Pragmatism*. Minneapolis, Minn.: University of Minnesota Press, 1982.

———. *Philosophy and the Mirror of Nature*. Princeton, N.J.: Princeton University Press, 1979.

Sartre, Jean-Paul. *Les chemins de la liberté*. 3 vols. Paris: Gallimard, 1945.

———. *L'être et le néant*. Paris Gallimard, 1943. *Being and Nothingness*. Translated by Hazel E. Barnes. New York: Philosophical Library, 1956.

———. *L'existentialisme est un humanisme*. Paris: Nagel, 1946. *Existentialism Is a Humanism*. Translated by Hazel Barnes. New York: Philosophical Library, 1947.

———. *La nausée*. Paris: Gallimard, 1980. *Nausea*. Translated by Lloyd Alexander. Norfolk, Conn.: New Directions, 1946.

Saussure, Ferdinand de. *Course in General Linguistics*. Translated by Wade Baskins. New York: McGraw-Hill, 1966.

Scheler, Max. *Der Formalismus in der Ethik und die materiale Wertethik*. 2d edition. Niemeyer, 1921. *Formalism in Ethics and Non-Formal Ethics of*

Values. Translated by Manfred S. Frings, Roger L. Funk. Evanston, Ill.: Northwestern University, 1973.

———. *Gesammelte Werke.* Edited by Maria Scheler. Bern: Franche, 1963.

———. *Die Stellung des Menschen im Kosmos.* Berne: Francke, 1928. *Man's Place in Nature.* Translated by Hans Meyerhoff. New York: Noonday, 1962.

———. *Vom Ewigen im Menschen.* Berlin: Neue Geist, 1933. *On the Eternal in Man.* Translated by Bernard Noble. London: SCM, 1960.

———. *Wesen und Formen der Sympathie.* Bonn: Cohen, 1923. *The Nature of Sympathy.* Translated by Peter Heath. General introduction by W. Stark. London: Routledge & Kegan Paul, 1954.

Schrag, Calvin. *Radical Reflection and the Origin of the Human Sciences.* West Lafayette, Ind.: Purdue University Press, 1980.

Schrödinger, Erwin. *My View of the World.* Translated by Cecily Hastings. Cambridge: At the University Press, 1964.

———. *Nature and the Greeks.* Cambridge: At the University Press, 1954.

Schumacher, E. F. *Small Is Beautiful.* New York: Harper & Row, 1975.

———. *A Guide for the Perplexed.* New York: Harper & Row, 1978.

Sherrington, Sir Charles. *Man on His Nature.* New York: Doubleday, 1953.

Šimsa, Jan. *Úzkost a naděje.* Prague, 1968.

Singer, Peter. *Animal Liberation.* New York: Avon, 1975.

———. *Animal Rights and Human Obligations.* New York: Prentice-Hall, 1976.

———. *The Expanding Circle: Ethics and Sociobiology.* New York: Farrar, Straus & Giroux, 1981.

Skinner, B. F. *Beyond Freedom and Dignity.* New York: Knopf, 1972.

———. *About Behaviorism.* New York: Knopf, 1974.

———. *Reflections on Behaviorism and Society.* Englewood Cliffs, N.J.: Prentice-Hall, 1978.

Stern, Wilhelm. *General Psychology of the Personalistic Viewpoint.* Translated by Howard Davis Spoerl. New York: MacMillan, 1938.

Stirner, Max. (Schmidt, John Kasper, pseud.) *Der Einzige und Sein Eigentum.* Leipzig: Otto Wigand, 1845. *The Ego and His Own.* Translated by S. T. Byington. Introduction by J. L. Walker. New York: Boni and Liveright, 1918.

Teilhard de Chardin, Pierre. *The Phenomenology of Man.* Introduction by Sir Julian Huxley. New York: Harper, 1961.

———. *Sur la souffrance.* Paris: Edition du Seuil, 1974.

Thoreau, Henry David. *The Selected Works of Thoreau.* Edited by Walter Harding. Revised edition. Boston: Houghton Mifflin, 1975.

Tillich, Paul. *The Courage to Be.* New Haven: Yale University Press, 1952.

———. *Systematic Theology.* 2 vols. Chicago: University of Chicago Press, 1951–57.

Titchener, E. B. *Experimental Psychology.* New York and London, Macmillan; 1901–5.

Tolstoy, Count Leo. *The Complete Works of Count Tolstoy.* 24 vols. Translated and edited by Leo Wiener. New York: AMS Press, 1968.

Troeltch, Ernst. *Der Historismus und seine Probleme.* Tübingen: J. C. B. Mohr (Paul Siebeck), 1922.

———. *The Absoluteness of Christianity and the History of Religions.* Translated by David Reid. Richmond: John Knox Press, 1971.

Ueberweg, Friedrich. *A History of Philosophy.* Translated by George S. Morris. First Engl. edition, 1872. Freeport, N.Y.: Books for Libraries Press, 1972.

Unamuno, Miguel. *The Tragic Sense of Life.* Translated by J. E. Crawford Flitch. New York: Dover, 1954.

Untermeyer, Louis. "Modern American Poetry." In *Modern American and British Poetry.* New York: Harcourt, Brace, 1950.

Van der Leeuw, Gerardhus. *Religion in Essence and Manifestation.* Translated by J. E. Turner. London: Allen & Unwin, 1938.

Watson, John Broadus. *Behaviorism.* New York: Norton, 1970.

Whitehead, Alfred North. *Adventures of Ideas.* New York: Macmillan, 1933.

———. *The Concept of Nature.* Cambridge: At the University Press, 1964.

———. *An Enquiry Concerning the Principles of Natural Knowledge.* Cambridge: At the University Press, 1919.

———. *The Function of Reason.* Boston: Beacon Press, 1958.

———. *Nature and Life.* Chicago: The University of Chicago Press, 1934.

———. *Principia Mathematica.* 2d edition. Cambridge: At the University Press, 1927.

———. *Process and Reality: An Essay in Cosmology.* Corrected edition. Edited by David Ray Griffin and Donald W. Sherburne. New York: Free Press, 1978.

Windelband, Wilhelm. *Geschichte der Philosophie.* Freiburg: I. B. Mohr, 1892. *A History of Philosophy.* Translated by James H. Tufts. New York: Macmillan, 1893.

———. *History of Ancient Philosophy.* Authorized translation by Herbert Ernest Cushman. From 2d German Edition. New York: C. Scribner's Sons, 1899.

Index of Names

Index of Topics